HARPERCOLLINS COLLEGE OUTLINE

Understanding Computers

Gerald A. Silver
Los Angeles City College

Myrna L. Silver

HarperPerennial
A Division of HarperCollinsPublishers

An American BookWorks Corporation Production
Production Manager: Mary Mooney
Editor: Margaret Tuttle

Library of Congress Cataloging-in-Publication Data

Silver, Gerald A.
    Understanding Computers / Gerald A. Silver, Myrna L. Silver
       p. cm.
    Includes bibliographical references and index.
    ISBN 0-06-467163-1
    1. Computers.   2. Computer software.   I. Silver, Myrna.
    II. Title.
    QA76.S5178   1994   93-11670
    004—dc20

94 95 96 97 98 ◆/RRD 10 9 8 7 6 5 4 3 2 1

Understanding Computers

Contents

Preface

Courses in computer literacy are taught in hundreds of schools and colleges across the country. These courses teach the student how the computer functions and how it is used in business, government, educational, and domestic applications. They impart a basic knowledge of a tool that has changed the face of most business, private, and public institutions.

This outline is written for the introductory computer literacy course that is offered to majors and nonmajors alike. Students from a diversity of backgrounds and disciplines take this course to learn how to use the computer.

The subject matter is presented in a clear and understandable form. The authors have taken care to present concepts and ideas in an easy-to-understand literary style. This is particularly important in the computer discipline because so many technical terms are involved. The outline explains the fundamentals of word processing, databases, spreadsheets, graphics, and communications.

This outline addresses the newest computer technology, including discussions of hardware and software, such as optical character recognition (OCR), scanners, desktop publishing, artificial intelligence, expert systems, networks, and laser storage devices. It can be used as a supplement or quick reference to any of the introductory texts or can serve as a stand alone book, providing a survey of fundamentals.

Gerald A. Silver
Myrna L. Silver

1

Computers in Today's World

*P*icture a factory producing color television sets. Each set begins as an electronic chassis that is stamped out and then moves down the assembly line. As each circuit board is finished, it is tested and then mounted in place. After the picture tube has been plugged in, the set is turned on and some precision adjustments are made. Then the test pattern disappears and a perfectly balanced color picture flashes on the screen, complete with sound. The set is inspected and found to be working properly. It is carefully placed in a shipping carton with packing, and the box is taped closed. Finally, a shipping label is typed and glued to the side of the carton. The set is then sent on its way to a retail store somewhere in the Midwest.

As you look around the factory, you become aware of a startling fact. There are no people here—only machines. The entire process of assembling, testing, packing, and even shipping the sets is completely automated, untouched by human hands. There are a few people employed in the plant. But they sit in a glassed-in control room, drinking coffee as they watch robots do all the work. Does this picture of a computerized manufacturing plant predict a world in which people are superfluous and jobs nonexistent?

In this opening chapter we will review how computers impact our lives. We will look at robotics, voice synthesizers, communications, fault-tolerant computers, and computer-aided design and manufacturing. Our objective is to show the impact the computer has on schools, offices, and industry, which sets the stage for following chapters that explore the inner workings of the computer, computer software, systems, and applications.

AUTOMATION

A decade or two ago some experts predicted that computers and automation would cause mass layoffs and unemployment. *Automation* is the application of computers to the manufacturing process by shifting control from people to machines.

The computer has brought with it many benefits and expanded opportunities, particularly for people entering the job market today. Consider the new vistas opened by the invention of robotics, artificial intelligence, voice synthesizers, and modern communications. These technologies, and others still on the drawing boards, hold out the promise that our work will become less tedious and more challenging, shops and offices more productive, and society better educated and able to cope with its problems.

In the last decade the unemployment rate has risen and fallen sharply due to many factors. The computer, however, has created more jobs than it has eliminated.

Although it is true that jobs have been lost because of computers and information technology, the benefits far outweigh the disadvantages. In some instances workers have been forced to upgrade their skills to remain employed. Clerical employment has increased, largely due to the computer's ability to handle a large volume of work. The computer has generated entire new industries that manufacture, sell, install, and repair computer and information processing equipment.

IMPACT ON EDUCATION

All levels of education—elementary, secondary, college, and university—as well as instructional, curricular, and administrative processes, are being affected by the computer. The computer is used for many administrative tasks, such as processing student records, counseling, and reporting grades. Classrooms, laboratories, lecture halls, admissions offices, libraries, study halls, and dormitories around the country are more and more frequently equipped with computers.

The computer supplements, or in some cases replaces, the teacher. It provides drill work, exercises, remedial material, enrichment material, and tests. It simulates a dialogue with the student. This raises many questions. Will the teacher of the future continue to interact directly with students through computerized lessons? Will the human aspect of the instructional process be affected if people are replaced, even in part, by machines? Will the teacher continue to create the material he or she presents or substitute packaged programs delivered by machine? What will the next generation of students be like if they have been trained, educated, influenced, nurtured, and stimulated by computer-based instruction?

Other questions sparked by the use of computers as educational tools concern the future curriculum and content of course work. What kinds of knowledge will students need to survive in our future society? Computer technology changes so fast that textbooks may be obsolete by the time they are printed. Learning about the computer itself may be one of the most important aspects of education. The computer-literate student will need to know how the computer works, how to program it, and how to use it as a general-purpose problem-solving tool.

EXPANDING AREAS OF COMPUTER USAGE

Let us look at some of the new technologies that show great promise and opportunity precisely because we have computers at our disposal. These include conversational languages, robotics, fault-tolerant computers, and lasers in communications.

Conversational languages

Much time and effort is being spent on developing *conversational languages* for programming computers. Languages more like natural communication and everyday English will allow people to communicate with computers in a comfortable style, greatly increasing the utility of the machines.

Presently computers are programmed using languages that require close adherence to rules of spelling, syntax, and language structure. The development of English-like conversational languages will mean that individuals with little or no programming skill will be able to direct computers to perform many unique personal tasks. Conversational languages are growing in importance, promising new jobs and employment opportunities as the computer finds wider applications at home and in business.

Artificial intelligence

A number of computer manufacturers are spending research funds on developing computers that simulate human intelligence. These systems are sometimes called *expert computers* and are part of a growing field known as *artificial intelligence*.

It is possible to build computers and write software that mimic human reasoning, allowing machines to perform tasks normally done by people. For instance, the complex task of evaluating a patient's condition could be turned over to a computer for help with diagnosis and treatment. This process would simulate a doctor's or nurse's logic and training.

Expert computers are taking over such tasks as scheduling complex production jobs. They can follow goods during the manufacturing process, order raw materials, schedule employees and equipment, and even type up shipping labels and send out bills without human intervention.

Expert computers are able to track satellites and create complex service and maintenance schedules, allowing a satellite to be taken out of service while another takes its place without any interruption in communications. Computers follow logical rules of system behavior and report solutions to a human observer.

Artificial intelligence is a rapidly growing field of research and development, offering many new jobs and employment opportunities. This work will involve equipment and system design and applications in business, schools, and industry for expert computers.

Voice communication with machines

A great deal of research is being done on *voice synthesizers and recognition devices*. The purpose is to enable computers to accept data input by the human voice rather than through a keyboard. The computer will then output data by simulating ordinary speech, making output systems more flexible and greatly expanding computer applications. Voice recognition will allow people to direct machines without hands-on control and make possible such things as typewriters that will respond to the human voice or automobiles that will be guided and controlled by speech.

Data will be entered into information processing systems by speaking into voice recognition machines. This will save data entry time by eliminating the need for keyboarding. In the not-too-distant future you may be able to call someone on the telephone by simply speaking the numbers, or perhaps the name of the individual you wish to call, into the instrument, and the telephone will do the rest. Homes and businesses will screen employees in secure areas through voice recognition, and toys and games will be activated by the human voice rather than the hand. Applications such as these are particularly helpful for the blind or handicapped.

Major applications of voice recognition are in the fields of security, home appliances, data entry, and toys and games. Voice recognition will control appliances, such as microwave ovens; perhaps in the near future you will be able to turn your television set on and off and change channels from your easy chair by just talking to your voice recognition television set.

Desktop publishing

The introduction of page makeup software and laser printers has fostered the industry of *desktop publishing*. Small businesses or individuals can lay out, design, and produce documents using desktop computers and laser printers.

As the price of laser printers continues to drop, many more computer users will turn to desktop publishing to create newsletters, reports, and other publications. Many jobs that are sent out to commercial printers may now be done in-house. Scanners and electronic artwork supplied on floppy disks can enable individuals with little or no artistic talent to create professional-looking drawings and artwork for inclusion in documents. The shift from commercial printers and typesetters to desktop publishing means that computer users will need to learn page design and principles of typography.

Desktop publishing will speed up the pace with which organizations can produce professional-looking documents. It will be possible to generate high-quality publications quickly and at lower cost. Publishing professionals predict that improvements in page makeup software and hardware will make it possible to create lengthy books for distribution to as few as ten or twenty individuals. Documents of this length are presently too expensive to produce in small quantities. Desktop publishing continues to change the economics of publishing.

Micro-computers

In the years ahead millions of small computer systems will be installed in homes, schools, automobiles, and small offices. This high level of use will cause an enormous demand for marketing, repair, and maintenance of these small systems. It will also stimulate software services including writing, distributing, and retailing new types of programs.

The microcomputer will become smaller and integrated into more and more systems. Almost daily, new uses for the computer are found in laboratories, medical research, and in the discovery and investigation of new compounds, materials, and processes. The research on superconductivity and the progress made in the transmission of electrical currents at low temperatures would be almost impossible without the computer.

Not only will more applications be found for microcomputers, but their design and structure will change as well. Computers will become *fault-tolerant*. These machines will incorporate redundant circuitry and software. Fault-tolerant computers will continue to function even though hardware failures occur and will be able to diagnose faults even before they occur. This will virtually eliminate "hard failures," where the computer simply stops functioning.

New computer storage devices are entering the marketplace. Recently, high-capacity optical storage drives (CD-ROM and laser disk drives) have become available. They are capable of storing and retrieving almost one billion characters of information almost instantly. One disk will hold the contents of dozens of sets of encyclopedias. A lawyer could carry an entire law library on one optical disk in his or her vest pocket.

Robotics

It has been said that machines should work and people should think. Business and industry executives are continually searching for machines to do the physical work of humans, freeing people to do more creative tasks. *Robots* are suited for use in hazardous or hostile environments or for monotonous, repetitive tasks. Robots are especially useful in the assembly of small quantities of complicated goods and the handling of precision parts. Industry analysts project that robotic devices will find their way into large and small businesses and perhaps even some homes in the next few years.

A number of American and Japanese companies are manufacturing robots. These companies specialize in machines that can assemble, sort, construct, or handle goods during the manufacturing process. This industry is growing as many new applications are found for robots. The greater use of robots may well create more jobs than it eliminates because as automated production lowers manufacturing costs (and selling prices in turn), more people will buy goods. This will boost demand and create a market for more robots. In addition, robots must be installed, serviced, and replaced when new and better machines come along, creating even more jobs.

Robots have become so important that the U.S. Census Bureau now collects data on the number and type of robots in service. The Department of Commerce will use this information to report the number of robots produced, their economic impact on U.S. industry, and the number of foreign robots imported into this country.

Communications

The breakup of the American Telephone and Telegraph system into regional companies, the growth of closed circuit cable television, the expansion of satellite communications, and the development of *fiber optics* have begun to greatly change the *communications* industry. *Laser* communications, the technological basis of the industry, is the subject of much current research and development. A laser beam can transmit hundreds of telephone calls, data, and television pictures over a single fiber optic strand of glass at one time.

These innovations profoundly affect the way voice and data are transmitted and are bringing communications to more people in more places than ever before.

The computer makes possible the operation of new communications services, for example, a new type of mobile phone service using the *cellular telephone* (Fig. 1.1). Cellular telephones provide better telephone service from moving vehicles and make many more channels available on one frequency. As the cellular telephone system is improved and its usage price falls, more businesses will be able to afford this computer-managed telephone service.

Much of the growth in data communications will be in the field of *local area networks (LANs)* (Fig. 1.2). LANs, discussed in a later chapter, will link computers in homes and offices together and allow computers in specified geographic areas to serve multiple users. Existing schools, hospitals, government buildings, office buildings, and apartment houses are being

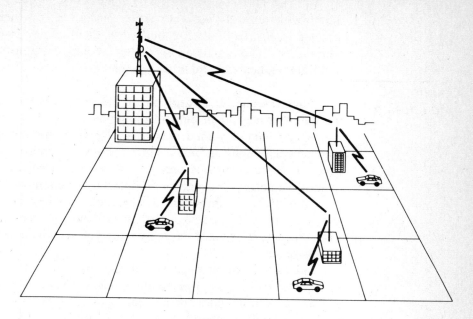

Fig. 1.1—Cellular Telephone

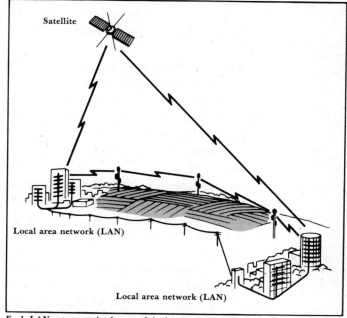

Each LAN may contain dozens of devices connected into a local system. These local systems in turn may be tied together through a satellite, microwave relay, or telephone line network.

Fig. 1.2—Local Area Network (LAN)

wired with coaxial cables to serve LANs. As new buildings are constructed, LAN facilities are built into them. These *smart buildings* are equipped with communications circuits, computer-controlled air conditioning, lighting, heating, and other services.

Computer-aided design

Much research and development has gone into how computers can aid the engineering and design of equipment as well as the manufacture of goods. In *computer-aided design (CAD)* the computer prepares and tests mechanical designs and makes engineering drawings. CAD eliminates the need for manual drawing and drafting and increases both the quality and quantity of designs that can be produced by an engineer.

Computers are important design tools in many industries. In graphic arts, they are used to design trademarks and produce artwork. Computers generate action-oriented computer art for television titles, movies, and commercials.

Once a new product has been designed, *computer-aided manufacturing (CAM)* can be used to produce the goods. CAM deals with process control, inventory control, and work scheduling. One of the most important areas of CAM is *numerical control (N/C)*. For example, in N/C a computer is connected to metalworking machines and directs equipment to grind, mill, punch, or cut metal, plastic, or other materials. Parts can be produced with greater precision and without the need for a human operator to guide each motion of metalworking machines.

Banking and credit

The computer is widely used in the finance, credit, and banking industries. Using a computer, employees can easily process deposits, commercial and consumer loans, revolving charge accounts for banks and department stores, prepare credit card statements, and maintain trust accounts. The computer is the heart of modern electronic banking. Without it, *electronic fund transfer systems (EFTS)*, such as Visa and MasterCard, would not be possible.

As the growth of the credit economy expands, bank managers will rely more heavily upon computers to handle banking and credit transactions. These systems will be expanded worldwide to process transactions, move debits and credits, and handle credit purchases from virtually any location.

Modeling and planning

The computer has become an important business *modeling and planning* tool, and its use in this area will continue to grow. For example, business conditions can be analyzed and reduced to a mathematical model that is entered into the computer. Then different sets of trial data can be fed in and the computer prints out results. When mathematical models are accurate, companies can be spared the time and expense of actual marketplace testing.

For example, a manufacturer may want to produce a food product of specific nutritional value, but not want to exceed a given cost or specific number of calories per ounce. The product must contain specified vitamins and a given amount of protein. It is difficult to decide on the proper formula since there are many ingredients that can be combined to make the product. With proper programming, the computer can quickly figure out all the possibilities and determine the best combination of components to produce the desired result at the lowest cost. The computer prints out a list of ingredients and quantities that most closely meet the desired specifications.

Supercomputers, giant high-speed computers, process vast quantities of information, such as meteorological data fed to them from points around the world. Large machines such as these will continue to expand and control the nation's communications, air traffic control, pipeline, traffic, and waterway facilities. Truly, the computer is only limited by our ability to create and understand its capabilities and put them to use.

Telecommuting

A new worker, known as the *telecommuter*, is emerging. The telecommuter does not go to work on the 8:15 A.M. express and return to the suburbs on the 5:42 P.M. train. Instead, he or she works at home, performing a full day's work without ever leaving the house. Using personal computers, modems, and communications software, telecommuters are able to perform data entry, accounting, management, and other tasks. Students will be able to attend classes, turn in assignments, and do other course work without ever leaving home.

The next decade is likely to see a great increase in the number of telecommuters as traffic jams roads and jobs continue to shift from production and manufacturing to service and clerical. Telecommuting will have societal impact. For instance, businesses may need to provide less office space and fewer parking facilities. More part-time work and job-sharing opportunities may arise. Telecommuting allows employees flexibility in setting their work hours and may simplify child care arrangements.

Some real estate experts predict that telecommuting will have a profound impact on the real estate market. As more and more cities adjust their zoning laws and companies employ telecommuters, demand for downtown office space will lessen. These experts believe that, given enough time, a substantial percentage of the workforce will perform services out of their homes and virtually eliminate downtown rush hour traffic.

The future of computers is here, and the student who understands the impact of this technology will have a competitive advantage. The computer-literate citizen of tomorrow will be more secure in the labor market and better able to cope with the broad social changes that the computer will inevitably bring.

Automation is the application of machines and computers to control their own operation. The computer has affected the way in which people are taught and the curriculum offered by schools on all levels of education. Areas of new technological development include conversational languages, artificial intelligence and expert computers, voice communication with machines, microcomputer expansion, robotics, communications, computer-aided design (CAD), and computer-aided manufacturing (CAM).

Conversational languages are more like natural communication and allow people to communicate with computers in a comfortable style. Expert systems are a rapidly growing area of computer usage. Voice recognition allows people to direct machines without hands-on control. It is used in security, telephone, appliance, data entry, and other applications. Robots are suited for use in hazardous or hostile environments, or for monotonous, repetitive tasks. Lasers and fiber optics have had great impact on the communications industry. There will be expanded use of cellular telephones and local area networks (LANs).

Desktop publishing will make possible the production of lengthy documents for distribution in small quantities. Desktop publishing enables small businesses and individuals with limited artistic skills to create attractive documents, including drawings and artwork.

Products are designed using computer-aided design (CAD) and then produced using computer-aided manufacturing (CAM). Using numerical control (N/C), computers are able to direct metalworking machines without the aid of human operators. The computer is finding new applications in modeling and planning. It helps manufacturers find the best mix when combining components in a product. Computers are used to design trademarks and artwork for the print media. There will be an increase in telecommuting, where employees, using personal computers and modems, perform their work from their homes.

Selected Readings

Long, Larry *Computers*, Prentice-Hall (1993). Chapter 1.

Parker, Charles S. *Understanding Computers and Information Processing*, Dryden Press (1992). Chapter 1.

Hutchinson, Sarah E. *Computers*, Irwin (1992). Chapter 1.

REVIEW QUESTIONS

True or False Questions

1. Little development has been done on conversational languages.
2. No applications for voice communication with machines are under consideration.
3. Fault-tolerant computers tend to be reliable.
4. Tedious and repetitive jobs are best suited for computer-controlled robots.
5. Many areas of communications have been affected by the computer.

6. The computer is frequently used as a design aid.

7. The computer has not been used as an aid in manufacturing.

8. New innovations in communications include the laser.

9. The computer is widely used in the banking and credit industry.

10. The computer is not suitable for modeling and planning applications.

11. Artificial intelligence is one of the newest applications for the computer.

12. Educators are finding numerous applications for the computer in the classroom.

13. Computer-assisted instruction is not suitable for classroom use.

14. The computer has had little influence in the job market and the types of skills required.

15. There has been a reduction in the reliance on optical storage systems.

Completion Questions

1. _____ has enabled small businesses to produce artistic documents.

2. _____ has become a commonly used means of teaching students.

3. _____ is often used in product design and manufacture.

4. _____ are best suited for use in noisy or dangerous applications.

5. Artificial intelligence seeks to mimic the _____ thought process.

ANSWER KEY

True or False Questions

1. F
2. F
3. T
4. T
5. T
6. T
7. F
8. T
9. T
10. F
11. T
12. T
13. F
14. F
15. F

Completion Questions

1. desktop publishing
2. computer-assisted instruction
3. CAD/CAM
4. robots
5. human

2

How the Computer Works

*F*rom time to time significant events occur, shaking society to its foundations. The discovery of fire, the invention of the wheel, and the domestication of animals were experiences that changed the world forever.

In the eighteenth century the world was once more transformed, this time by the Industrial Revolution, which created the factory system. The dawn of the machine age relieved men and women of much arduous physical labor. Many industries, which had been conducted in the home or on a farm, were abandoned as people flocked to the cities where factories were located. Virtually no one in the developing countries was left untouched by the Industrial Revolution.

In this century another life-changing revolution has taken place. The increasing use of computers and information systems has transformed the way people live, think, conduct business, and communicate with one another. The computer freed the human mind from tedious mental tasks in much the same way that machines freed the human body from physical drudgery.

Four decades ago the computer was an expensive scientific wonder, understood by only a handful of researchers and mathematicians. Today the computer is indispensable in scientific research and in business. Microprocessors, a primary element of microcomputers, have become so small that they can be incorporated into automobiles, toys, and home appliances. Microcomputers can be kept on a desktop or carried about in a briefcase.

WHAT ARE COMPUTERS?

In general terms a computer is any instrument that computes, calculates, or reckons. Thus, the abacus, the adding machine, and the hand-held calculator are all forms of computers. However, for our purposes we need a more precise definition of a computer. A *computer* is an electronic device capable of receiving input, storing instructions for solving problems, and generating output with high speed and accuracy (Fig. 2.1).

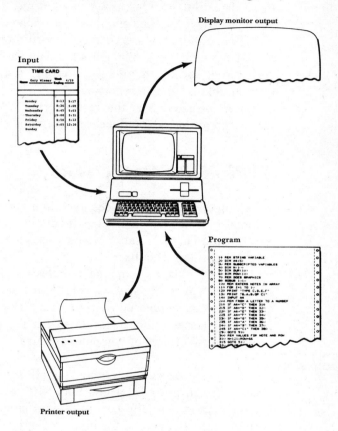

Fig. 2.1—Computer Systems Follow a Program

Computers are composed of switches, wires, and printed circuit boards, transistors, or integrated circuits. They may include display monitors, keyboards, printers, magnetic tape and disk drives, and other devices. These components, described later in greater detail, are wired together into a unit called a computing system, better known as a computer.

The ability of computers to manipulate data gives them their power. *Data* are items of information valuable to an individual or an organization. They are factual material, such as measurements or statistics, used as a basis for discussion, decision making, and calculation. Data are compiled to form reports, letters, figures, records, or documents.

In a narrower sense data consist of numbers or letters that may be manipulated, processed, or reordered by computers to increase their value or utility. Technically, data are the factual material processed by the computer, and information is the knowledge derived from the manipulation of these data. But popular usage has blurred this distinction. Many people today use the terms data and information interchangeably.

Thus, *data processing* is the restructuring, manipulating, or reordering of data by computers to increase the data's usefulness. Processing includes classifying, sorting, merging, recording, retrieving, calculating, transmitting, summarizing, and reporting.

Word processing is the restructuring or reordering by computers of words and phrases to produce reports or documents.

TYPES OF COMPUTERS

Computer systems are designed in a variety of sizes and prices. Small computer systems with limited input/output capacity may cost less than $100, while large, versatile systems with a variety of input/output devices can cost millions of dollars.

Figure 2.2 shows some general classes of computers, and how systems have been reduced in size. Generally, the smaller systems, such as microcomputers, are purchased outright. Larger systems, on the other hand, are frequently leased rather than purchased. The systems described below represent general classes of computer systems.

Microcomputers

Microcomputers are systems that are small enough to sit on a desktop. They range in price from less than $100 to several thousands of dollars. Microcomputers usually have a limited number of input/output devices—perhaps only a keyboard for input, a floppy disk or hard drive for storage, and a display monitor. Computers in this category are suitable for home and business use.

Workstations and RISC

A group of high performance microcomputers have come into use that serve as *workstations* for performing graphics and other applications. Workstations are high-speed microcomputers designed to be used by one person to accomplish tasks that require many complex computations or color visual imaging. These workstations are based upon systems with a special design called *reduced instruction set computers (RISC)*. These high-powered computers are able to process millions of instructions per second because of their specialized internal design. This extra speed makes these systems particularly suited for engineering, scientific, and software development users.

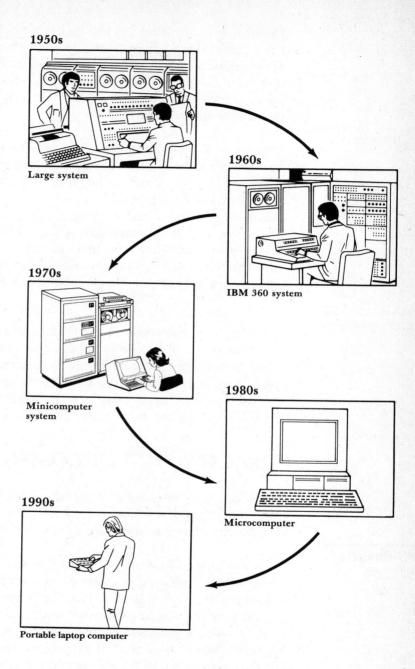

1950s

Large system

1960s

IBM 360 system

1970s

Minicomputer
system

1980s

Microcomputer

1990s

Portable laptop computer

Fig. 2.2—Changes in Computer Size

Minicomputers

The next larger machine is classified as a minicomputer. A *minicomputer* is a general-purpose computing device, either mounted on a rack or placed on a desktop. Minicomputers cost from under $10,000 to well over $50,000, fully equipped. They do not require special air conditioning to keep their components cool nor do they need a protected environment. Often several users share one minicomputer.

Mainframes

A typical *mainframe computer system* usually includes several printers, optical character scanners, display monitors, disk and tape storage devices, and a large main memory section, and it may require special air conditioning and highly skilled operators.

Mainframe computers are used by retailing firms, factories, government agencies, and schools and universities. They may serve hundreds of users at one time. Common applications include order processing, payroll, inventory, and billing activities. Mainframes are often linked with other computers to provide computing power in a large network of machines.

Supercomputers

Even larger computers, manufactured by Control Data Corporation, Cray, and others, are in a category called *supercomputers*. These machines cost millions of dollars and provide enormous computing power. They can process billions of instructions per second and simultaneously serve thousands of users. Such systems are used by large business firms, universities, government agencies, and the military.

CHARACTERISTICS OF COMPUTERS

Computers possess qualities that make them highly suitable for processing information. Let's look at some of these characteristics to better understand why these machines have gained such importance.

Self-direction

A computer is *self-directing* (that is, it is able to direct its own activities) because it can follow a program. A *program* is a series of instructions or statements recorded in a form that can be processed by a computer. These instructions direct the computer through a series of steps that are designed to solve a problem. Programs may be written by professionals, called *programmers*, or by users of the computer who have a specific problem to solve. Programmers lay out each step and enter the instructions into the computer.

Once the program is in the computer, the machine carries out each step in sequence, performing actions and making comparisons or calculations. Human intervention is not needed during the program run. After a successful program has been written and tested, the computer can process different sets of data with the same program.

High speed

The modern computer can execute tens of thousands of instructions in only a fraction of a second. A program containing a sequence of millions of instructions can be processed in a second on a fast computer.

Computers can be compared on the basis of their speed. One means is to compare the number of instructions each machine can process per second. Computers are rated in *millions of instructions per second* or *MIPS*.

Another means of comparing computers is based upon their internal electronic speed. Modern computers are rated in *nanoseconds*. One nanosecond (ns) is equal to one-billionth of a second. Earlier computers processed thousands of data items in microseconds. One *microsecond* (μs) is equal to one-millionth of a second. The machines that used punched cards processed information in *milliseconds*. One millisecond (ms) is equal to one-thousandth of a second.

The high speed of a computer becomes obvious when it is compared to manual methods of processing data. Manual methods, using the human hand or eye, are measured in seconds. Obviously, machines which can move data in billionths of a second are vastly superior when high speed is important.

High accuracy

Modern computers are devices with few moving parts. They contain *solid state* electronic equipment manufactured on chips of silicon without filaments that are prone to burn out. They have built-in error checking systems to detect malfunctions. A computer can add millions of figures without error. No other device yet invented possesses this high degree of accuracy.

Of course, the accuracy of the results can be no higher than the accuracy of the information supplied and the accuracy of the processing instructions. The common saying *Garbage In-Garbage Out (GIGO)* expresses the fact that the quality of the result can be no better than the quality of the information input. Many errors blamed on the computer are really caused by incorrect data entered by a human operator.

Reliability

Electronic computers are highly reliable. Since they involve almost no moving parts, computers do not have mechanical failures nearly as often as other machines. They can function year in and year out with long periods between failures or breakdowns. However, mechanical devices, such as disk or tape drives or printers, may malfunction, causing the failure of the entire system. A computer system is no more reliable than its weakest component.

Low cost per unit of data processed

Because computers move data in the form of electronic pulses, they are able to handle vast amounts of information at an extremely low cost.

Although large computers are expensive to install, once they are in operation the cost to process a given unit of data is very low.

HARDWARE COMPONENTS

Hardware comprises the physical devices, machines, and equipment for handling data. Hardware includes keyboards, disk drives, printers, and other machines. The computer receives data through a keyboard or other input device. It processes information in its central processing unit (CPU) where it performs mathematical calculations and makes logical decisions. When it exceeds its internal storage capacity, it may call on external storage devices for help. The computer is self-directing to the extent that it can follow a set of instructions, process data, and output or store results without human intervention.

The computer is made up of several subsystems. Each subsystem is a functioning system in its own right, and each functions as part of the larger system (Fig. 2.3). The major subsystems that make up a computer are:

> *Input*
> *Central processing unit (CPU)*
> *Secondary storage*
> *Output*
> *Internal bus*

The related input and output devices, such as optical character readers, video monitors, or printers, are called *peripheral devices*. The exact function of these devices is explained more fully in later chapters. Peripherals are any input or output devices associated with a computer but not part of the central processing unit. The abbreviation *I/O* is often used to refer collectively to input and output devices.

Input system

The *input system* of a computer reads data (in the form of printed characters on a page, bar codes, or magnetized areas on magnetic tapes or disks) and converts them into electronic pulses. It then transmits these pulses through wires to the central processing unit.

A computer may use one or several input devices, each handling a different form of input. The most common devices are:

KEYBOARD

Keystrokes on a keyboard cause electronic pulses to be sent to the central processing unit.

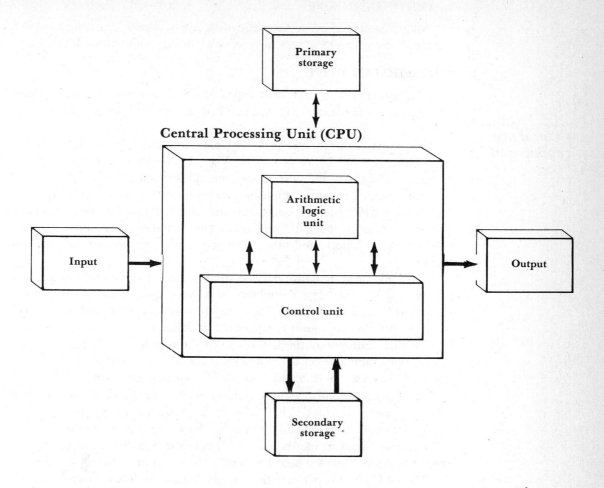

Fig. 2.3—Computer System Components

LASER BEAM SCANNER

Bar codes or symbols are scanned and translated into electronic pulses.

OPTICAL CHARACTER READER (OCR) AND MARK-SENSE READER

Handwritten, typewritten, or printed character forms or penciled-in bubbles on a page are scanned and translated into electronic pulses.

MAGNETIC INK CHARACTER READER (MICR)

Magnetically coded characters on a page are scanned and translated into electronic pulses.

MAGNETIC DISK DRIVE

Magnetized bits on a magnetic disk are scanned and translated into electronic pulses. (These may also serve as storage and output devices.)

MAGNETIC TAPE DRIVE

Magnetized bits on magnetic tape are scanned and translated into electronic pulses. (These too may also serve as storage and output devices.)

Central processing unit

The most complex and powerful part of the computer is the *central processing unit (CPU)*, or processor. The CPU is the heart of the computer system. It integrates and coordinates overall operation. Although the number and types of input or output devices may differ among computers, all must have a CPU. In microcomputers the CPU is housed in the system unit. This box includes the CPU and other components. Keyboards, magnetic tape devices, printers, and other system components are wired to the system unit.

The CPU or system unit may be small enough to be carried or as tall as a person. CPUs in large computers may have control panels with many lights, buttons, and switches. They may also have a keyboard for entering instructions and a monitor to display information.

On microcomputers the CPU is a Very Large-Scale Integrated (VLSI) circuit chip mounted on a main board, called a motherboard, with other chips. This chip set is located inside the system box. These chips may include memory control circuits which enable the CPU to communicate with peripheral devices. The circuitry is designed to move, store, and manipulate data electronically, but it has no moving parts. Only electronic pulses move about inside the CPU. All controls and directions to the CPU are made through the keyboard, and no CPU lights or switches are present.

The CPU circuits perform three major functions. They control the overall operation of the computer and coordinate its parts, perform arithmetic calculations and make logical decisions, and store the programs and data being processed.

Software in the CPU's *control unit* monitors the printer, tape drives, and other peripherals and provides a system for storing and remembering the instructions in programs. It opens and closes the circuits that feed data to and from storage.

Another section of the CPU, called the *arithmetic and logic unit (ALU)*, performs mathematical calculations, compares numerical values, compares nonnumerical values (such as letters), and makes logical decisions. For example, the computer can be instructed to branch to one of three operations, depending on whether a value being tested is greater than, equal to, or less than another value.

Primary memory, sometimes called primary storage, is another element of the computer. Modern computers use semiconductors and integrated circuits to provide primary memory.

Primary memory is a reusable, fast storage medium, directly accessible by the control unit. Each storage cell is capable of storing one bit of data. A *bit*, short for binary digit, is the smallest unit of information that can be held in memory. Bits are used in *binary notation*, a numbering system which relies upon two digits, 0 and 1, to represent two states. The binary system differs from decimal notation, which relies upon the digits 0 through 9. Binary notation is particularly suited to computers, since it can represent a switch that is on or off, a transistor that is conducting, or a bit of information stored on a magnetically coated surface.

Bits of binary data are generally stored in groups called bytes. A *byte* is a group of bits (pulses) that form a character—a digit, letter, or symbol. Typically, a byte consists of eight bits.

Primary memory capacity varies from one computer to another, ranging from a few thousand to over one billion bytes. Storage capacity is one of the measures used to compare computer systems. The letter K (derived from the prefix kilo, meaning one thousand) is used to represent 2 to the tenth power or 1,024 units.

The student should be alert to the various forms that are used in the industry to refer to one thousand bytes. The letter K may stand for 1,024, as in 4K bytes to express 4,096 bytes. Kilobytes may be abbreviated to KB instead of K, as in 4KB; but it is never written 4KB bytes. Further, a megabyte is one million bytes (or one thousand kilobytes, or 1,000 x 1,024 bytes). Megabyte is abbreviated to M or MB (4M bytes, 4M, or 4MB).

Secondary storage system

The CPU uses its *secondary storage* system to store data that exceed its primary storage capacity. Secondary storage allows billions of numbers or characters to be stored until needed.

Data can be fed to and from primary storage in only a few billionths of a second, but it takes several thousandths of a second to retrieve a piece of data from secondary storage. Therefore, secondary storage is used for large files of data where selected data need not be accessed continually, such as files of accounts receivable, accounts payable, inventory, and payroll records.

Most computer systems use a combination of primary and secondary storage media. The two most common forms of secondary storage currently in use are magnetic disk and magnetic tape.

MAGNETIC DISK

A *magnetic disk* is a metal or plastic disk, similar to a phonograph record without grooves, that is coated with a ferromagnetic material. Data are recorded on the disk for storage. They can be read out many times and will remain on the disk until they are erased. Disks can be reused, erased, and written upon repeatedly.

There are several forms of disk storage. On large computer systems a *rigid disk* system, generally referred to as a hard disk system, is most common. Similar smaller sized disk storage systems are used on microcomputers.

On microcomputers *floppy disk* storage systems are prevalent. A floppy disk, sometimes called a *diskette*, is a thin, flexible, plastic disk housed in an envelope or rigid plastic sleeve. These inexpensive disks hold hundreds of thousands or millions of bytes of data which can be accessed at random. An added feature of the floppy disk is that it can be easily filed, stored, or mailed, thereby greatly increasing its convenience and usefulness.

MAGNETIC TAPE

Magnetic tape is a plastic ribbon, similar to the tape used on home tape recorders, that is coated with ferromagnetic material. It is wound on reels of varying length or mounted in plastic cartridges or cassettes. Data are placed on tape by magnetizing small areas of the coating. These areas represent bits of data. It is a process similar to recording information on a home tape recorder except that data are encoded.

Output system

The computer's *output system* reports the results of processing by the CPU. Output is an essential step and unless it is provided, processing has little value. Reporting and outputting may be done on a variety of devices, such as a printer, video monitor, or voice synthesizing unit. The most common types of computer output are listed below.

DISPLAY MONITOR

Electronic pulses from the CPU are converted into a graphic display on a screen via a cathode ray tube. Drawings, illustrations, graphs, and tables can be displayed in black and white or color.

PRINTER

Electronic pulses from the CPU are converted into readable characters on a printed page. Printers output large volumes of data such as multipage reports.

PLOTTER

Electronic pulses from the CPU are converted into graphic designs, plots, or line drawings on a sheet of paper.

AUDIO SYNTHESIZER

Electronic pulses from the CPU are converted into sound. The devices are equipped with electrical circuits and amplifiers that can synthesize the human voice, musical tones, or other audible sounds.

MAGNETIC DISK DRIVE

Electronic pulses from the CPU are stored as magnetized areas on a magnetic disk. The information on the disk may be stored and retrieved as necessary.

MAGNETIC TAPE DRIVE

Electronic pulses from the CPU are recorded as magnetized areas on magnetic tape. The information may be stored and retrieved as necessary.

Remote terminals

A *remote computer terminal* allows the user to gain access to a computer from a site different from that of the computer. Data are transmitted from the terminal to the computer, and the results of processing return through the terminal. Long-range communications links, such as telephone or telegraph wires or microwave transmission, tie the terminal to the central computer.

Remote terminals make it practical to process data that would be slow and expensive to send by other means. For example, remote terminals are used by large and small retailers to handle accounting, bookkeeping, and credit, by insurance companies to process claims, and by hospitals to process patients' records.

Internal bus system

The *internal bus system* is an integral part of all computers. It is comprised of the wires and circuits that tie all the input, output, and storage devices into a functioning whole. The internal bus system is much like the human nervous system. It provides pathways over which signals, data, and instructions can be moved. The internal bus system can also be linked to several computers and remote terminals to form a network.

Internal wiring integrates the computer's local devices. More elaborate and sophisticated circuits, involving telephone lines, satellite links, or microwave transmission systems, enable data to be moved between computers and to and from remote terminals located thousands of miles apart.

SOFTWARE COMPONENTS

Software includes the programs—codes, sets of instructions, languages, and commands—that enable a computer to perform its functions. As computers evolved, it soon became apparent that software was as important as hardware in producing results from a system. Because of the large number of computers now in use, thousands of programs have been and are being written. Many software companies are currently in the business of developing and selling applications programs and software for large and small computers. In addition, users exchange programs and information through computer user groups.

User interface

An important area of software development has been the *user interface*. The user interface is the means by which a user interacts or communicates with the computer software. Some user-friendly interfaces are designed for the novice user. These involve simple commands or visual images that enable the inexperienced user to direct the computer, with little or no training. Interfaces for expert users are designed to make the full power of the computer available to professionals and experienced operators.

All computer programs can be divided into two categories: applications software and system software. Applications software performs such duties as keeping track of payments, computing customer balances, or generating letters and memos. System software is designed to manage the resources of the computer, to enable programs to be copied from one device to another, or to keep a log of jobs handled by the computer. These two types of software are described below.

Applications software

Applications programs are designed to meet a variety of needs. They are written by computer manufacturers or software companies for a general purpose or by users to solve a specific, or local, problem. Examples of applications programs include programs to prepare payrolls, perform accounting or financial functions, compute business ratios or profits, manage personnel files, or keep track of inventory. Businesses buy computers so that they can run an applications program to solve a problem, perform a task, or carry out a function that might otherwise be performed by a human operator.

Applications programs are often sold as packages. These include (1) instructions entered on a disk and ready for use in the computer and (2) program *documentation*, that is, instructions for users, flowcharts, sample input data, output specifications, program listings, and other written material that describe and explain the program. Some of the most popular applications packages are graphics, word processing, communications, database management systems (DBMS), and spreadsheet analysis.

System software

A second category of software, called *system software*, is an essential part of computer operations. System programs do not solve end user problems. Instead, they manage the resources of the computer, automate its operations, and facilitate programming and testing. Most applications programs run under the control or direction of a system program.

System software is generally provided by the computer manufacturer or a firm specializing in system programs, rather than written by the user. The writing of system software requires a great deal of technical knowledge of specific hardware details. These specialized programs may take thousands of hours to write and cost hundreds of thousands of dollars to develop.

Once finished, a piece of system software may be used by many computer owners. It enables them to run applications programs that in turn solve local problems.

WHAT THE COMPUTER CAN DO

Computers are able to store, structure, and manipulate vast files of information and can compute results of complicated scientific problems. Some of the most important uses of the computer involve *database management systems (DBMS)*. Database management systems, discussed in more detail in a later chapter, allow government agencies, businesses, and other institutions to quickly and easily maintain and manage files containing millions of records. Database software enables users to alphabetize, sort, sequence, or update thousands of records in only a few seconds.

The telephone, the telegraph, satellite relay stations, microwave circuits, and other forms of *data communications* are important parts of computers and information processing. Through data communications, one computer can exchange data with another thousands of miles away; it can send and receive data to and from hundreds of terminals located at distant points. Data communications enables large files of information to be accessed by many users over great distances and allows conferences to be conducted over communications circuits. We will study computer networks and data communications in more detail in a later chapter.

Computers can scan hundreds of records in a minute or less. They can store millions of names, addresses, telephone numbers, or other information and keep it ready for immediate retrieval. Computers can solve all sorts of mathematical problems, ranging from the simple addition of a column of numbers to working out complex equations involving thousands of steps. Computers print out digital information, such as numbers, or text material, such as words or phrases. They can also draw pictures and plot curves or graphs. High-level activities such as these are actually accomplished in the computer with elementary mathematics, simple logic, and basic comparisons. Complicated programs are built up using these elementary tools.

Computers are not able to reason or think in the same sense as human beings do. Computers cannot set long-range goals or exhibit creativity and imagination. They are not capable of emotion and feelings, though their printouts may reflect the feelings and emotions of their human programmers.

HOW COMPUTERS MEET BUSINESS NEEDS

Computers were originally developed for scientific and mathematical applications and are still widely used in these disciplines. Because of the specialized nature of early computers, they were impractical for business use. However, the introduction of low-cost models and the development of more versatile programming languages have greatly increased their practical value to the ordinary business. Computers owe much of their success to their ability to meet many of the demands placed on businesses operating in a highly competitive marketplace.

Time factor

To be of the greatest value to an enterprise, data must be available at specific times in the business cycle. The success or failure of many businesses depends on this time factor. For example, credit data delivered after a transaction is completed is of little use to the sales manager who has already extended credit to a customer who turns out to be a bad risk.

The pace of modern business often requires the almost instantaneous processing of large volumes of data. Important decisions may have to be made on short notice. A big sale may hinge on a salesperson having current inventory or the price of goods at his or her fingertips. Because the computer is capable of immediate record processing, such up-to-the-minute information is available.

Cost factor

The realization of cost savings has led many firms to shift their information processing to computers. In the past sales could be written up and orders filled, with the bills and records of the transactions all prepared by hand. However, manual methods are now too expensive for most firms. The computer provides an inexpensive means of processing transactions.

Accuracy factor

Large investments in equipment, inventory, and other assets and the need to manipulate large sums of money require accurate information processing. In business decisions that involve millions of dollars a mistake in one calculation can be disastrous. Computers are a valuable business tool because of their high accuracy and low rate of error. Banks, for example, can post hundreds of thousands of deposits and withdrawals to customer accounts and make all figures balance at the end of the day because of the computer's accuracy.

Better control of data

Many organizations have experienced increases in the number of transactions that must be processed. Without the computer it would be virtually impossible for stock exchanges to process the millions of buy and sell orders placed each week. Consider the dilemma the Internal Revenue Service and the Social Security Administration would face if they had to handle the staggering number of tax returns, checks, and reports without computers.

Business people need precise control of the volumes of information processed. The computer can restructure a list of data in many different forms. For example, it can print out a list of the previous day's sales in chronological order. It can then reorganize the list by type of merchandise sold, by salesperson or by department. This added flexibility gives the business manager more information and more control.

Better utilization of resources

Business firms have millions of dollars invested in buildings, equipment, inventory, and personnel. The computer enables managers to control and allocate their resources much more efficiently.

Improved service

Computers help businesses provide individualized attention and better service to customers. For example, a department store with 25,000 accounts can process sales, returns, payments, and other charges and have the information immediately available at sales counters and credit offices.

Mechanization

It is said that machines should work and people should think. Many business people believe that human resources should be applied to those tasks for which humans are uniquely qualified. Routine transactions and calculations should be done by machines, thus freeing people for more creative activities. Electronic information processing makes such a division of labor more attainable.

Computers are indispensible in outer space exploration, manufacturing, weather forecasting, economic modeling, scientific research, the production of motion pictures, radio and TV broadcasting, and many other areas of endeavor.

In this chapter we have mentioned a few of the applications for which computers are used. We have also introduced you to a few unfamiliar terms. As you read on you will discover many more interesting applications for the computer. You will also learn many more terms that make up the rich vocabulary of computers and information processing. Becoming familiar with these new terms will be an asset in communicating with others.

A computer is an electronic device composed of switches, wires, integrated circuits, and other parts capable of input, storage, the ability to follow a set of instructions called a program, and output. Microcomputers are small systems that may fit on a desktop and are suitable for home or business use. Minicomputers may be rack mounted machines and are larger than microcomputers. Mainframe computers are large systems with many printers, monitors, and input/output devices. Supercomputers are even larger machines with enormous computing power.

A computer is self-directing because it can follow a series of instructions, containing the steps for the solution of a problem, without human intervention. The major characteristics of computers are high speed, high accuracy, reliability, and the ability to process large volumes of data at low cost. The speed of modern computers is measured in millions of instructions per second (MIPS). Computers move data about in nanoseconds (ns). A nanosecond is one-billionth of a second. A bit is the smallest unit of information that can be held in memory. A group of bits is called a byte and represents one character.

Input systems send data to the computer. The central processing unit (CPU) manipulates data and contains the arithmetic and logic unit (ALU) and the control unit. It also accesses primary memory. Secondary storage is provided by magnetic disk and magnetic tape. Printers, video monitors, and other devices provide output for the system.

Data are items of knowledge of value to an individual or business. Information is the result of processing data. Data processing is the restructuring, manipulation, or reordering of data to increase its usefulness and value. The major manipulations include classifying, sorting, merging, recording, retrieving, calculating, transmitting, summarizing, and reporting. Word processing is the manipulation of words and phrases to generate letters, memos, and reports. Applications programs are designed to solve a variety of local problems. System software manages the resources of the computer and controls its operations. Computers are used in many aspects of business including sales, marketing, accounting, inventory control, word processing, and personnel management. They are also used in banking and credit, in the manufacture of goods, and for modeling and planning business systems and products.

Selected Readings

McKeown, Patrick G. *Living With Computers*, Harcourt Brace Jovanovich (1993). Chapter 2.

Mandell, Steven L. *Computers and Information Processing*, West Publishing Company (1992). Chapter 4.

O'Brien, James A. *The Nature of Computers*, Dryden Press (1993). Chapter 7.

REVIEW QUESTIONS

True or False Questions

1. The term computer refers to an electronic device which can be programmed.
2. The term self-directing means that a machine does not require a program.
3. The terms word processing and data processing are synonymous.
4. Computer speeds are rated in MIPS.
5. A bit is a group of bytes.
6. A computer program is a set of instructions in machine-readable form.
7. The time factor is of little importance in information processing.
8. Most businesses have little use for devices that process data or use microcomputers.
9. Applications software is the same as system software.
10. A mainframe is a major type of computer.
11. Most computers do not use secondary storage.
12. The user interface is a means of communicating with software.
13. Microcomputers are not able to meet business needs.
14. GIGO means Gigabytes In-Gigabytes Out.
15. The function of the computer's input system is to print out reports.

Completion Questions

1. A set of instructions that tells a computer how to perform a task such as balancing a checkbook is known as a _____.
2. Reports are printed out on the computer's _____ system.
3. A(n) _____ monitor shows images on the screen of a cathode ray tube.
4. A(n) _____ program is designed to solve a local problem.
5. To be of value, data must be available at specific times in the business _____.

ANSWER KEY

True or False Questions

1. T
2. F
3. F
4. T
5. F
6. T
7. F
8. F
9. F
10. T
11. F
12. T
13. F
14. F
15. F

Completion Questions

1. program
2. output
3. display
4. applications
5. cycle

3

Brief History of Computers

Some inventions, such as the light bulb, sewing machine, and telephone, can be attributed to the genius of one person. But the modern electronic computer did not spring from the mind of a Thomas Edison or Alexander Graham Bell. It is the result of countless inventions, ideas, and developments made by many men and women. In this chapter, you will learn about the ideas, events, and inventions that led to the computer as we know it today.

To successfully and meaningfully process information, three elements must be present: hardware, software, and personnel. A computer has no value without people and programs to direct its efforts. Once programmed, however, the computer becomes self-directing, able to follow instructions without further human intervention.

HARDWARE AND SOFTWARE

Computer *hardware* consists of the physical equipment, that is, the machines and devices, used in information processing. Laser printers, computers, and display monitors are examples of hardware. Computer *software* includes the programs, computer languages, and sets of instructions used in information processing. A computer program giving the steps to be taken in preparing and printing out payroll checks is an example of software. The language used to communicate with the computer and a diagram of the flow of information in a program are also software.

Computing requires knowledgeable *personnel*. Modern computer installations employ hundreds of people as operators, programmers, librarians, systems analysts, and maintenance personnel.

Early efforts to develop computers focused on hardware. But people soon realized that computers and other equipment could not be used effectively without adequate software. Early software was crude and limited. The first computer languages were difficult to learn and to use, and no systems were available to schedule jobs efficiently for the computer. The machines had to be made more versatile, efficient, and compatible with the skills of their human operators.

New methods of instructing the computer and new programs to expand its range of applications were developed. Much of the growth and change in computers in the last two decades has been in software and programming. At the same time it has become widely recognized that a skilled staff of trained computer personnel is just as important to an organization as its investments in hardware or software.

New information processing inventions are finding their way into industry more and more rapidly. One could safely say that as many new ideas and techniques have been introduced in the last two decades as in the entire preceding history of computers.

Information processing methods and technology have evolved through three major eras from primitive manual methods to modern electronic computers (Fig. 3.1). The manual era began when people first started counting. The second major era started at the end of the nineteenth century when unit record processing became widely used. The invention of the computer in the 1940s ushered in the electronic data processing era.

THE MANUAL ERA

Throughout history human beings have used their creative powers to invent and develop devices and systems to help them in their tasks. The manipulation and recording of data are no exception. Manual data processing, although still in use because of its simplicity and convenience, has largely been replaced by automated methods.

Human fingers were the first counting aids used to process data. Methods such as piling rocks or gathering sticks were used to help in figuring larger quantities. Mathematical systems advanced with written notation and the invention of Roman numerals. In A.D. 512, Arab mathematicians took a giant leap forward with the introduction of Arabic numerals, the concept of zero, and the development of long division, logarithms, square roots, and trigonometric functions. In 1340, the Italians contributed double entry bookkeeping, still used today. Principles of higher mathematics were the "software concepts" that enabled humans to perform complex computations and to solve difficult problems.

FIFTH GENERATION

1990   Laptop, notebook computers,
desktop publishing,
user-friendly software packages

1980   Microcomputers, personal computers,
artificial intelligence, robotics,
local area networks (LANs)

1970   FOURTH GENERATION
Monolithic circuits, large scale integrated
circuits, Pascal language

1960   THIRD GENERATION
Multiprogramming, teleprocessing, OCR, MICR, BASIC
language, minicomputer, audio response unit

1950   SECOND GENERATION
Magnetic tape and disk, transistor,
FORTRAN language

FIRST GENERATION
ENIAC, stored program, EDVAC, EDSAC, punched-card
processing

1900   Monroe calculator
Hollerith code
Key-driven multipliers
Felt's comptometer

Babbage's Analytic Engine and Difference Engine
1800   Jacquard punched-card loom

1700

Leibnitz's calculator
Pascal's numerical wheel calculator
1600   Slide rule (analog computer)

1500

1400

Double-entry bookkeeping system

1300
PAST   Abacus
Decimal system
Finger counting

(Left margin labels, top to bottom: ELECTRONIC INFORMATION PROCESSING ERA; UNIT RECORD ERA; MANUAL ERA)

Fig. 3.1—Information Processing History

Early hardware

The *abacus* was one of the first mechanical devices developed to perform mathematical tasks. Although its origin is uncertain, the abacus was used by many civilized peoples including the early Chinese and Romans. It is still common today in some parts of the world.

The abacus consists of a frame with beads strung along parallel rods. The beads are moved to represent quantities. Addition and subtraction and other arithmetic operations are performed by manipulating the beads. Similarly, the Romans moved pebbles, called *calculi*, in slots to perform computations.

In 1617, John Napier, a Scottish mathematician, invented a device later called *Napier's bones*. Napier's bones are rods engraved with numbers. By rotating the rods, the user can perform multiplication, division, and square root problems.

The *slide rule* is an early example of an analog computer. Analog systems process data on a continuum rather than by using discrete letters or numbers. The slide rule appeared in several forms during the seventeenth century. Gunter's scale, approximately two feet long and used to perform multiplication, was one form of the slide rule.

In 1642 the French philosopher Blaise Pascal successfully built a *numerical wheel calculator*. This device performed calculations by means of wheels and cogs indexed to represent different quantities.

In 1671 the German mathematician Gottfried Leibnitz completed a machine that could add, subtract, multiply, and divide. The Leibnitz *calculator* operated by means of notched wheels and ratchets, features still found in some mechanical desk calculators.

Nineteenth-century hardware

The next step in the evolution of computers was the development of a device completely unrelated to early calculators and slide rules. In France in 1801, Joseph Marie Jacquard perfected an automatic system for weaving patterns into fabric. He used cards with punched holes to guide the warp threads on his loom. The holes in the card controlled the pattern that was woven into the fabric. The *Jacquard card* was the forerunner of the punched cards used in unit record systems. Instead of the holes representing patterns or stitches, the holes in punched cards represent data. A hole represented the digit 1 and the absence of a hole the digit 0.

About ten years later in England, Charles Babbage, a visionary mathematician, began work on a mechanical calculator that would perform extremely complex arithmetic functions and calculations. Babbage spent part of his life and fortune attempting to build his *Difference Engine*. Later, he abandoned this machine in favor of a more complicated one called the *Analytic Engine*, which would perform arithmetic functions on data read in from punched cards. Neither device was ever completed. The technology of the day was too limited. However, a prototype was built many years after Babbage's death which proved the validity of the device.

Charles Babbage earned his place in the history of information processing as the man who attempted to construct the first complex computer long before the theory of electricity was understood. Babbage was far ahead of his time in envisioning a stored program. The hundreds of drawings and plans he left served as an inspiration and education to the inventors and mathematicians who came after him.

Although a century would go by before such a complex computer would finally be built, many small steps toward the goal were taken during the next few decades. The era of industrialization and mechanization had begun. American inventors were actively pioneering new machines and devices. Nineteenth-century inventors successfully developed machines that performed some of the operations Babbage had conceived for his Analytic Engine.

In 1872 Frank Stephen Baldwin built a calculator that performed all four basic mathematical functions. This marked the beginning of the calculating industry in the United States. In 1887 Dorr E. Felt patented a *comptometer*. This machine opened the way for adding multidigit numbers mechanically.

No discussion of computers would be complete without a mention of George Boole. Boole pioneered a two-state form of algebra, using 1s and 0s, which became known as Boolean algebra. Boole's concepts laid the foundation for the computer logic and programming that followed generations later.

THE UNIT RECORD ERA

In the 1880s Herman Hollerith, an employee of the U.S. Census Bureau, successfully combined the concepts of Jacquard's cards with data recording and manipulation. He devised a coding system in which holes punched in cards could represent numbers and letters. Hollerith's system was designed to handle the large increase in data processed by the bureau. This method is called the *unit record system*. Each punched card, according to Hollerith, should contain information on only one household and could not contain collective data, hence the term unit record.

The unit record system was used to process the 1890 census, and the job was done in one-fourth the time it took to do the 1880 census. Calculating machines manipulated cards containing data and eliminated tedious manual tallying. The Hollerith coding system became the standard data representation method for the unit record system and for the modern computer.

Hollerith left the Census Bureau to manufacture and sell his data processing machine. The company he founded merged with two others to become the International Business Machines Corporation, or IBM, which later became a leader in the production of electronic data processing machines.

The capability of the calculating machine was expanded in 1892 when W. S. Burroughs developed a 90-key model that could process up to nine decimal digits and again in 1914 when Jay R. Monroe and F. S. Baldwin designed and built the Monroe calculator.

About 1908 James Powers, a statistical engineer at the Census Bureau, developed a series of unit record machines that used holes punched into cards. These machines were used to process the 1910 census. Powers left the Census Bureau and in 1911 founded his own company to manufacture unit record machines. The Powers Accounting Machine Company merged with other companies to become part of the Sperry Rand Corporation, which went on to produce and sell the UNIVAC computer.

The *wiring board*, consisting of a wiring panel with terminals and groups of jumper wires, was used to program unit record machines. To program the system, the operator physically connected the appropriate terminals with the computers to form electrical paths that directed the machine to carry out various functions. Errors in programming were hard to locate with this method, and programs were not easily transferred from one machine to another.

From 1930 to the 1960s the punched card and electrical accounting machines were the major means of processing data for large firms. Today they have been largely replaced by computerized systems.

THE ELECTRONIC INFORMATION PROCESSING ERA

The first true digital computer was conceived by John Vincent Atanasoff, working at Iowa State College with Clifford Berry, a graduate assistant. In 1939, they constructed a device called the *Atanasoff-Berry computer*, or just *ABC*. It used vacuum tubes and was capable of internally storing a set of instructions.

For many years the Princeton mathematician John von Neumann was given credit for developing the concept of the first stored program computer, which was built in 1946. But after years of litigation, in 1974 the courts recognized that it was actually Atanasoff and Berry who came up with the first true *internally stored program* computer, making the machine self-directing and setting it apart from others.

Internal program storage, discussed later in this chapter, eliminated the physical wiring of instructions in the computer. New programs could be input quickly to replace old ones, without the tedious task of rewiring. This improvement greatly increased the machine's general-purpose capabilities.

In 1944 Howard G. Aiken, a physicist at Harvard University, perfected the *Automatic Sequence Control Calculator, Mark I.* The Mark I was an electromechanical calculator composed of numerous telephone relays and rotating mechanical wheels. Punched paper tape and punched cards were used to provide data input. Although Aiken had the assistance of IBM in his venture, this machine is not considered a true computer because it lacked the ability to internally store a set of instructions.

Shortly after the Mark I was introduced, two electrical engineers were working to solve ballistics problems for the Army. In the process John W. Mauchly and J. Presper Eckert of the University of Pennsylvania, along with their colleague Leslie Groves, developed a prototype device called the *ENIAC*, or *Electrical Numerical Integrator and Calculator*. It differed from Aiken's device in that it used 18,000 vacuum tubes instead of telephone relays and therefore operated much more rapidly than the Mark I. The ENIAC was fully electronic and had no moving parts.

The early computers were limited because they were programmed by an external set of instructions, usually a wiring board. A device was needed that would store a set of instructions internally, thereby greatly increasing its flexibility.

The stored program

The ENIAC became obsolete when the internally stored program—a concept basic to all modern computers—was developed. John von Neumann, who had developed a computer for the Institute for Advanced Studies at Princeton, joined Eckert, Mauchly, and others in designing a machine, the *Electronic Discrete Variable Automatic Computer (EDVAC)*, that would accept and store a set of instructions (a program). While the EDVAC was being constructed, another device, the *Electronic Delay Storage Automatic Calculator (EDSAC)*, was completed at Cambridge University in England in 1949. EDSAC was a practical machine that operated according to an internally stored program.

These machines took advantage of the fact that information could be stored electronically in a system of vacuum tubes and relays. Early programmers were able to write data into electronic storage (which came to be known as the machine's primary memory system) and replace it with new information as needed. Electronic memory quickly became much more efficient than unit record storage.

One method of storing information is with binary numbers. The binary number system makes use of only two digits, 0 and 1, each called a bit (short for binary digit). Any number in the decimal system may be represented as a binary number. For example, 8 is 1000 when converted to the binary system. If a closed electrical relay is thought of as representing a 1 and an open relay a 0, then one closed relay followed by three open ones represents the binary number 1000 or the decimal number 8. Since many electronic components have only two possible states (open/closed, conducting/nonconducting, on/off), binary numbers are most efficient for storage of numerical data in electronic memory. Various conventions have been devised for representing letters of the alphabet and other symbols as patterns of 1s and 0s.

Von Neumann's internally stored program concept, with instructions read into the machine on punched cards, replaced the inconvenient wiring board. These instructions directed the machine to carry out a sequence of steps. The internally stored program gives the computer much of its power. Its advantages are:

1. The computer can be reprogrammed by entering instructions from another set of records, instead of rewiring or using different wiring boards.

2. The program may be written and tested before the actual data are available.

3. The program makes the machine self-directing; a human operator does not have to guide each step.

Mauchly and Eckert were also involved in designing and building the *Universal Automatic Computer (UNIVAC I)*. The company they formed eventually became the UNIVAC division of the Sperry Rand Corporation. The UNIVAC I was the first American computer to be sold commercially. It was also one of the first machines to use magnetic tape as a means of data input and output. The UNIVAC received national attention in November 1952 when data it processed predicted Eisenhower's victory over Stevenson in the presidential election.

First generation computers

Computer development is sometimes classified in generations, or major periods of development. The first generation of computers operated with vacuum tubes and relays and could store a program internally. These computers received their input data through paper tape or cards. The machines were large and often unreliable because the many vacuum tubes overheated and burned out. First generation machines date from the late 1940s. They proliferated in the mid-1950s, until the introduction of the transistor made them obsolete.

First generation software

The development of the stored program meant a major change in the way computers could be directed to perform tasks. Instructions in a program could now be read into memory locations and stored inside the machine. At first storage was accomplished by a system of relays and switches. Later, magnetic core storage systems were developed which used ferrite rings that could be magnetized to store data.

First generation computer programming was done in *machine language*. Machine language is the only language a computer can directly understand. The instructions are coded in the form of 0s and 1s to represent the two-state characteristic of the electronic components involved: off or on, low or high, right or left. For example, 1011 may mean to add, while 0101 might mean to move data. Programming in machine language is time consuming and tedious. At the time, each brand of computer had its own machine language, and thus the exchange of programs between computers was greatly limited.

The need for more efficient software led to the development of *assembler language*. In assembler language, instructions are given to the computer in symbols or abbreviations called *mnemonics*. These mnemonics, such as ADD, OR, and PACK, are translated into 1s and 0s and tell the machine to perform certain functions.

Assembler language is specific to a particular machine. It is much easier than machine language for the programmer to use because it involves words or word-like symbols rather than 0s and 1s. Because computers operate in machine language, assembler language has to be translated by a special program stored in the machine. This program converts the mnemonics into machine language. Most modern computers can still be programmed in assembler language, if desired.

Second generation computers

The invention of the *transistor* in 1948 led to the development of smaller, more dependable second generation computers. These computers not only had greater speed and storage capacity than first generation machines, but they were more compact and cost less. Data were input by paper and magnetic tapes or, most often, by punched cards. By the late 1950s and early 1960s these machines were widely used.

At the same time, faster, more efficient, and larger-capacity means of data input, output, and storage were developed. *Magnetic disk storage* was introduced, giving the computer vastly improved storage characteristics.

Second generation software

In the second generation *problem-oriented languages (POLS)* were developed. These languages stressed problem-solving features, were more like ordinary language than the symbolic assembler language, and eliminated many of the programming details required in machine and assembler languages. Program languages that more closely resemble spoken language are called *high-level languages*.

Instructions written in these problem-oriented languages still have to be translated into machine language before the computer can execute them. This is done by a *compiler*. A compiler converts programming instructions into machine-executable form. A different compiler was developed to translate each problem-oriented language into machine language and each machine needed to have its own specific compiler. Still, this method was more efficient than machine or assembler language.

FORTRAN (FORmula TRANslating system), developed by John Backus, was one of the first problem-oriented languages. It became one of the major languages and still remains important for mathematics and science applications. Other languages created in this period were ALGOL, LISP, and COBOL.

Special programs, called *operating systems*, were written to replace the human element in scheduling work. Operating systems start programs, stop them when they do not run properly, and deal with error conditions and interruptions efficiently without stopping the computer. Virtually all modern computers are equipped with operating system software.

Third generation computers

The development of *microelectronics* led to the appearance of third generation computers in the mid-1960s. Third generation computers were characterized by further reductions in size, lower cost, and improved methods of storing data. These machines used the Integrated Circuit (IC), a microelectronic device in which hundreds of components are integrated onto a single small "*chip*."

The minicomputer was a major development in the third generation. The minicomputer appeared during the 1960s and its use spread in the early 1970s. Minicomputers are desktop or rack-mounted computers possessing some but not all the features of large machines, at a much lower cost. They are often used for small business and office applications and sometimes as part of a larger computer system. Today, minicomputers are being widely replaced by microcomputers.

Third generation software

Third generation computers required new languages and better means of scheduling work. Early computer programs were set up and run one at a time, while an operator stood by to handle errors and problems. If an error appeared, the computer had to be stopped. This procedure was satisfactory as long as only a few programs had to be run. But as the volume of work increased, the need for a better method to schedule loads became imperative.

COBOL (Common Business Oriented Language), another POL developed during the second generation of computers, became widely used during the third generation. Because COBOL uses terms from everyday business English, it brought programming within the reach of business people. It has become one of the major languages for large business computer systems.

Other languages developed or widely used during the third generation were *RPG (Report Program Generator)* and *PL/I (Programming Language I)*. These languages, together with COBOL, are designed to run programs that handle data fed to the computer in batches and are referred to as *batch programming languages*.

In the 1960s new ways were being found to use the computer. Improvements in operating systems further expanded the computer's utility by allowing *multiprogramming*. Several programs could be processed at the same time by sharing the computer's available resources. Many computer terminals could be connected to one computer so that many programmers and devices could use the system at the same time. This concurrent use of one machine by several people or devices is called *time sharing*.

As the computer became more available through time sharing, programmers began to want to interact directly with the computer rather than having to wait for their job to be run in a batch. As a result, operating systems were improved to allow *interactive programming*. This led to the invention of languages suited to interactive programming. The most popular interactive languages developed during the third generation were *BASIC (Beginners All-Purpose Symbolic Instruction Code)* and *APL (A Programming Language)*.

Fourth generation computers

Fourth generation machines appeared in the 1970s and utilized still newer electronic technology that made them even smaller and faster than computers of the third generation. Many new types of terminals and means of computer access were also developed in the 1970s.

One of the major inventions that led to the fourth generation was the *Large-Scale Integrated circuit (LSI)*. The LSI is a small chip, measuring perhaps only 1/8 inch square and containing thousands of small electronic components that function as a complete system. In effect, an entire computer can be manufactured on a single chip no larger than a fifty-cent piece. One chip may perform the functions of an entire computer, calculator, or control device.

Another advance was the *Very Large-Scale Integrated circuit (VLSI)*. VLSIs contain thousands or millions of electrical components and hundreds of complex functioning circuits which formerly would have required dozens of LSI chips.

This new microelectronic technology led to the introduction of the modern *microcomputer* and revolutionized the computer industry. The technology made it possible to manufacture smaller computers that ran with greater speed, reliability, and capacity for lower cost. At first, hobby computer kits came on the market using microprocessor chips like the Intel 8080. A *microprocessor* is a complete computer central processing unit (CPU) manufactured on a single chip of silicon. These chips were used in such machines as the Altair, a home computer kit. The Apple I was developed by Steven Wozniack and Steven Jobs in 1977. The Apple I was built around the Mostek 6502 microprocessor.

Tandy Corporation began selling the popular TRS-80 microcomputer, which was followed by other systems, including the Atari and the

Commodore. When IBM introduced its personal computer, the PC, in 1981, the microcomputer market took off. Soon other companies began producing desktop personal computers following the open architecture design, using Intel, Mostek, and other chips. The open architecture concept, used by Apple Computers, IBM, and others, relied upon readily available off-the-shelf components.

These new computers spawned a need for more improved storage and output systems. During this period the *floppy disk* storage system came into widespread use. It allowed hundreds of thousands of characters to be stored on a small plastic disk weighing only a few ounces. Faster, more efficient output devices, such as laser printers and color screen displays, entered the market. *Color graphic computers* and *audio synthesizing machines* came into use.

In 1984, Apple Computers introduced the Macintosh. This user-friendly machine included a mouse, a hand-held pointing device used for input. The Macintosh gained immediate acceptance and became widely used because of its excellent, consistent graphical user interface, which incorporated the mouse. The 1980s saw improved models of the Macintosh enter the market, as well as new IBM PCs, including the IBM AT and PS/2. The PS/2's internal design departed from IBM's earlier PCs, primarily in its use of IBM's new microchannel architecture.

Fourth generation software

A major language to gain popularity during the fourth generation was *Pascal*, developed by Niklaus Wirth of Zurich. It was named for the French mathematician and philosopher Blaise Pascal. This language was designed to make *structured programming* easier. Structured programming, discussed later, is an improved, more orderly means of designing and writing programs. Among the benefits of Pascal and structured programming techniques is greatly simplified programming error detection.

In addition to the intrinsic merits of its orderliness, Pascal became popular because of its compact compiler, allowing the language to be used on the small and microcomputers, which by this time were proliferating rapidly. Although not widely used in business, Pascal is used in education and is well known by computer science students.

During this time, new operating systems were developed, some specifically for microcomputer applications. One such operating system, *MS-DOS (Microsoft—Disk Operating System)*, and a similar version developed by IBM, *PC-DOS (Personal Computer—Disk Operating System)*, became the standard for IBM PCs and compatibles (computers based on the same design and chips).

Windows, an operating environment that runs on DOS, was developed by Microsoft Corporation. This graphic interface for the PC uses a mouse and *icons*, small pictures used as symbols on the screen, to direct the computer. This system was similar to the graphic interface Apple had earlier developed for its Macintosh computers. IBM later introduced OS/2, an operating system specifically aimed at its new line of desktop machines, the PS/2.

American Telephone and Telegraph continued to develop an operating system called UNIX, an operating system with special telecommunications characteristics, used on many PCs and minicomputers.

The late 1980s and early 1990s saw a proliferation of user-friendly software packages. These include such spreadsheet programs as Lotus 1-2-3 and SuperCalc5, database managers such as dBase III and IV, and word processing programs such as WordStar, WordPerfect, and Microsoft Word. These packages greatly expanded the capability of the desktop computer, providing electronic spreadsheet, database, and word processing capability while easing the burden on the computer user.

The last several years have seen the introduction and growth of the desktop publishing market, with such programs as Aldus PageMaker and Ventura Publisher. These applications programs enable newsletters, reports, and other typeset documents to be designed on a desktop computer and printed using a laser printer.

The next page is yet to be written on computer hardware and software. We are entering the fifth generation. Research is being conducted now on vastly improved memory systems that will allow millions of characters to be stored in a cube a fraction of an inch square. Computers that mimic human intelligence are being developed. These *artificial intelligence (AI)* machines will operate and reason much as human beings do without the structure required on earlier computers. Robots driven by "expert" computers will begin to act and think more like people. The field of *robotics* will come into its own. New computer network and communications programs and systems are being designed to link large and small computers into integrated national networks.

New technology has allowed powerful computers with hard disk storage drives to be manufactured in the form of lightweight laptop computers. Even smaller notebook computers, little larger than a textbook and easily carried, are entering the marketplace in large numbers. Computers now on the drawing boards promise even greater breakthroughs in smaller size, higher speed, and lower cost.

The machines, devices, mechanisms, and other physical equipment used to process data, such as printers, computers, and display monitors, are hardware. The programs, computer languages, procedures and sets of instructions used to process data, are software. The language used to communicate with the computer and the diagram of the flow of information in a program are also software.

Information processing has evolved through three major eras. The manual era relied upon human calculation and problem solving aided by simple devices. Hardware of the manual era included the abacus, Napier's bones, slide rules, and mechanical calculators. Babbage's Difference Engine and Analytic Engine were the first plans for a complex computer but they were never constructed.

The unit record era relied upon punched cards. The unit record machine was designed by Herman Hollerith in the 1880s. It was based upon concepts used in the Jacquard loom and became the principal means of processing data from the 1930s through the 1960s.

The electronic information processing era relies on the computer. The first electronic computer was designed and built by Atanasoff and Berry. Later machines were designed by Mauchly and Eckert. Early machines included the EDVAC, EDSAC, and UNIVAC. These machines relied upon the stored program to hold data and instructions.

First generation computers were constructed from vacuum tubes and relays and were programmed in machine language or assembler language. A compiler, a program stored in the machine, translated instructions into machine language. Second generation computers were constructed using transistors and were smaller and more reliable. They were programmed in problem-oriented languages (POL) such as FORTRAN. They utilized magnetic tape and disk storage. Third generation computers were constructed from integrated circuits (ICs). Minicomputers were developed at the end of this era. COBOL, a POL, came into widespread use. Improved operating systems allowed time sharing and interactive programming. BASIC and APL are popular interactive programming languages. Fourth generation computers are based on large-scale integrated circuits (LSIs) which allowed the introduction of microcomputers, including the Macintosh and the IBM Personal Computer. During this period color graphics, audio synthesizers, structured programming, and new operating systems came into use. The late 1980s saw a proliferation of user-friendly software packages.

Research is now under way on improved memory systems, artificial intelligence, robotics, and data communications.

Selected Readings

Floyd, Nancy A. *Essentials of Information Processing*, Irwin (1991). Chapter 1.

Kidder, Tracy. *The Soul of a New Machine*, Avon Books (1981).

Mandell, Steven L. *Computers and Information Processing*, West Publishing Company (1992). Chapter 2.

Manes, Stephen. *Gates*, Doubleday (1993).

Slotnick, Daniel L. *Computers and Applications*, D. C. Heath (1990). Chapter 2.

REVIEW QUESTIONS

True or False Questions

1. Hardware includes the software that directs the computer.
2. No major developments in information processing techniques took place before 1900.
3. A stored program has the advantages of allowing the computer to direct itself.
4. A major development in the first generation of hardware was the floppy disk.
5. A major development in the second generation of hardware was the punched card machine.
6. A major development in the third generation of hardware was the IC.
7. Major developments in the fourth generation of hardware were the LSI and VLSI.
8. No major changes in software took place between the first and third generation of computers.
9. Microcomputers are used in most unit record machines.
10. Machine language does not differ from assembler language.
11. Problem-oriented languages offer no advantages.
12. Desktop computers are used for home and business applications.
13. High speed was a characteristic of the manual era of data processing.
14. A seventeenth century data processing innovation was the Felt comptometer.
15. The Census Bureau first used unit record machines.

Completion Questions

1. Pascal and Leibnitz made contributions to data processing in the _____ century.
2. Contributions were made by _____ to data processing in the nineteenth century.
3. Transistors, resistors, and integrated circuits are _____ which are used in the manufacturing of computers.
4. A computer language is a piece of _____.
5. _____ programming techniques were designed to make programming easier.

ANSWER KEY

True or False Questions

1. F
2. F
3. T
4. F
5. F
6. T
7. T
8. F
9. F

10. F
11. F
12. T
13. F
14. F
15. T

Completion Questions

1. eighteenth
2. Jacquard/Babbage/Felt/Boole
3. components
4. software
5. structured

4

Input/Output Systems

In this chapter you will learn about data input and output devices. All data, whether quantities or numbers, names, or codes, must be converted into a form the computer can read before they can be processed. These data may originate from many sources. Payroll records, inventory reports, time cards, price tags, sales slips, shipping memos, and telephone order forms all create data which must be conveyed to the computer.

There have been many innovations in recent years in methods of collecting and entering data into the computer system. These new methods automate data input and reduce or eliminate the need for human operators.

In this chapter we also look at the variety of media used by the computer as output. This includes the display of characters or graphics on a display monitor, printed reports and graphics, and sounds or spoken words. There is a great similarity between input and output machines, and computer users sometimes refer to these devices collectively as I/O devices. Since input is the first step, we will look at it first.

DATA INPUT FUNDAMENTALS

A *source document* is created at the time of a transaction. It is the original recording of the data. A source document may be a time card filled out by an employee, a list of parts prepared by an inventory clerk, or an order taken over the phone by a salesperson. Sales, returns of goods, deliveries, shipments, goods on order, checks received, bills paid, or other transactions may generate source documents.

Regardless of the form of the source document, if the information it contains is to be processed by a computer, that information must be readable by the computer. A source document printed in machine-readable type is suitable for direct input to the computer. A casually handwritten time card, containing smudges and erasures, would probably only be readable by people and must be converted into machine-readable data by keyboarding before it could be processed by the computer.

INPUT MODES

The two primary means of data input are transaction-oriented processing and batch processing. These two modes are described below.

Transaction-oriented processing

In *transaction-oriented processing* the computer receives information from a terminal at the time a transaction takes place. There is no delay between the time the information is entered and its processing by the computer. This method is sometimes called *real time processing*.

Information can be entered from automated devices that read bar codes or scan optical or magnetic characters on a tag or card. It may also be entered by a human operator who keyboards the data.

One advantage of transaction-oriented processing is the speed with which data can be entered or retrieved. A clerk at an airline ticket counter may enter a request for a customer's seating preference or for a change in a ticket by keying data into a terminal. The computer will acknowledge the request immediately and process the information accordingly. A second advantage is the elimination of the need for an intermediate storage step, such as recording data onto disks.

Batch processing

In *batch processing*, data generated by a transaction are recorded on magnetic tape, floppy disks, or other media. At some time after the data have been recorded, the computer processes them. Batch processing is sometimes referred to as *off-line processing*, since the information is gathered away from the computer.

Batch processing was widely used before transaction-oriented processing systems were introduced. It is still used when information does not have to be acted on immediately or when stored data do not have to be kept up-to-date with every transaction. For example, a bank might record transactions at a branch throughout the day. The information is then relayed to a central point and processed at night when there is less load on the computer. Bank checking accounts are usually processed in a batch. The checks are processed as they are received at the bank, but then they are collected in a file and mailed to account holders in a batch with a statement at the end of the month.

DATA INPUT REQUIREMENTS

Whether transaction-oriented (real time) or batch (off-line) methods are used, three major factors, accuracy, cost, and speed, are usually considered in judging the usefulness of a data input system.

Accuracy

The data input method must accurately reflect the details of the transaction and report information without error. Some methods, such as bar code scanners and magnetic ink readers, are very accurate; they may read millions of pieces of information without an error. Other methods, such as keyboarding, involve human operators who can make mistakes. The operator must read and interpret handwritten or printed characters and then type the correct characters.

To reduce the chance of error, various accuracy checks are used, such as hash totals, check digits, and redundancy checks. These systems use mathematical routines to check data accuracy or provide duplicate information to ensure correctness of data.

Cost

Cost is a major factor in data input. Automated input methods are designed to read bar codes and specially coded tags or to scan source documents such as checks without human operators. Such automation reduces labor costs.

Speed

The amount of time required to input information into a computer is another important factor. In batch processing data is entered over a period of time and processing is delayed. Where immediate return of results is necessary, transaction-oriented systems are generally used. When a jumbo jet is sitting at a passenger gate, the ticket agent must be able to determine immediately how many seats are available. The delays inherent in a batch system would not serve the needs of the airline's ticketing process.

ON-LINE DATA INPUT DEVICES

A variety of *on-line* data input processing methods have been developed. On-line devices are wired directly to the computer and support transaction-oriented processing. Input devices for remote mainframes include dumb terminals and smart terminals; input devices for all types include voice recognition devices, Touch-Tone (R) input, mice, and digitizers.

Dumb terminals

Some computer terminals relay data directly to the computer and have no processing capability of their own. These devices are called *dumb terminals* because they are unable to manipulate or process data. They rely upon a remote computer for formatting, error checking, and data storage. Dumb terminals serve only to collect data and forward them to the computer for processing.

Smart terminals

When inexpensive microprocessors were introduced, it became practical to construct terminals with their own built-in computers. These were called *intelligent* or *smart terminals*. Smart terminals can process data locally, reformat information, and check logic or accuracy before forwarding the information to the computer.

Smart terminals simplify data input because they can cue the operator by asking for information. Some have diskette storage devices attached. This enables the terminal to keep a record of data sent to the main computer. In the event of a loss of information at the main computer, the smart terminal can reconstruct the information.

Voice recognition devices

Voice recognition devices are capable of deciphering commands given by a human voice and converting them into pulses that are sent to the computer for processing or for display in digital form. This ability to interpret voice patterns eliminates the need for more direct data input methods such as keyboarding.

Voice recognition devices convert analog waveforms of human speech to digital form. The end point of each word is determined by silence and pauses. A computer then compares the resulting pattern to patterns of words stored in the machine. If a match is found, the word is displayed on a display monitor or printed on a page. If a match cannot be found, the computer prompts the speaker to repeat the word or to use a synonym.

Several different forms of voice recognition equipment are now on the market. The simplest is a machine that is programmed for a particular speaker and can recognize only that speaker's voice pattern using pitch and volume. Such a system is called *speaker-dependent*. A *speaker-independent* system is able to interpret the speech of many different people.

Voice recognition machines can decipher only a limited vocabulary of isolated words or short phrases. The ideal voice recognition equipment would be able to interpret continuous speech and be independent of the speaker. However, to date no device has been built that can handle strings of sounds without pauses to identify words, words that sound alike, and the wide range of human voices. Researchers are investigating methods of recognizing series of words spoken in different tones, inflections, accents, and dialects to make communication between people and machines easier.

Touch-Tone terminals

The widespread use of the Touch-Tone telephone has led to the development of *Touch-Tone terminals*. Touch-Tone terminals are devices that emit sounds that are picked up by a telephone transmitter and sent over the line. Sound transmission eliminates the need for connecting wires between the telephone and the terminal.

Using a Touch-Tone input system, for example, a field salesperson may dial his or her office computer and then enter order information through a portable Touch-Tone terminal. As keys representing letters or numbers are pressed, the Touch-Tone terminal emits audible tones. There is no physical connection between the Touch-Tone terminal and the telephone line. In effect, every telephone becomes a point at which data can be entered.

Mice, digitizers, and other devices

Another means of direct input is a device called a *mouse*. The mouse is moved about on a tabletop to direct a pointer on the screen. The mouse has a ball mounted in it which can rotate. When the mouse is moved, optical sensors in the device detect the rotating motion of the ball and direct the pointer to various figures, or *icons*, displayed on the screen. For example, the operator may wish to select a color from a list of colors displayed on the screen. The user moves the mouse to direct the pointer on the screen to a color on the list and then presses a button on the mouse to make the selection. This eliminates the need for a keyboard and typing skills.

Input can also be accomplished through the use of *digitizers*. The digitizer consists of a digitizing pad or tablet, a paper or preprinted form to be used on the pad, and a conventional ball-point pen or other pointing device. The operator draws pictures or traces lines on the form which is placed on the digitizer pad. As lines are drawn, the pad generates x-y coordinates describing the lines and sends the coordinates to the computer. The information is processed and the lines are displayed on a screen or printer. No keyboarding is involved.

A variety of other devices are used to input data. A *joystick* enables data to be input by hand movements and does not require typing skills. These devices position a pointer on the screen. They can also be used to detect operator responses. Many popular video games use joysticks or paddles along with the display monitor. A *trackball* is a round ball that is rotated by the fingers and used to input x-y coordinates to the computer.

The *light pen display console* is another form of input. A unique feature called a light pen is used to change or replace data displayed on the screen. When touched to the screen, a light beam from the pen modifies the data as desired. Data remain on display until replaced by new output from the computer or until the unit is turned off. No hard copy is generated. Similarly, *touch-sensitive screens* detect the touch of a human finger or other object.

SOURCE DATA INPUT

Source data input, sometimes referred to as *point-of-sale (POS) input*, is the gathering of information at the time a transaction takes place. This type of input is widely used in retailing and banking. The most common source data input systems are bar code scanning, optical scanning, and magnetic ink recognition.

Point-of-sale (POS) terminals

Point-of-sale (POS) terminals convert data entered from a sales clerk's keyboard into electronic pulses that are sent to a computer for processing. They are commonplace in retail stores and provide a convenient means of preparing invoices and receipts, updating inventory files, and checking credit at the time a sale is made.

Each terminal is provided with keys for entering information, such as a product code or price. The computer locates the product code in an information file (often stored on magnetic disk or tape) and processes the sale. It may adjust the inventory to reflect the purchase, post the sale to the customer's account or record the payment, and print out a receipt at the terminal showing the items purchased, price, and sales tax.

Laser beam scanners

Laser scanning is a fast, accurate method of reading data from a product label for point-of-sale processing. The *laser beam scanner* uses a beam of coherent light to read bar codes or symbols on a product or package. Coherent light beams do not spread as ordinary light beams do. Instead they form a tightly focused, narrow ribbon of light. Items are moved across the fixed scanner beam or scanned by a hand-held wand to input data to a computer.

Laser beam scanners are used in supermarkets for checking out goods. Most canned goods and articles sold in drugstores and supermarkets now carry the *Universal Product Code (UPC)* (Fig. 4.1). Soft goods, such as vegetables or bulk goods, cannot be labeled with bar codes. For such items, the clerk inputs the data from a keyboard associated with the scanner.

Fig. 4.1—Universal Product Code (UPC)

Optical sense readers

Optical sense readers are devices that are capable of interpreting pen or pencil marks, bars, or filled-in areas from cards, tags, or packages. They do not decipher printed letters or numbers. The marks are converted into an electronic pulse that is sent to the computer for processing.

Optical sense cards are used to record test scores, prices, order numbers, or stock inventory directly in the field. These source documents are then read by the optical sense reader directly. A card or other optical sense form and an ordinary pencil or pen become a convenient source of data input. However, accuracy does depend on the marks being made properly. Marks that are not solid or heavy enough may be misread.

Optical character readers

Optical character recognition (OCR) machines read data optically and convert them to electronic pulses. *Optical character readers* are designed to read certain handwritten, typewritten, or printed numbers, letters, and special characters from orders, cash register tapes, adding machine tapes, utility bills, telephone bills, tickets, and similar source documents. They can be programmed to read selected areas on a bill or order form. For example, they can read a price column, a total, a printed form number, or a hand-printed message.

Scanners are frequently connected to desktop computers. With appropriate character recognition software, these machines are able to read typewritten or printed pages and convert them to text files that can be manipulated by word processing programs. Systems such as these are beginning to be used by law firms, publishers, and other businesses who need to convert many printed or typewritten documents to files that can be edited and revised once they are on the computer.

In the field, OCR provides a convenient means of recording data without keyboarding. A salesperson, secretary, or stock clerk can write each character in a separate block on specially printed forms while observing a few simple rules for letter shaping.

Magnetic ink character readers

Magnetic ink character recognition (MICR) devices read data printed in ink containing particles of magnetic material. The most common magnetically inscribed documents in use today are checks, deposit slips, and bills. Specially shaped characters are printed on the documents in magnetic ink. Data can also be encoded magnetically on strips, such as on credit or debit cards.

MICR readers include a document hopper, a read station, and a stacker. Hundreds of documents can be read and sorted in one minute. The machine can read documents of different sizes and thicknesses, such as might occur in a collection of checks from many different banks. As the documents move through the MICR device, they are scanned for the special ink images. The magnetic images on the page affect a magnetic field in the machine, which sends electronic pulses to the computer for processing.

DATA OUTPUT

When you go to the supermarket, you must give the clerk something, either a check, a credit card, or cash, that is in a physical form suitable for use in the ordinary business world. Similarly, data output by the computer is of little value unless it is in a form comprehensible and usable by people.

All data output devices perform the same basic function: they convert the electrical pulses processed by the computer into a usable form. Early computers used a modified electric typewriter as their sole form of output. These devices could output a couple of lines a minute. Modern laser printers can output over 20,000 lines a minute. In addition, modern computers can output spoken words, or characters and images on a screen.

The major categories of computer output media include printers, plotters, and display monitors. *Hard copy* output devices such as printers and plotters generate a permanent paper copy or printout of the data that may be read by humans and may be filed, duplicated, mailed, or otherwise processed manually. Examples include printed reports and forms. Generally, hard copy output devices operate more slowly than other devices. Because they require paper and other supplies, they are more expensive to run.

By contrast, display monitors can output large volumes of data quickly and at a low cost, but because there is no hard copy, their usefulness for certain applications is limited. Computer systems often include a combination of hard copy and other devices that can be switched in and out as the work in process requires.

CHARACTER OUTPUT SEQUENCE

There are several techniques for creating output in the form of character images. Characters are output in two modes: serial and parallel. In *serial output*, characters are struck one at a time. For example, a line of 100 characters would be printed character by character, usually from left to right. The ordinary typewriter follows this principle. Generally, the serial mode is not used for high-volume computer output. Because it is economical from a machine design standpoint, it is often used for low-cost or low-volume output systems.

In *parallel output*, all characters on a line are struck at the same instant. The type wheel printer uses this principle. To produce a line 100 characters wide, the output device turns 100 type wheels across the page so that the desired character is in position to be printed. At a signal 100 hammers strike the page at the same instant. Naturally, parallel printing is much faster than serial printing.

Impact printers

The *impact printer* uses a principle similar to a typewriter. A type element forms the images by striking a ribbon which imprints on a sheet of paper. In this system, each character is in relief. A set of numbers and characters (called a font) is molded on each type element. To print a character, the element is indexed to the proper position, that is, moved to bring the proper character into position, and struck against the ribbon onto the page. Type element printers can produce up to fifty characters per second—too slow for high-volume computer output. The advantages of the type element are that type sizes and styles can be changed by substituting elements, and the print quality produced by these devices is better.

Several kinds of printers use this principle. The *daisy wheel* printer uses a daisy wheel which consists of a set of spokes arranged in a flat, circular pattern around a central core, similar to the arrangement of the petals of a daisy. Each spoke contains a different character. The wheel rotates to bring the desired spoke into position to be struck by a hammer so that the character is imprinted on the page. Daisy wheel printers produce high-quality images at speeds up to fifty characters per second.

A slightly different design that works on the same principle is the *thimble* printer. The thimble is constructed of molded plastic curved spokes, each with a different character on it. As the thimble rotates, a hammer strikes an individual spoke against a sheet of paper. Thimble printers are used on personal computers because of the high quality images they produce and their economical design.

Printed characters can also be generated with a *dot matrix* printer. A group of wires or rods is arranged in a one by seven or other matrix pattern. Each rod prints a dot when struck. Characters are formed by patterns of dots (Fig. 4.2). To print the digit 4, for example, the rods that form the image of the number are struck from behind and forced against the paper. A ribbon inserted between the rods and the page provides the ink.

Fig. 4.2—Dot Matrix Image

Sometimes several passes of the print head may be needed to create near letter-quality images. The greater the number of pins in the matrix, the better the print quality. A twenty-four-pin dot matrix printer is capable of producing a better quality image than a nine-pin printer.

Dot matrix printers are less expensive than other impact machines and are fast, capable of outputting several hundred characters per second. These machines are programmable, allowing different sizes of characters or foreign language characters to be generated. Some can create multicolor output, including graphics and illustrations.

A faster means of output is the *drum printer*. The drum is a metal cylinder around which characters are cast. It contains as many bands of letters around its perimeter as there are print positions. Each band contains all the characters in the font. The drum printer is equipped with a ribbon transport mechanism and an impact hammer. As the drum rotates, the hammer moves down the length of the drum, striking the appropriate letters to form the line of printed characters. Drum printers are faster than daisy wheel or dot matrix printers. However, the type faces cannot be changed easily because the drum is permanently mounted in the machine.

High-speed output is possible with a *band printer*. Type letterforms are stamped on a steel band that is mounted around two moving pulleys. The pulleys move each letterform into printing position. A ribbon is placed between the page and the band. To print a character, a hammer behind the paper forces the sheet up against the moving type band. When the sheet is brought into contact with the moving band, a letter image is transferred to the paper. Band printers can produce up to 3,000 lines per minute. The bands may be changed to provide different typefaces.

Thermal printers

The *thermal printer* produces characters by using heat and heat-sensitive paper. Character forms are generated by heating selected rods in a matrix with an electronic heating element. When the ends of the selected rods touch the heat-sensitive paper, the image is generated. Although only a limited number of papers are available (and are more expensive for this printer) the printer is very quiet, making it suitable for use where noise is undesirable.

Ink jet printers

Ink jet printers are becoming widely used because they can output black and white or color images quickly and inexpensively. Many different types of ink jet printers are manufactured. These can output lines of text through to full-color graphic images, including drawings, figures, and illustrations. The simplest ink jet printer, sometimes known as a drop-on-demand device, contains a print head that has a group of ink jets formed into a matrix. A piezoelectric crystal is used to energize the system. When the crystal receives a pulse, it vibrates, causing a small droplet of ink to leave the jet and squirt onto the page. The letter is formed by a combination of ink jets simultaneously squirting the pattern of the letter onto the page. Different colors of ink may be used, and in combination they can create a variety of additional colors. The ink sets quickly upon touching the page.

More sophisticated ink jet printers form the image from a continuous stream of ink droplets sprayed across a page (Fig. 4.3). The ink droplets, which have been charged, move between another set of plates which deflect the stream as it moves across the page. These devices are capable of

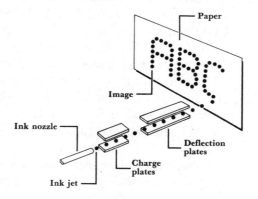

Fig. 4.3—Ink Jet Printer

forming images on many different materials, such as paper, plastic, and fabric. Up to 200 characters per second are produced from a stream of more than 100,000 droplets per second.

Laser printers

One of the fastest printers is the *laser printer*. These machines can produce up to 20,000 lines per minute. They are capable of outputting lines of text as well as drawings and figures. These devices operate on a principle similar to a Xerox copying machine. A laser beam sweeps back and forth across the length of a drum. The beam is switched on and off as it sweeps across the drum. The drum, which has been electrostatically charged, responds to the moving light beam, causing areas of the drum to lose their charge. The drum then rotates past a brush, which transfers a toner to selected areas of the drum. Much like an ordinary office copier, the toner, now forming an image, is transferred to a sheet of plain paper. Finally, the paper passes under fuser rollers which permanently set the image.

These printers can combine computer output with a predesigned form and produce both enlarged and reduced images. Working with collating, punching, and binding machines, laser printers can turn computer-generated information into finished booklets or manuals.

Computer output microfilm (COM)

Computer output microfilm (COM) units transfer output data from the computer to microfilm media. A magnifying viewer is used to display the images. Common forms are microfilm, microfiche, and aperture cards. *Microfilm* is a strip of film containing extremely small photographic images. *Microfiche* is a single piece of film, four by six inches, holding dozens of images. The *aperture card* is a punched card upon which a microfilm image is mounted in a window cut into the card. COM has several advantages over paper output. It requires substantially less storage space, it is easy to mail, and data can be retrieved easily.

COM output machines print nearly 14,000 lines of data per minute. A one-inch stack of microfiche records may contain the same amount of data as 25,000 pages of computer printout. COM costs approximately one-tenth as much as line printer output and is generated approximately ten times as fast. However, COM requires microfilm readers in order for people to be able to read the small images. The microfilming process also calls for film processing equipment and supplies.

Plotter output

Plotters convert data sent from the computer into graphic shapes, such as lines, curves, drawings, charts, and diagrams. The plotter is equipped with a movable pen and carriage mechanism and a chart paper holder. The carriage, holding one or more pens, moves across the page. In a *drum plotter* the paper is mounted on a drum that rotates to move the paper at the same time the carriage is moving. In a *flatbed plotter* the paper is held in a stationary position and only the carriage moves.

Digital information received from the computer causes the drum to rotate or the pen to move. These movements create a line representing the output data. Precise charts, lines, and drawings can be prepared because the CPU provides exact horizontal (x) and vertical (y) coordinates to direct the position of the pen.

Drum printers can produce plotter charts of just about any length. Flatbed plotters are limited to the size of sheet that can be conveniently positioned under the carriage mechanism.

The plotter is used to plot many different kinds of business and scientific data, such as stock market curves, utility price curves, and analog waveforms and to construct figures, symbols, pie charts, and bar graphs.

Display monitors

The *cathode ray tube (CRT)* is frequently used as a display monitor. The process is similar to the process of forming images on an ordinary television screen. An electron beam is scanned back and forth across the face of a phosphor-coated tube at high speeds. The beam is modulated (turned on and off) as it swings back and forth. When the beam is on, it activates the phosphor coating on the inside of the tube, causing it to glow. The glowing spots on the tube create patterns visible from the front of the tube. Letters, numbers, tables, curves, lines, and other figures can be generated in this manner.

The *display monitor* resembles an ordinary television screen. Monochrome monitors convert electronic pulses into visual images and display them in one color on a cathode ray tube. Such devices may display several thousand characters on the screen at one time and can load a screen with characters in a fraction of a second. They are virtually silent. Formatted images, blank forms, and operator cues can be displayed. Display monitors are widely used where formatted data or an inquiry and response are to be displayed.

COLOR GRAPHICS MONITORS

The *color graphics monitor* has a screen capable of displaying a variety of lines, shapes, curves, and printed letters in full color. These monitors allow drawings, illustrations, graphs, charts, and moving images to be created from data input by the user and displayed on the screen as output. On some units the images appear to be three-dimensional or holographic. Images can be rotated as they are displayed on the screen. The user interacts with and directs the monitor from a console keyboard. Associated software routines allow the user to edit output from the keyboard by inserting, deleting, adjusting, and changing the color of displayed elements.

Color images can be displayed in two different modes: the raster pattern and the vector display. The *raster pattern* is the method used to create images on an ordinary television set. As an electron beam swings back and forth across the face of the screen, light and dark spots are created by variations in the beam's intensity. Each spot or dot that makes up an image is called a picture element or *pixel*. In the *vector display*, a continuous electron beam is directed in straight lines over the face of the screen. This lays down a pattern of lines or shapes, creating the image.

The advantage of the raster pattern is its ability to generate high-resolution color graphics. The more pixels making up the final image, the greater its detail or resolution. The principle is the same in reproducing photographs in print media in either color or black and white. If you look at a photograph in this book under a magnifying glass, you will see that it is made up of many small dots. Each dot, corresponding to a pixel, blends with the others to create a final image. Compare this photograph to a photograph in a newspaper and you will see how the number of dots per square inch affects the quality of the image.

The advantage of a vector display is speed. Images can be displayed more quickly when patterns are described as vectors rather than as collections of pixels.

Liquid crystal display (LCD)

Liquid crystal display (LCD) uses a liquid suspended in an electrical field. A voltage applied across the liquid causes a change in its optical characteristics. By applying a voltage selectively, an image, in the form of characters, can be made to appear. You are familiar with a liquid crystal display if you own a pocket calculator or digital watch. LCDs are inexpensive and rugged compared to cathode ray tubes and other forms of output, but they lack the brightness and intensity of a CRT. LCD images change slowly as the screen contents are modified, making them unsuitable for rapid display changes.

Audio synthesizer

The *audio synthesizer*, sometimes referred to as an audio response unit, converts data output by the computer into an audible signal. It can output data as spoken language, musical tones, or other audio signals. The device synthesizes the human voice or the sound of a musical instrument using an oscillator and data stored in the computer's memory system.

Audio synthesizers are particularly useful in conjunction with a Touch-Tone telephone. A caller can dial a computer from a Touch-Tone telephone and key an inquiry into the system. The computer will respond to the inquiry and then synthesize a verbal reply that is sent back over the telephone line. Audio synthesizers are especially valuable for blind people.

In this chapter we have described many different input and output methods—from scanners and OCR devices to the mouse, joystick, and digitizer. Improvements and innovations in input and output methods broaden the means by which data can be transferred to and from the computer. Perhaps in the near future you will be able to sit down before a computer and simply speak in a conversational style in order to generate a neatly typed letter or report, properly spelled, punctuated, and formatted. But until this becomes a reality, you still need not only some keyboard and typing skills, but also a knowledge of how to use the input and output devices now available.

A source document is the original record generated at the time a transaction takes place. In transaction-oriented processing, there is no delay between the entry of information and its processing. In batch processing, data are recorded on a storage medium and then processed at some time after the original transaction takes place. The major factors to be considered in evaluating data entry systems are accuracy, cost, and speed.

Dumb terminals have no built-in logic. Smart or Intelligent terminals can process data before they are transmitted to the computer because these terminals are equipped with microprocessors. Voice recognition devices are capable of deciphering commands given by the human voice and convert-

ing them into electronic pulses for processing. Touch-Tone terminals relay tones over a telephone line for processing and do not require hard wire connections. The mouse, digitizer, joystick, and touch-sensitive screen are input methods that increase the ways information can be entered into computers.

Point-of-sale (POS) input, used in retail establishments, records a transaction at the time it takes place. POS devices include point-of-sale terminals, bar code scanners, and optical scanners. Laser beam scanners use a beam of coherent light to scan bar codes or symbols from products or goods. Optical sense readers sense pencil marks or filled-in areas. Optical character recognition (OCR) devices convert letters or numbers into pulses for processing. Magnetic ink character recognition (MICR) devices convert magnetic ink characters into pulses for processing.

Hard copy output devices generate paper copies. Characters may be output in serial fashion, with one letter struck at a time, or in parallel fashion, with all characters in the line struck at the same instant. Types of non-impact printers include thermal, ink jet, and laser printers. Common types of impact printers are daisy wheel, thimble, dot matrix, type drum, and band. Computer output microfilm (COM) units include microfilm, microfiche, and aperture cards. Other output devices include plotters and audio synthesizers. Display monitors use an electron beam to scan a phosphor-coated tube to display characters. The output images of color graphics monitors are formed from a series of dots called pixels. In liquid crystal display (LCD) characters are formed by a liquid suspended in an electrical field.

Selected Readings

Capron, H. L. *Essentials of Computing*, Benjamin Cummings (1992). Chapter 4.

Hutchinson, Sarah E. *Computers*, Irwin (1992). Chapter 3.

Parker, Charles S. *Understanding Computers and Information Processing*, Dryden Press (1992). Chapter 5.

REVIEW QUESTIONS

True or False Questions

1. Lack of delay is an advantage of transaction-oriented processing over batch processing.
2. The system used for reading magnetic ink characters relies upon optical characteristics.
3. The presence of a microprocessor is the difference between dumb and smart terminals.
4. The production of permanent copies is the advantage of hard copy output.
5. Serial printing is faster than parallel printing.
6. Magnetic inking is the principle used in laser printers.

7. Reduced image size is an advantage of computer output microfilm.
8. Plotters are able to display information as charts and graphs.
9. Monochrome monitors differ from color graphics monitors in their ability to display charts and graphs.
10. Impact printers image a page by striking a letterform against the paper.
11. Raster and vector displays image the screen in the same way.
12. Audio synthesizers produce sound output.
13. A laser printer is an example of data input.
14. A source document is the same as a computer printout.
15. Voice recognition devices function on the principles of serial output.

Completion Questions

1. Hard copy output devices tend to be _____.
2. _____ terminals are often found in markets or department stores.
3. A printed letter is an example of _____ computer output.
4. Printers that output a matrix of dots are known as _____ matrix printers.
5. Department stores and banks often use _____ processing.

ANSWER KEY

True or False Questions

1. T
2. F
3. T
4. T
5. F
6. F
7. T
8. T
9. F
10. T
11. F
12. T
13. F
14. F
15. F

Completion Questions

1. slow
2. Point-of-sale
3. hard copy
4. dot
5. transaction-oriented

5

Secondary Storage

A little over five hundred years ago Gutenberg printed his first Bible. His masterpiece weighed over twenty pounds. Today the entire contents of the Bible could be stored, with room to spare, on a floppy disk weighing only a few ounces. Since business enterprises must store millions of records generated by marketing, personnel, inventory, production, distribution, and financial operations, secondary storage plays an important role in file management.

In a previous chapter we discussed the computer's primary memory capability. Primary memory is easily accessible storage from which data can be retrieved quickly, but its capacity is limited. In this chapter we will look at secondary storage and see how magnetic disk, tape, and other storage media are used to supplement the computer's primary memory.

SECONDARY STORAGE CONCEPTS

Secondary storage systems give the computer enormously expanded memory capability. Most computer systems have several different forms of secondary storage media. Information flows back and forth between the computer and the secondary storage devices. Without such systems, computers would have to rely totally upon their primary memory to store information.

The capacity to store large amounts of data in a small amount of space has increased substantially over the past several decades. A measure of storage capacity is *recording density*, or the number of bits per square inch. Three decades ago it required a magnetic surface about the size of a double bed to store a million bytes of data. Today the same amount of information can be stored on a magnetic surface the size of a postage stamp. By the year 2000, industry experts estimate that the same amount of data will fit on a surface the size of a grain of salt, representing roughly a 3000-fold increase in storage density.

ADVANTAGES AND LIMITATIONS OF SECONDARY STORAGE

Secondary storage is an efficient, cost-effective means of storing millions of characters ready for retrieval or further processing. Storing a million bytes of data in secondary storage, such as on a magnetic disk, costs substantially less than putting the same data in primary memory semiconductors.

Secondary storage is much like a giant electronic scratchpad available to the computer. Data can be written into secondary memory at the rate of millions of characters per second and later read out or erased. Because it relies upon expandable or erasable media such as a tape or a disk, the capacity is limited only by the size and number of secondary storage devices.

Secondary storage devices simplify the moving and storing of data. Thin plastic disks or reels of tape can be sent through the mail or conveniently stored in file cabinets. Information is easily exchanged with other data centers or computers by exchanging reels of tape, floppy disks, or disk packs. Backup files can be generated and stored in a safe place. Duplicate files may be distributed to many computer users simultaneously. Disks and tape may be sent where they are needed much more easily than bulky physical records, documents, checks, tax reports, and other items printed on paper.

One limitation of secondary storage is that its retrieval time is slower than that of primary memory. It takes more time for a computer to retrieve data from a rotating disk or reel of tape than from directly accessible semiconductor memory. Another limitation is that some secondary storage devices require delicate and precisely positioned moving parts. In addition, fingerprints, dust particles, or especially the presence of magnetic fields can destroy valuable data (Fig. 5.1).

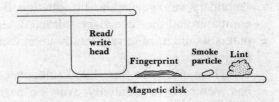

Fig. 5.1—Contamination on a Recording Surface

ACCESS TIME

The time required to locate and retrieve a given piece of data from storage is known as the *access time*. To illustrate, estimate how long it would take you to find a particular piece of information in your class notes. If your notes are with you in class and they consist of only a few pages, it will take less time than if they are at home and they fill several notebooks. Access time is a function of (1) the location of the data, (2) the amount of data to be searched, and (3) the speed of the hardware.

Primary memory is directly accessible to the CPU. Since it is limited in capacity, it usually contains fewer data than all the secondary memory in a system. Primary memory is usually solid state electronic, whereas secondary storage is electromechanical or optical in nature, usually involving slower moving parts. These factors combine to make primary memory faster than secondary storage.

Access times differ among secondary storage devices according to the medium and retrieval mechanism used. A piece of data located at the end of a reel of tape, for example, will take longer to locate than a piece at the beginning of the tape. The greater the volume of data to be searched, the longer the time necessary to retrieve the data. If the memory system requires positioning a magnetic head over a disk or track, if time elapses while the disk rotates until the information moves under the head to be read, or if a tape must be repositioned, then access will be slowed down.

ACCESS METHODS

Several different methods are used to access information from secondary storage. These include sequential access devices, direct access storage devices, and indexed file systems.

Sequential access

Devices that locate a given piece of data in a file by searching the storage medium in sequence from beginning to end are called *sequential access devices*. Magnetic tape is a commonly used form of sequential access storage. Data are stored on magnetic tape in the order in which they were recorded. They need not be in any logical order. To find a piece of data, the computer rewinds the reel of tape to the beginning and checks each item on the tape until it finds the specified data.

Direct access

Direct access storage devices (DASD) can retrieve data directly from storage without searching in sequence. The storage medium is divided into storage locations, and each location is given an address. Each piece of data is assigned to one of these addresses as it is written into storage. Given the address, the computer can locate a specific piece of data without searching through every item in the file. It can go directly to the item.

Of course, data stored on direct access devices can be accessed sequentially as well. Magnetic disk systems are common direct access devices. Understandably, direct access devices are faster than sequential access systems.

Indexed file access

Indexed file access is a combination of sequential and direct access. In this method, each record (for example, an individual's name, address, and phone number) in the file is stored sequentially. Each record has a primary key. The *primary key*, which may be a social security number, part number, or other identification, serves as a file or record locator number. Within a given sequenced block of data, specific records may be stored at random. An index at the beginning of each block is used to locate a group of records. To access a specific or target record, the computer uses the primary key or record locator number. The computer then proceeds to search sequentially for the target record, which is not stored in sequence, eliminating the need to search all records in the entire file and allowing both sequential and direct access of the same file.

To help understand the concept, suppose a group of college students is to be seated in alphabetical order in twenty-six rows. All students whose last names begin with A are seated in the front row of the class. Those whose last names begin with B are seated in the second row, and so on. Within any given row students are not necessarily seated alphabetically. In this arrangement, one might locate a specific student by directly accessing the correct row and then searching sequentially to find the specific name.

MAGNETIC TAPE STORAGE

Magnetic tape is a sequential access storage medium. One or more tape units may be connected to the CPU to give the computer access to data stored on more than one reel of magnetic tape at a time.

Tape reels

Magnetic tape is 1/2-inch-wide plastic ribbon that has been coated with a thin layer of ferromagnetic material and wound on reels. The two most common reel sizes are 10-1/2 inches in diameter, holding 2,400 feet of tape, and 8-1/2 inches, holding 1,200 feet.

Each reel of magnetic tape contains two indicator marks, the *load-point mark* and the *end-of-reel mark*, which note the beginning and end of usable recording tape on the reel. The indicators are small pieces of reflective foil bonded to the edge of the tape so that they can be sensed by photocells in the drive mechanism.

The tape reel is equipped with a special plastic ring, called the *file protection ring*. When the ring is in place on the hub of the reel, new data can be recorded or old data erased from the tape. When the ring is removed, no new data can be recorded over the existing bits of information. The removal of this ring protects against accidental destruction of important data because it requires a deliberate act by the computer operator to replace the ring. In other words, "No ring, no write."

Recording data

Data are recorded by magnetizing areas of the coating as the tape passes under a write head. The head converts electronic pulses (representing alphabetic and numeric characters) into magnetized areas on the moving tape. Data are read from the tape by a reverse procedure. The read head senses the magnetized areas on the tape, induces a current in a pickup coil, and converts the magnetic fields to electronic pulses. These pulses, representing coded data, are sent to the computer for processing. The same head may be used for both writing and reading and is often referred to as a *read/write head* (Fig. 5.2).

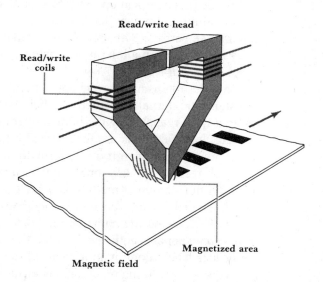

Fig. 5.2—Recording on Magnetic Tape

File organization

Files on a tape are organized into records. A tape record is a group of bytes relating to a single transaction—for example, a part name and part number. Tape records can be either fixed or variable in length. A record can be only one byte or as many as several thousand. Each record on the tape is separated by a 0.6-inch-wide space, called the *interrecord gap* (IRG).

When a computer reads a file, the tape drive comes to a stop after each record, starts again, moves to the next record, stops again, and so on. Approximately 0.6 inches of tape—the IRG—will go by during the time required for the drive to go from a stopped position to the proper speed for reading or writing.

Interrecord gaps occupy space on the tape that cannot be used for data storage. One method of avoiding this loss is to combine several records into a *block* without IRGs. Blocks are separated by an *interblock gap (IBG)*. Records within the block are separated by a *group mark* inserted during recording.

File identification

A reel of tape may contain all or part of the records for one or more files. Because of this, in any file maintenance procedure care must be taken to see that the correct files are being processed. For example, updating the wrong inventory file or posting charges to the wrong list of customers would cause serious problems. A file identification system is especially important in secondary storage systems, where data are stored in a magnetic code that a human operator cannot read to verify identification.

Labeling techniques have been developed to identify files accurately and prevent errors. The labels are similar to a book's table of contents. They contain information on the contents and location of the files stored on a reel of tape or a disk.

In order to ensure that the correct reel of tape is loaded for processing, a system of external and internal labels is used. The *external label* is written in a form readable by the human operator. It is applied to the outside of the reel. Internal labels are magnetized bits of information recorded on the tape. They contain identifying information that is readable by the computer.

Each reel of tape has three types of internal label. It has a *volume label* just after the load-point mark to indicate the number of that reel. Before each file on the reel is a *header* or *file label* that identifies the file and gives information such as the file name and the date after which it can be erased. The *trailer label* appears at the end of each file and gives the same information as the header label, along with a count of the blocks of records that are in the file. This is used during processing to ensure that all records are processed.

Processing tape files

Magnetic tape can be used for both input and output during processing and to generate backup files. Often *transaction* or *detail files*, recorded on magnetic tape or disk, will be merged with a *master file* recorded on magnetic tape, and a new, updated master file will be output on another magnetic tape. A tape drive is required for each tape file involved.

Figure 5.3 illustrates the updating of a master file for department store charge accounts, where both the master and detail files are on magnetic tape. The input master file contains the master records, each of which

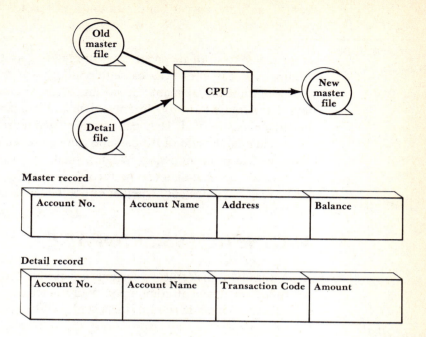

Master record

Account No.	Account Name	Address	Balance

Detail record

Account No.	Account Name	Transaction Code	Amount

Fig. 5.3—Tape File Processing

includes an account number, name, address, and a balance amount. The account numbers are in sequential order. The input detail file contains records of transactions that have occurred during the month. Each record shows the account number and name, the kind of transaction, and the amount. Some accounts may have more than one transaction to be posted; others may have none. The records in the detail file are also in sequential order by account number (having been previously sorted and merged in another operation), with records for the same account grouped together.

The program will merge the two input files and produce a new master file. Documents such as reports or statements could also be produced at this time. Because tape is a sequential access medium, each record must be read in turn before the next one in line can be read.

The computer first reads a record from the old master file and one from the detail file into primary memory and checks to see if the account numbers match. If they do, the transaction is posted. The next detail record is read and the account numbers checked. After all transactions for that account have been posted, the new updated master record is written onto the output tape file. If the account numbers do not match, it is assumed that no transactions have occurred within the month and the old master record is copied onto the new master file. In either case the next master record is read in and the process continues until all records have been posted and written.

Magnetic tape cassette

Another form of magnetic tape storage is a system that uses common Phillips-type cassettes. The cassette contains a reel of 1/8-inch-wide tape (3.785 millimeters), capable of storing several hundred thousand bytes of data. *Cassette tape storage* is convenient and inexpensive. Cassettes can be mailed and easily filed. They can be erased and reused.

Accidental erasure of the cassette can be prevented with a system similar to the file protection ring. When a small plastic tab is broken off from the cassette, no new data can be recorded over the existing contents. Data can be read out repeatedly whether or not the tab is in place.

MAGNETIC DISK STORAGE

A variety of disk storage systems are used for secondary storage. These are found on personal computers, mainframes, and supercomputers. The most common include rigid, Winchester, and flexible (floppy) disks.

Rigid disks

Rigid disk storage systems are a common means of storing files on many mainframe and microcomputer systems. Rigid disk drives may be of two types, with either removable or permanently mounted rigid magnetic disks. The *rigid magnetic disk* is a round metal plate with a thin coating of ferromagnetic material. Each disk is approximately fourteen inches in diameter and has from 200 to 500 concentric *tracks* on each surface. Data are recorded one byte at a time along each track. Depending on the system used, from 3,625 to 7,294 bytes of data can be recorded on each track. Each track holds the same amount of data. Rigid disks are sometimes known as hard disks, particularly on microcomputer systems.

A *disk pack* is a collection of two or more disks (usually six) that cannot be separated. All are mounted on a common shaft. The vertical alignment formed by tracks in the same position on all disks in the pack is called a *cylinder*. A *disk drive* rotates the pack at 2,400 revolutions per minute. Each disk pack weighs about ten pounds and can be removed from the drive mechanism and stored in a filing cabinet. Disk packs can store up to 1,260 million bytes of data, depending on the particular system. The rate at which data can be moved from the disk to the CPU ranges from 806,000 bytes per second to three million bytes per second.

Recording and accessing data

Data are recorded on both the top and bottom surfaces of each disk, except for the top and bottom surfaces of the pack. A disk pack with six disks has ten recording surfaces.

Read/write heads attached to either movable or fixed arms record and read data on the disk pack. In the *movable head* system, the arms move back and forth across the surfaces of the disks. Two read/write heads attached to one arm service the bottom of one disk and the top of another.

In the *fixed head* system, a single read/write head is positioned over each track. Data are recorded or read as the track rotates beneath the stationary head. Average access time in this arrangement is five milliseconds or less. Although the movable head system is more economical to manufacture than the fixed head, its access time which is thirty milliseconds, is slower.

Disk storage is a direct access medium. To locate a given piece of data, the arms advance across the disks to the appropriate track. A read head senses the magnetized areas on the revolving disk and converts them into electronic pulses. Average access time to locate a given record ranges from twelve to eighteen milliseconds, depending upon the equipment.

Winchester disks

Winchester technology is a system in which data are recorded on one or more permanently mounted revolving disks. The 14-, 8-, 5-1/4-, or 3-1/2-inch-diameter metal disk is sealed in a tamper-proof and contamination-free metal or plastic case. The Winchester is named after the Winchester 30-30 rifle, because the earliest model, developed by IBM Corporation, stored thirty megabytes in each of two drives. Many desktop computers are equipped with these hard disk systems and are able to store from as little as twenty megabytes to over several hundred megabytes.

Data are recorded on the revolving disk in much the same way as other disk systems. The disks may have up to a thousand tracks each. High recording densities are possible because the distance between the recording head and the disk can be reduced to less than a thousandth of an inch. Dust or dirt that would normally collect between the disk and the recording head is eliminated by the protective case.

Flexible (floppy) disks

The *floppy disk*, sometimes called a *diskette*, is a thin, flexible plastic disk, 5-1/4 or 3-1/2 inches in diameter, with a coating of ferromagnetic material. It is housed in a square plastic envelope with an aperture that allows a read/write head to access the disk with the envelope in place.

Floppy disks are similar to phonograph records. They can be removed from the disk drive, filed, mailed, or otherwise easily handled. Their low cost makes them competitive with other storage media.

When floppy disks were first introduced, they were eight inches in diameter. But these were relatively bulky and have been largely supplanted by smaller disks and drives. The floppy disk drive rotates a disk under a read/write head. Typically, data can be transferred at rates up to 625,000 bytes per second. The average access time is approximately forty milliseconds. Floppy disk drives are smaller and more economical to manufacture than rigid disk or Winchester systems.

Many new desktop computers, including the IBM PS/2, come equipped with 3-1/2 inch floppy disk drives. These drives are able to read and write data from the 3-1/2 inch floppy disk. The 3-1/2 inch floppy disk is able to store up to 1.44MB of data. It is equipped with a write-protect system. Instead of a notch, the disk has a write-protect block located in the upper right corner of the disk. When the block is in the protect position, data can be read from the disk but cannot be written on it. When the block is moved to the enable position, data can be written on the disk. A stainless steel slider is provided that covers the recording window. This slider is moved aside when the disk is inserted in a drive so the read/write head can access the disk.

To record data, the disk, still in its plastic protective cover, is inserted in a drive. The disk rotates within the envelope at approximately 300 revolutions per minute, and data are recorded by a read/write head through an aperture in the envelope. The upper right corner of the disk has a write-protect notch. When this notch is covered over with a patch of tape, data can be read from the disk but cannot be written on it. This protects the disk from accidental erasure, in much the same way as does the file protection ring on a reel of magnetic tape.

Records and files are organized and processed on floppy disks in a manner slightly different from rigid disk systems. Since floppy disks use a single disk, data cannot be written in cylinders as on a disk pack. Instead, the floppy disk is formatted with a group of forty or eighty concentric tracks. The tracks, in turn, are subdivided into sectors. There may be eight or nine sectors per track. It is common to store 512 bytes of data on each sector. This enables the drive to retrieve data by positioning the read/write head to a specific track and sector.

MASS STORAGE DEVICES

Many computer systems must store hundreds of millions of records, each containing thousands of bytes of data. Examples are extensive social security, driver registration, and income tax files. Thousands of floppy disks would be needed to store that amount of information. Therefore, *mass storage* systems have been developed specifically for storing extensive files where instantaneous access is not critical.

Cellular mass storage

The IBM 3850 is a mass storage device based on *cellular* (or honeycomb) *storage*. Data are stored in specially designed cartridges that are housed in cells in a honeycomb. Strips of magnetic tape are mounted on a length of flexible plastic which is placed in the cartridge. The cellular drive positions itself in front of a cell, withdraws a cartridge, and positions it under a read/write head. These systems can store fifty megabytes of data per cell. Average access time is about ten seconds. Its large capacity and slow access time make this system suited for large files where pieces of data are not accessed frequently.

Magnetic bubble storage

Other mass storage systems use the *magnetic bubble* principle discussed under primary memory, although the physical devices are different. The medium used is a garnet substrate coated with a thin magnetic film. In magnetic bubble storage the presence or absence of a bubble-shaped magnetic domain represents either a 1 or a 0. The bubbles representing data are read from the substrate using specially constructed magnetic pickup coils. One system developed by Intel Corporation uses cassettes that hold a comparable amount of data to a floppy disk and provide nonvolatile mass storage.

Optical disk storage

Laser beams are used to record and read data encoded on a revolving plastic or metal disk. The system is similar to video disks used to play back television and motion picture features. Information is written onto the disk by a process that uses a laser beam to melt holes in a tellurium surface or by a system that heats up the surface of the disk, causing gas bubbles to deform the surface layer. The information is read from the disk by scanning the changed reflectivity of the surface in the presence of a reflected laser beam.

Since laser systems rely upon optics, they are not prone to erasure from magnetic fields as are magnetic disks or tapes. Optical disk storage has the advantages of random access, permanence, low cost, and great storage capacity, with up to four billion bytes of data stored on a single twelve-inch disk.

Many mass storage applications are satisfied by optical storage systems that are able to write data once and then read it many times. These systems, known as *Write Once Read Many (WORM)*, can store large files of data that can be accessed many times but cannot be repeatedly written upon. Other optical disk systems are erasable and allow new data to be written on them. Much research and development is going into WORMs and other optical mass storage systems.

COMPARISON OF STORAGE MEDIA

An organization that has millions of records to be filed needs a large secondary storage system. In choosing storage media the user must consider whether files are in sequential or random order, cost of hardware, data access speeds, and primary storage capabilities. Most computer installations use a combination of media to provide high-speed access for certain files and high-capacity storage for others.

A reel of magnetic tape, which weighs about four pounds, will hold an amount of data equivalent to what could be stored in a set of encyclopedias. A reel of magnetic tape about 2,400 feet long costs less than $20. Printed pages to store the same amount of data would cost hundreds of dollars. There is far less chance of a record being lost or damaged on tape than on paper. Magnetic tape can be erased and reused.

Magnetic tape is, however, subject to damage, is limited to the sequential access method, and has a much slower access time than a magnetic disk. Magnetic disks can be accessed sequentially or directly, are less apt to be damaged, and have a fast access time. Floppy disks are lightweight and are easily filed and mailed. They are suitable where a relatively small amount of data must be stored or transmitted.

Winchester disk storage systems are convenient to use and suitable for desktop computers. Cellular storage, bubble memory, and optical disk technologies have proven to be effective methods of mass storage. The specific storage system should be selected on the basis of the user's needs, budget, and capacity requirements.

Now that we have completed our discussion of the computer and its peripheral devices, we will want to see how the computer is integrated with other machines in a network. The next chapter discusses networks and data communications.

The computer's secondary storage system is designed to supplement primary memory capacity using magnetic disk, magnetic tapes, or other media. Access time is a function of the location of the data, the amount of data to be searched, and the speed of the hardware. In sequential access a file is searched record by record. In direct or random access data are retrieved directly from storage, without searching in sequence, by using location addresses.

The indexed file access method uses a primary key to locate a record. Within a given sequenced block of data, specific records may be stored at random. A magnetic tape reel may contain up to 2,400 feet of tape. The tape on each reel has a load point mark and an end-of-reel mark. A file protection ring prevents accidental erasure of data. Records are grouped together, or blocked, to save space on the tape. Records are separated by an interrecord gap (IRG), and blocks by an interblock gap (IBG). Reels of magnetic tape include volume, header, and trailer labels.

Cassette tape storage uses 1/8-inch-wide tape stored in a plastic case. Data are stored on magnetic disks in concentric tracks. A disk pack is a collection of two or more disks mounted on a common shaft. Data are orga-

nized in cylinders on disk packs. The Winchester technology uses a permanently mounted revolving disk protected by a sealed case.

The floppy disk system uses a thin, flexible disk housed in a plastic envelope. Floppy disks are equipped with write-protect notches or sliding blocks that prevent data from accidentally being erased from the disk. In cellular mass storage specially designed cartridges are housed in honeycomb storage compartments. Other mass storage systems are magnetic bubble memory and optical disk storage. WORMs are devices able to Write Once but Read Many times.

Selected Readings

Long, Larry *Computers*, Prentice-Hall (1993). Chapter 6.

McKeown, Patrick G. *Living With Computers*, Harcourt Brace Jovanovich (1993). Chapter 8.

Mandell, Steven L. *Computers and Information Processing,* West Publishing Company (1992). Chapter 6.

REVIEW QUESTIONS

True or False Questions

1. Primary and secondary storage systems offer similar advantages.
2. High speed retrieval is a use for secondary storage.
3. Virtually unlimited storage capacity is an important advantage of secondary storage systems.
4. Average access time is an important factor in judging speed.
5. Floppy disks are good examples of sequential access media.
6. Direct access storage has no advantage over sequential access storage.
7. A purpose of labeling files is to identify information in storage.
8. Direct access devices work on the principle of searching in sequence.
9. Indexed file access is an example of primary access.
10. Secondary storage is slower than primary memory.
11. A tape record is a group of transactions.
12. External labels are readable by humans.
13. Internal labels are readable by machines.
14. Reels begin with a header or file label.
15. Master files update detail files.

Completion Questions

1. Looking up five words in the dictionary would be an example of _____ access.
2. Average access time is a measure of _____ it takes to find a piece of data.
3. A 5-1/4 inch floppy disk contains a _____ protect notch.
4. A 3-1/2 inch floppy disk contains a write-protect _____.
5. A Winchester storage devices is an example of _____ storage.

ANSWER KEY

True or False Questions

1. F
2. F
3. T
4. T
5. F
6. F
7. T
8. F
9. F
10. F
11. F
12. T
13. T
14. T
15. F

Completion Questions

1. random
2. how long
3. write-
4. block
5. secondary

6

Networks and Data Communications

When Alexander Graham Bell exclaimed over a twisted cable to his associate in the next room, "Watson, come here! I want you!" he almost certainly did not foresee that his invention would one day be part of a worldwide communications system. He could not have imagined today's communications network that links hundreds of millions of telephones, business and home computers, and television sets.

In this chapter we will look at the field of telecommunications. We will see how satellites, microwave electronics, fiber optics, and telephone networks are being integrated into a vast computer system that moves data and information, human voices, and television pictures.

WHAT IS TELECOMMUNICATIONS?

Telecommunications is the process of moving data, audio information (sound), and video information (pictures) over long distances by means of transmission lines such as telephone cables, microwave channels, and fiber optic circuits.

Telecommunications has three major domains (Fig. 6.1). One domain is audio transmission, that is, the transmission of sounds, including the human voice, by telephone through long distance lines, local circuits, or private board exchanges (PBX). A second domain is video transmission, or the moving of pictures, using airwaves or cable access television (CATV). The third domain is *data communications*, or the transmission of information in digital form through a network of computers, terminals, and transmission lines.

The first efforts at telecommunications involved transmitting sound; then video and data transmission came on the scene. Today, the three domains are merging into a single technology, with pictures, voice, and data transmitted interchangeably.

Information processing is primarily concerned with data communications. Data communications systems process data remotely and may involve computers, terminals, transmission lines, telephone or telegraph lines, or microwave circuits to transmit digital information. Data communications makes teleprocessing possible. *Teleprocessing* is the remote processing of data using communications circuits.

An integral part of the data communications system is the *communications link*, the physical means of connecting elements of the system in order to transmit and receive information. The communications link consists of the hardware and circuitry that integrate one or more computers and one or more terminals and permit the flow of data between them.

EVOLUTION OF TELECOMMUNICATIONS

Before the age of modern data communications, how was information moved from one place to another? It was usually physically carried; papers, cards, record books, or tapes were moved from point to point to be processed. The invention of the telegraph and the telephone made the movement of data easier. With these technologies, information could be converted into electronic signals and sent over wires. During the past hundred years, homes and offices across the United States and throughout the world have become linked through the development of a vast network of telephone lines.

Data communications took a step forward after World War II with the military's development of Semi-Automatic Ground Environment (SAGE) in which telephone lines and later radio circuits were used to send information from remote terminals to a computer. This availability of real time data processing increased the military's ability to make rapid, accurate air defense judgments.

Seeing the success of military data communications, business firms began to use data communications as a tool for solving business data processing problems. One early system was Semi-Automatic Business Research Environment (SABRE), which processed airline reservations. A listing of available seats was stored in a central computer. Terminals were placed in airline ticket offices. Ticket agents could query the system to learn the number of unsold seats on any given flight. This reliable and highly successful method of handling seat reservations pointed the way toward other data communications applications.

During the 1960s the Advanced Research Projects Agency of the U.S. Department of Defense established the *ARPA network*. This network, known as ARPANET, tied together the computers of several dozen university and research institutions in the United States and Europe. UCLA, Stanford, MIT, and other schools were able to transmit data through ARPANET. Today, this network, now known as Internet, has expanded to include a worldwide base of users.

At the same time a video network began to emerge. *Cable access television (CATV)* became a major force in bringing television to millions of homes throughout the country. These television cables originally served areas that could not be reached by ordinary television signals. Soon cable networks expanded to other areas. They continue to grow and now offer such diverse services as electronic newspapers, teletext, home security monitoring, and shop-at-home ordering.

During the 1970s several government and private communication satellites were put into orbit, allowing radio, television, voice, and data to be transmitted around the world. Such firms as Satellite Business Systems, RCA, Southern Pacific Communications, and AT&T now offer services via satellite.

Today, data communications is invaluable to businesses with big inventories or a large flow of data from remote points and makes possible new processes such as electronic metering, monitoring, and mail. Much of the recent growth in data communications has been in point-of-sale (POS) terminals. These terminals are connected to a central computer via a communications link. As we have seen, POS terminals are already widely used in retail establishments. Their applications will continue to increase as more retail establishments install them.

In the 1980s hundreds of thousands of microcomputers were installed in homes, schools, and offices across the country. At first they were confined to local processing, but then users began requesting access to large databases such as those offered by Dow Jones, CompuServe, and others. Access to these databases became available through ordinary telephone lines.

The next step in the evolution of telecommunications seems to be the integration of video, voice, and data transmission. It is likely that the computer, telephone, and cable television will eventually be merged into a single networked system, tying together almost every home and office in this country as well as many nations around the world.

DISTRIBUTED DATA PROCESSING

The availability of the low-cost microcomputer changed the direction of data processing markedly. The installation of low-cost computers in businesses across the country reduced the need for large central computer installations. Businesses moved toward a new concept called *distributed data processing (DDP)*. In distributed data processing, large central computers are replaced by a network of small, stand-alone processors. The smaller computers can communicate with each other through data communications circuits.

Advantages and limitations

Networks of computers that distribute data processing resources over a large geographic area have both advantages and limitations.

Data communications makes real-time processing applications available to almost any business. It does away with the need for physically carrying records or data to a computer center. Many users can share the same system or the same database, thereby reducing costs. Since several computers can be integrated into one system, each user has access to greater available resources. The load on the system can be controlled and balanced to get the most out of all computers in the network.

Distributed data processing systems cost less to operate than central systems without the need to install large computers with extensive secondary storage systems. A total network breakdown or failure is less likely because processing is spread among many small computers. Response time can be reduced, with users accessing local information rather than large central computers located some distance away.

But distributed systems are not without their problems. Although a total system failure is less likely, the use of many communication links increases the chances of subsystem failures. Telephone lines, microwave links, and relay satellites do break down.

When data are stored and processed at many points, it is more difficult to maintain security and protect the integrity of the system. Measures must be taken to keep unauthorized users from querying the system or accessing files.

Cost accounting procedures must be designed to handle and control usage on the system. Without controls, information processing costs can rise substantially because of the many users who have access to the system.

DATA COMMUNICATIONS APPLICATIONS

Before discussing how data are transmitted through a network, let us look at some of the more common applications for which data communications is used. Data communications is a vital and rapidly changing technology, and new applications are being discovered almost daily. Here are some major applications of data communications systems.

Electronic banking

The entire banking industry has benefited from data communications. *Electronic funds transfer (EFT)* systems are becoming widely used, with funds, debits and credits, and charges and payments electronically routed between banks and their customers. EFT is fast. It eliminates delays associated with sending hard copy documents and can handle the large volume of transactions generated by the banking industry. Data communications adds flexibility to banking. Using home terminals, customers will soon be able to transfer funds, pay bills, or ask about the status of their accounts. *Automated teller machines (ATMs)* using communications links are being installed in shopping centers and storefronts, allowing individuals to make deposits or withdrawals from their accounts twenty-four hours a day.

Information retrieval systems

Data communications networks make large databases of information available to users all over the country. Stock market information, wire service news reports, or comprehensive banks of statistical data can be accessed from remote terminals. For example, an individual can use a personal computer and telephone to access the Dow Jones database for information needed on the history and earnings of a given stock in order to make an informed purchasing decision.

E-mail

By the use of data communications, letters are sent electronically rather than through the mails. Either a facsimile of a document is sent using a fax machine, or a data file composed on a computer is transmitted. In this instance, the sender sits at an electronic terminal and keyboards the date, time, and person to whom a message is directed and the message itself. The system automatically routes the message to the recipient. At the receiving end a hard copy may be printed out or a signal may flash indicating that a message is waiting for the recipient.

Electronic mail, known as E-mail, or fax messages can be sent simultaneously to many people. Data can be received at one point, revised or updated, and sent on to other points. Electronic mail eliminates time delays and other problems associated with physically delivered mail.

Electronic word processing

Electronic word processing, which came into its own with the advent of the personal computer, has benefitted from modern data communications. Business people can write letters, memos, and reports using word processing systems. Then, using remote terminals located in homes, offices, or automobiles, they can send documents virtually anywhere in the world. For example, a sales representative can compose a letter on a per-

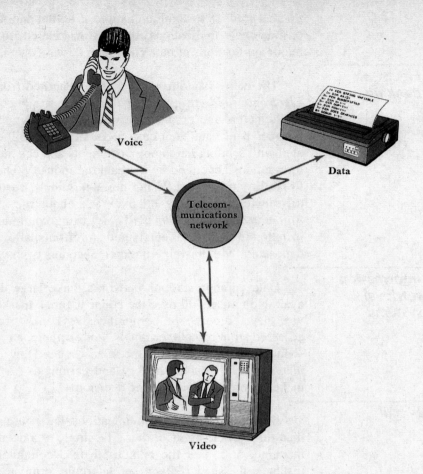

Fig. 6.1—Domains of Telecommunications

sonal computer, which may be connected to a data communications network. A supervisor can access the draft, make changes, and then electronically forward it to a division manager for checking. After other interested people have reviewed and revised the letter, a finished hard copy, incorporating all the changes and revisions, can be printed out.

Electronic shopping

Computer terminals located in homes or offices can be tied to closed circuit cable systems through which customers can see and order goods. Shopping from home is now available in many communities. Such a system is of great use for shut-ins and invalids.

Value-added networks

Many data communications users access value-added networks (VANs) to obtain data and information. CompuServe, for example, maintains large databases of information on many topics that are easily accessed by users. Airline flight schedules, theater reviews, magazine articles, and even entire encyclopedias are available on-line. Other more specialized systems, such as Lexis, make available court decisions and law articles, simplifying legal research. Other databases provide information on the stock and bond markets and other financial news.

Teleconferences

A *teleconferencing network* using hard copy printers, video terminals, or picture phones allows participants at different locations to have access to the same information, to make individual contributions to the meeting, and to interact. Such conferences are easier to arrange and much less expensive than flying individuals around the country.

Teleconferencing may take several forms. In a voice-only conference, information is exchanged through a conference telephone call. In a data communications conference, participants interact through a network of terminals. Video techniques may involve the transmission of still pictures, graphics, or full-motion video to each member of the conference. In the most elaborate system all the participants are linked together through real time circuits enabling the exchange of voices, illustrations, full-motion pictures, and data.

Monitoring and metering

Many homes, businesses, and factories are equipped with digital communications monitoring equipment that reports fire, break-ins, flood, or other emergency conditions to a central agency or police department. Other equipment measures use of utilities. Consumption of gas, water, or electricity is metered and reported to a central billing computer through closed circuit cable.

DATA TRANSMISSION PRINCIPLES

In a data communications system, data are transmitted between terminals and computers or between several computers over telephone or telegraph lines or fiber optic, microwave, or radio wave circuits. The transmission mode selected for a teleprocessing system depends upon what the user needs.

Data transmission circuits

Communication lines or circuits for teleprocessing systems are categorized according to the direction of data flow and volume of transmission.

DIRECTION OF DATA FLOW

Circuits can be categorized according to the direction in which data can flow through them. Three types of circuits are in common use. They are

(1) simplex circuits, (2) half-duplex circuits, and (3) full-duplex circuits (Fig. 6.2).

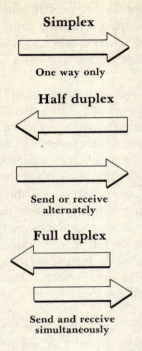

Fig. 6.2—Directions of Data Flow

In the *simplex circuit*, data can flow in only one direction. A line either receives or transmits data; it cannot do both. The simplex circuit is therefore a limited means of data transmission. A terminal coupled to a simplex circuit that only transmits data is called a *send-only terminal*. A terminal coupled to a simplex circuit that only receives data is called a *receive-only terminal*. An ordinary radio broadcast is an example of this type of circuit. One can hear signals but cannot respond.

A *half-duplex* circuit can receive and transmit data, but can do only one thing at a time. The half-duplex line can be shifted from one direction of data flow to the other, but its utility is still limited. If a terminal is transmitting data over a half-duplex circuit, the computer cannot interrupt the input flow to send back an important message. It must wait until the terminal shifts the circuit to the receive mode before delivering the information. In ship-to-shore radio only one voice is heard on the circuit at a time.

A *full-duplex* circuit is obviously the most efficient, because it allows a concurrent two-way transmission of data. A household telephone is an example of full-duplex. The telephone allows users on both ends of the line to speak simultaneously. Suppose an operator is entering data through a terminal to the computer and is unaware that the system's storage capacity has reached its limit. With a full-duplex circuit, the computer can signal the terminal to stop inputting data before the system becomes overloaded.

VOLUME OF DATA TRANSMITTED

Communication lines are also classified by the volume of data they can transmit. Of course, volume is the number of characters transmitted so it can be measured by the speed of transmission, or the number of characters transmitted per second. The grade of a line refers to its capacity for volume; the higher the grade of the line, the higher the volume carried.

The standard measure of line capacity or data transmission speed is *bits per second (bps)*. The higher the bps, the more data the line can move per given interval of time.

The three grades of lines used for data transmission are (1) narrow-band line, (2) voice-grade line, and (3) wide-band line.

Narrow-band lines have a maximum transmission speed of about 300 bps. These lines are not widely used. They are, however, less expensive to lease than other grades.

Voice-grade, or voice-band, lines can transmit more than 300 bps. They are called voice grade because they are commonly used for ordinary telephone conversations.

Wide-band lines are capable of transmitting data at 18,000 bps or higher. Of the three grades of lines, wide-band lines have the greatest capacity for moving data and are the most expensive to lease.

Thus, we see that the most versatile and expensive circuit would be a full-duplex, wide-band line. A simplex, narrow-band line would be less expensive, but more limited in capacity.

Transmission modes

Once a communication channel has been established, data can be transmitted in two modes. The *asynchronous* mode is the transmission of data character by character without any reference to a clock. Generally, a *start bit* precedes the transmission of the character and it is followed by a *stop bit*. Such systems require relatively inexpensive hardware, but they are limited in speed.

The *synchronous* mode is the transmission of information in a format that is synchronized to a clock at both the transmitting and receiving ends. Stop and start pulses are not used. Instead, the circuit transmits a signal precisely timed to when the receiver is ready to accept it. Synchronous transmission equipment is more expensive than asynchronous equipment, but it can transmit a higher volume of data per second.

Channels

Channels are the paths between terminals and computers or between computers. A computer that services ten terminals concurrently would require ten channels. In theory each channel would require a separate line, a considerable expense in setting up the system. Further complicating the problem are the differing speeds at which data are transmitted. It is inefficient and expensive to connect several slow-speed terminals to a distant computer on one line. They would not use the full capacity of the line or the computer. Methods have been found to allow many terminals operating at different speeds to share one line. Two devices that help solve these problems are data concentrators and multiplexers.

CONCENTRATORS

A device that makes it efficient for a slow-speed terminal to operate on a high-volume transmission line is a *data concentrator*. A data concentrator stores characters and then transmits them all at once over a line in a high-speed burst. High-volume transmission lines cost more money to operate and lease than lower bps lines. Organizations that have large amounts of information to transmit find it most economical to send the maximum amount of information possible over the line to take advantage of the line's capacity.

Data concentrators increase transmission efficiency through *buffering*. Built-in buffering circuits store up characters from a slow-speed device. When sufficient data are accumulated, they are sent over the line at once. Suppose four operators working at ordinary typing speed feed data to a computer over one channel. Each of the four keyboards is connected to one concentrator. The concentrator stores up the characters in a buffer and then transmits them in a burst. This process makes the best use of the facilities.

MULTIPLEXERS

Another means of sending data from several sources over one line is a *multiplexer*. A multiplexer interleaves data from several devices and sends them over a single transmission line. The multiplexer on one end sets up channels over which to transmit the data coming in from the terminals. The multiplexer at the other end of the line separates the data and sends them to the computer. This arrangement provides a low-cost means of coupling dozens of on-line terminals to a computer using only a single transmission line.

For example, four keyboard-speed devices can be tied to a single transmission line using a multiplexer. As each key is struck, an appropriate pulse is sent to the multiplexer. The multiplexer interleaves the pulses and sends them over the line. Thus, by rotating time slots all four keyboards can transmit data over one line concurrently.

Multiplexers differ from concentrators in their principle of operation. Concentrators save up characters in a buffer and then transmit them in a burst. Multiplexers interleave data on a circuit. Both multiplexers and concentrators allow more devices to share a single line. This enables many slow-speed devices to transmit data concurrently over a single circuit. It also greatly reduces line charges, since many devices can share the same line at no extra cost.

Communications media

The major media used to transmit data are telephone lines, private wire systems, coaxial cables, fiber optics, radio circuits, satellite, and microwave circuits. These are discussed below.

1. The most common medium for transmitting data is the ordinary *telephone line*, or *twisted pair*, as it is sometimes called. Lines are already in place in most businesses. There are wired networks of telephone lines in most countries. However, all instruments must be physically wired to the system.

2. There are networks of privately owned wires linking point to point. *Private wire systems* are expensive, since they are not shared by other users as is a telephone line.

3. A network of *coaxial cables* may be used instead of conventional twisted pair wiring. Data may be transmitted at low frequency and voltage (base band) or at high-speed radio frequencies (broad band). Coaxial cable systems may not be compatible with conventional circuits.

4. *Fiber optics* are cables made of bundles of glass or plastic fibers that are able to transmit light along their entire length. Each filament, or strand, of glass in the cable carries an individual data or voice transmission in the form of light (as a series of flashes). There are no interference problems, particularly from radio waves, and access is easily protected.

5. *Radio circuits* (AM and FM) are a major means of transmitting information. Possible problems include broadcast interference, sun spot interference, and security.

6. A system of orbiting *satellites* allows information to be relayed between points on the globe. Satellite transmission is subject to interference from sun spots and has security problems.

7. Data may be transmitted over *microwave circuits*. These systems transmit high-frequency radio signals from one antenna tower to another. Voice, data, and video information can be sent simultaneously. Wires or cables are not required. However, such transmissions are limited to line-of-sight applications.

Modems

A modem (MOdulator-DEModulator) is a device which connects a terminal or a computer to a telephone line (Fig. 6.3). Modems receive digital signals from a computer or terminal and convert them to analog signals for transmission over the telephone line. The process is known as *modulation*. At the receiving end of the line the analog signals are converted back to digital signals in a process known as *demodulation*. This system is necessary because digital signals cannot be sent over ordinary telephone lines.

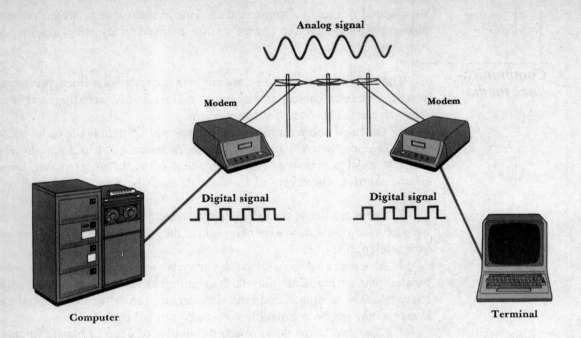

Fig. 6.3—Circuit with Modems

Modems are capable of sending signals from as little as 300 to over 19,200 bps. Modems are widely used by banks, insurance companies, or other organizations that must send data over telephone lines to remote locations. They are also used by hobbyists and others at home to access bulletin boards or other computers by sending and receiving data files over ordinary voice-grade telephone lines.

NETWORKS

A *telecommunications network* is an arrangement of communications facilities that links together users who may communicate voice, data, or video information. A telecommunications network may be limited to a few users at nearby points, or it may extend to thousands of users in local clusters or scattered around the globe.

A telecommunications network may be specialized, allowing the transmission of only one type of information—video, voice, or data. Some CATV networks transmit both video and digital information. Systems that combine both voice and data are more efficient and flexible. For example, some systems enable a telephone and data terminal to be serviced by a single existing telephone line.

In a data communications network users access the system through terminals or *workstations*. These are entry points to the system, referred to as *ports*. A group of local ports may be clustered about a point known as a *node*. Nodes are connected together through long-distance facilities called *long-haul circuits*. The switching, monitoring, and control of the network is done through a system of data communications computers.

Wide area networks

Wide area networks (WANs) are composed of computers and data communications equipment that can link users worldwide. Internet, one of the world's largest WANs, links schools, libraries, governments and private users from many distant points. For example, a student using Internet can access a library catalog in Australia, a file in a government computer in Washington, or skip across the Atlantic to send an E-mail communication to another user in Germany.

Network architecture

The structure, design, and layout of the network and transmission facilities are called the *system architecture*, or its *topology*. The architecture of systems takes many forms, depending upon the needs of the system users. There are five major topologies in use: tree, star, point-to-point, bus, and ring (Fig. 6.4).

1. In the *tree* or *hierarchical* configuration, all terminals are tied to, and communications are routed through, a central host computer. The host computer monitors and controls the movement of data throughout the network. It performs major information processing functions and serves as a backup computer. The terminals do not communicate with each other directly. The design resembles a tree with branches.

2. In the *star* design, all computers are tied to a central computer, but the major processing is done by the satellite processors rather than the host. All computers, including the central computer, are on equal level with all others on the system.

3. In a *point-to-point* design, all computers are tied to each other in a mesh of point-to-point wiring with no central computer.

4. In the *bus* configuration, all computers are tied together in a single line with no host computer. Each has access to the data on the bus.

5. In the *ring* design, computers are integrated into an active loop. Information is transmitted from station to station through a series of repeaters. There is a continuous flow of data around the ring.

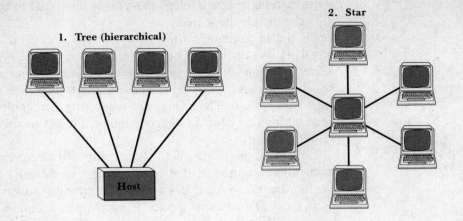

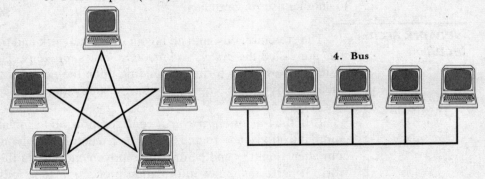

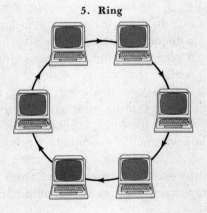

Fig. 6.4—Network Topologies

LOCAL AREA NETWORKS

A *local area network* (LAN) is a communications system that enables users in a geographically limited area to share computer resources and communications equipment. LANs are usually limited to five miles or less in range and rely upon coaxial cables. Users are added to or dropped from a system by connecting to or disconnecting from the coaxial cable. LANs are usually limited to users in one company or perhaps in a government agency or university.

One of the most successful LAN systems is called *Ethernet.* It was developed by Xerox Corporation in conjunction with Digital Equipment Corporation and Intel Incorporated. Ethernet is a standardized package of hardware, communications lines, and system software. Ethernet users are tied together through a single coaxial cable. A user can query other users on the network, move data from one point to another, or direct information to be output on printers throughout the system. Services on the system include EtherLink Exchange, EtherShare, EtherPrint, and EtherMail.

LANs can be interfaced with other LANs and other networks through bridges and gateways. Dissimilar LANs are connected to one another using a *bridge interface.* The bridge provides the connection that allows LANs of different types to communicate with one another.

If a LAN is to be connected to a non-LAN network, then a *gateway interface* is used. The gateway provides the circuits and software to allow a LAN to send and receive data over long-haul communications circuits. A user in one LAN who wants to communicate with a workstation in another LAN gains access through a port that in turn selects the appropriate bridge or gateway and long-haul circuit. The long-haul circuit may be a telephone, microwave, or satellite link. Information can be routed between workstations in different LANs as though they were in the same local network.

Data communications is one of the most dynamic areas of computers and information processing discussed so far. The breakup of AT&T into smaller competing companies and the entry of many new common carriers into the marketplace means new jobs and changing technology. Students who understand data communications and its impact have an advantage in the labor market of the future.

Telecommunications is the science of moving information by means of *transmission lines, telephone cables, microwave channels, or fiber optic circuits. The three major domains are audio or voice transmission, video transmission, and data communications or digital transmission. Data communications makes possible teleprocessing, where data are processed remotely.*

A communications link is the physical means by which elements of the system are connected and by which information is transmitted or received. Telecommunications was first used by the military and then adopted by airline, hotel, and other reservation systems. The point-of-sale terminal is an example of a teleprocessing application.

Distributed data processing (DDP) systems involve a network of small, stand-alone processors and data communications circuits that allow many users to share the same resources. Such systems are limited by communications costs and potential failure of communications links. Modern data communications applications include electronic banking, information retrieval systems, electronic word processing, electronic mail, electronic shopping, teleconferences, monitoring, and metering.

Three types of transmission circuits in common use are simplex, half-duplex, and full-duplex. The standard measure of data transmission speed is bits per second (bps). Three common grades of lines are narrow-band, voice-grade, and wide-band. A channel is a path between a terminal and a computer or between several computers. Data concentrators use buffering circuits to get maximum use of high-volume lines with slow-speed terminals. Multiplexers allow data from several sources to be sent over one line.

Major communications media include telephone lines, private wire circuits, coaxial cables, fiber optics, radio circuits, satellites, and microwave circuits. Modems connect terminals or computers to telephone lines. These devices are used by banks, insurance companies, home computer users, and others. A network is an arrangement of facilities linked by communications lines. They include workstations, ports, and nodes tied together through long-haul lines. Common network topologies are the tree, star, point-to-point, bus, and ring. Local area networks (LANs) use coaxial cables to link computers in a geographically limited area. National and international communications networks can be accessed by many users all over the country and abroad.

Selected Readings

Stamper, David A. *Business Data Communications*, Benjamin Cummings (1991). Chapter 8.

Silver, Gerald A. *Data Communications for Business*, Boyd & Fraser (1994). Chapters 6, 10.

Walrand, Jean. *Communication Networks*, Irwin (1991). Chapters 1, 2.

REVIEW QUESTIONS

1. The term telecommunications does not include video transmissions.
2. A major limitation of teleprocessing is its inability to handle digital information.
3. A major data communications application involves airline ticketing.
4. Teleprocessing differs from local processing in that data are processed at a remote site.
5. Data communications is synonymous with telecommunications.
6. Simplex, half-duplex, and full duplex are three kinds of transmission circuits used in teleprocessing.
7. Narrow-band lines can handle more data than wide-band lines.
8. Modems are frequently connected to desktop computers.
9. Fiber optic and microwave circuits are common communications media.
10. The evolution of telecommunications includes heavy military applications.
11. Local processing has no advantages over distributed data processing.
12. Word processing is usually done on an information retrieval system.
13. Teleconferences are conducted using at least one communications link.
14. Modems perform the same function as data concentrators.
15. Multiplexers are not usable on data circuits.

*Completion
Questions*

1. Stockbroker's offices, business firms, and small engineering companies often use _____ communications.
2. Modems are used to connect _____ to telephone lines.
3. Local area networks usually operate within a range of _____ miles.
4. _____ allow data from several sources to be sent over one line.
5. A system's network architecture is also known as its _____ .

ANSWER KEY

*True or False
Questions*

1. F
2. F
3. T
4. T
5. F
6. T
7. F
8. T
9. T
10. T
11. F
12. F
13. T

14. F
15. F

Completion Questions

1. data
2. computers
3. five
4. Multiplexers
5. topology

7

Computer Operating Systems

One of the most complex and important programs on any computer is the operating system (OS). The operating system integrates the overall operation of the computer. This software ties together the functions of the CPU, input, output, and secondary storage systems into an integrated whole.

In many respects the operating system performs functions that are invisible to the user, similar to services performed by the public utility that provides electricity to your home or office. You need not understand the inner workings of the power generation plant to take advantage of the electric power that is provided.

This chapter opens our discussion of computer software and focuses on operation systems. Later chapters cover fundamentals of graphics packages, word processors, spreadsheet programs, database managers, and others. This chapter explains operating system functions, the services operating systems provide, types of operating systems, and describes some of the major operating systems for mainframes and microcomputers.

TYPES OF COMPUTER SOFTWARE

Many different types of computer programs are used to create a functioning computer system (Fig. 7.1). Applications programs compose a cate-

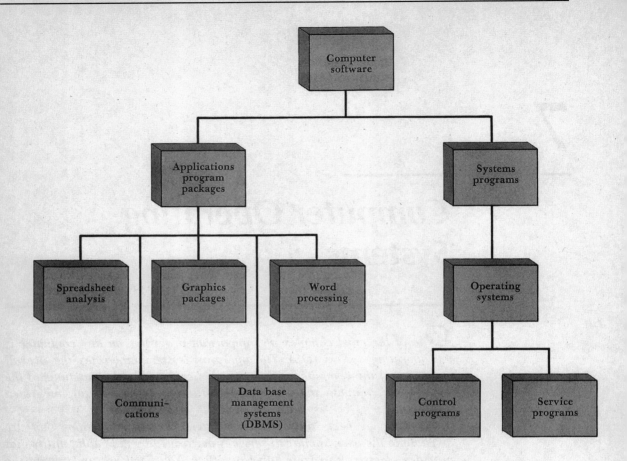

Fig. 7.1—Types of Computer Software

gory of software that includes word processors, spreadsheet programs, database managers, desktop publishing software, and others. They are used to meet specific end user information processing needs. Applications software is discussed in later chapters.

The second category consists of *systems programs*. Most important in this group are the *operating systems (OS)* essential to virtually every computer. Operating systems are master control programs that reside in the computer at all times and enable applications programs to perform their functions.

Operating systems differ from one another and are tailored to take into account features unique to a particular computer system. Operating systems are programmed for specific microcomputers, mainframes, or networks. Computer users need to understand the computer's operating system and its capabilities in order to fully use the resources of the computer.

FUNCTION OF OPERATING SYSTEMS

An operating system is a complex group of programs that resides all or in part in the computer's memory. An operating system controls the computer's overall functioning, manages its resources, monitors its status, handles interruptions, schedules its work in an efficient manner, and enables it to communicate with input/output devices. The operating system controls input/output devices, calls programs from storage, and links parts of programs together into larger programs. The operating system also includes language translators, programs that sort and merge files, and programs that assist in program developing and debugging, to name just a few.

Operating systems remove much of the detail and effort required on the part of the computer operator when running programs. They alleviate much of the routine and technical detail required to operate the computer properly. Some of the services provided by operating systems are:

Schedule input and output operations. Handles the transfer of information between keyboards, monitors, printers, and secondary storage devices.

Schedules jobs according to priority. Enables certain jobs to be run ahead of others.

Communicates with the human operator. Displays or prints messages for the operator.

Handles interruptions. Allows programs to be interrupted in a systematic manner.

Logs jobs in and out. Time and date stamps jobs that are run or files that are stored or updated.

Monitors system status. Ensures that necessary devices and facilities are operational and functioning properly.

Controls system access and data security functions. Prevents unauthorized access and limits users on a system.

Combines phases of a job into a complete run. Allows complex multipart programs to be run as a unit.

Facilitates debugging and locating of errors. Has routines that display contents of memory and assist in trouble shooting programs.

Provides multiprogramming capability. Allows several programs to be run concurrently.

Provides multiprocessing capability. Allows two or more computers to act together and coordinates their functions.

Loads compilers or language translators. Enables different computer languages to be run on the computer.

Maintains the computer's library of programs. Provides a directory of stored programs, including the date and time of generation.

EVOLUTION OF OPERATING SYSTEMS

Operating systems are provided by most computer manufacturers. Such software was not available on early computers. To appreciate its role, one need only look at how early machines were operated before its development. In the absence of an operating system, the operator had to read a set of handwritten instructions from the programmer for each job, load in the appropriate language translator, and then load the job and the data set. The operator then had to stand by, keeping a close eye on the machine while it ran the program.

If the program contained an error and stopped executing part way through, or if a printer ran out of paper, or an input device jammed, the operator had to diagnose the cause of the failure and decide what to do. The operator had to log all jobs in and out so that accounting records could be kept on usage and had to schedule jobs according to priority.

Operators, even with help, found it impossible to keep up with the hundreds of programs to be run through a computer in one day. Obviously, the weak link in the chain was the human operator. In the 1950s, computer engineers designed master control programs, called operating systems, to replace the functions of human operators. Operating systems have proven so successful that virtually all modern computers have them.

Early operating systems were designed for single large mainframe computers. In the 1970s, the introduction of minicomputers and, later, microcomputers led to the development of microcomputer operating systems. These included Control Program for Microcomputers (CP/M) and Microsoft Disk Operating System (MS-DOS). In the 1980s, the increased reliance upon networks brought about network operating systems such as Novell and UNIX.

RESIDENT STORAGE DEVICES

A nucleus of operating system instructions must always be stored in primary memory. However, the bulk of the instructions may occupy several hundred thousand bytes or more and thus is too big to be kept entirely in primary memory in many computers. It is therefore necessary to rely upon secondary storage, such as a disk or tape, to hold the main part of the operating system. The nucleus in primary memory can call special routines in from secondary storage as needed.

Two types of commands are executed by operating systems. *Internal commands* are those which may be executed immediately because they are resident within primary memory at all times. The internal command portion of the operating system is loaded as soon as the computer is started, and the resident routines are continually available for processing internal commands.

Less frequently used commands are stored outside of primary memory on a floppy disk or other secondary storage device, and are called *external commands*. When an external command is needed, the computer transfers the needed portion of the operating system from a resident storage device to primary memory. This allows the operating system to perform many complicated tasks without tying up primary memory with infrequently used instructions.

Operating systems are classified according to the nature of the storage device that holds the operating system. A *disk operating system (DOS)* stores the bulk of its commands on a magnetic disk. The DOS operating system is widely used on microcomputers.

A microcomputer may be equipped with several floppy disk drives, or one floppy disk drive and one hard drive. In the first instance, the internal DOS commands are loaded immediately from a floppy disk, and the external routines are called in from the floppy disk as needed. If a hard drive is available, as is more common today, the operating system's internal routines are loaded into memory when the computer is started and then the external commands are called in from the hard disk as needed.

STRUCTURE OF OPERATING SYSTEMS

At the center of the operating system is the *kernel* (Fig. 7.2). The kernel contains the core of the operating system. All or part of the kernel resides in the main memory at all times and calls in other routines. The kernel includes the routines that execute the internal commands. The external routines are located in the *shell* surrounding the kernel.

Programs in the shell are either *control programs* or *service programs*. They include compilers, interpreters, assemblers, editors, and program debuggers. *I/O driver routines* that program specific input/output devices are also located in the shell.

Surrounding both the kernel and the shell are the security and file protection programs. They prevent unauthorized users from accessing the shell or kernel programs. Database management systems (DBMS), word processing, desktop publishing, graphics, communications, and spreadsheet analysis programs may be available at this level. These are described in later chapters.

Control programs

Control programs manage overall operations, schedule work, communicate with the operator, log jobs, and monitor system status. These tasks are done using the following modules.

SUPERVISOR PROGRAM

The *supervisor program* controls the overall scheduling of the computer's operations. It pulls required routines from the resident storage device (disk, tape, etc.) and loads them into primary memory. It also conveys messages to the computer operator, indicating error conditions, I/O devices that need attention, and so on. The programs are located in the shell.

Interruptions caused by errors or input/output problems are processed in an orderly way to reduce time loss. If an error is detected, the computer prints out a message and goes on to the next job without delay.

The supervisor program keeps a list of jobs run and clocks them in and out. It records and prints out the elapsed compilation and execution time.

INPUT/OUTPUT CONTROL SYSTEM (IOCS)

Careful and efficient scheduling and operation of input/output and secondary storage devices are essential if the computer is to run at maximum processing speed and without interruption. In most computers the

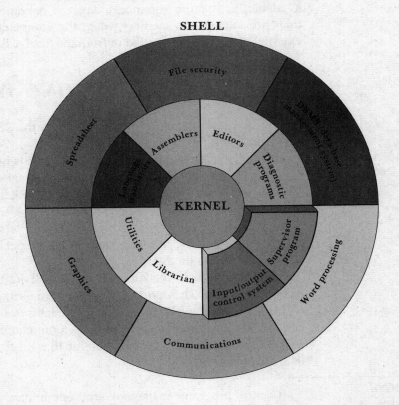

Fig. 7.2—Operating System Structure

input/output control system (IOCS) software performs these functions rapidly.

The IOCS continually monitors the I/O devices. If the printer is out of paper, for example, the IOCS sends a message to the operator. If a device malfunctions or is not available, it substitutes another device that is available so that processing will not be interrupted.

The IOCS readies input and output devices for use. For example, it checks identification labels and indexes reels of tape to the required point. It opens the circuitry that permits data to flow between the I/O devices and the CPU. It checks parity of data being transmitted in and out of the computer.

On some machines, such as microcomputers, the input/output control system functions are performed by *firmware*. Firmware consists of programming instructions stored in hardware, such as on a read-only memory (ROM) chip. Most microcomputers are equipped with a *Basic Input/Output System (BIOS)*. This BIOS chip implements the portion of the operating system that services input and output devices. Since they are implemented in ROM, the BIOS routines that are frequently used can be called in quickly without resorting to calls to a floppy disk drive or other external storage medium.

Service programs

Service programs are subprograms that perform frequently used routines and functions for the programmer. They save much programming time and effort by making a great variety of procedures available. The specific program needed is called out by the operating system as directed by the job control instructions.

The computer's ability to store and call out these service programs gives it much of its power and capability. Descriptions of some common service programs follow.

LIBRARIAN PROGRAM

The *librarian program* maintains the system library. It allocates a storage area in the computer system for any program or part of a program that a programmer wishes to save and keeps track of where that program has been stored for future use. A system library is usually kept on disk or tape.

The *system library* contains programs from many sources. Some are frequently accessed programs or modules cataloged by users; others are cataloged by the manufacturer. These programs have wide applications in the routine processing performed by many users.

UTILITY PROGRAM

Much computer work involves preparing and maintaining files that must be merged, updated, or sorted. Programs stored in the operating system that perform these common tasks are called *utility programs*. They are called out by job management commands. Sort and merge programs are usually general in nature and serve multiple functions. Other utility programs perform such tasks as transferring data from disk to disk or from tape to disk and reformatting data. The common COPY and DISKCOPY commands used on microcomputers are examples of utility programs.

LANGUAGE TRANSLATOR

Computers are able to execute instructions only if they are coded in machine language. Since most people prefer to write programs in a high-level language such as BASIC or Pascal, a *language translator* is necessary. A translator converts statements into instructions the computer can execute. A *compiler* is a translator that converts an entire program into machine instructions before the computer begins executing; an *interpreter* translates instructions into machine language line by line as the computer executes the program. In addition, an operating system may include an *assembly program* or *assembler* to convert programs written in assembler language into machine instructions.

Each translator can convert only one programming language into a form the machine understands, so a separate translator is needed for each language (Fig. 7.3). Some operating systems include only one or two language translators, such as BASIC or Pascal, while others are equipped with dozens of translators.

DIAGNOSTIC PROGRAM

A *diagnostic program*, or debugger, facilitates locating errors or bugs in a program. Some diagnostic programs check primary memory by writing information into memory, reading it out, and comparing it for accuracy. Others echo back characters from a keyboard or display them on a screen to verify that input/output devices are functioning properly.

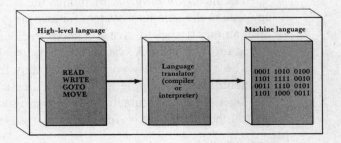

Fig. 7.3—Language Translator

TYPES OF OPERATING SYSTEMS

Many different types of operating systems have been developed for mainframes and microcomputers. Operating systems can be characterized as being batch, multi-user, real-time, or network.

Batch operating systems

As the name indicates, *batch operating systems* are designed to control batch processing. They accept and process jobs in sequence, without regard to priority. Although they can process several jobs concurrently, they do not allow computer terminals to share the computer's resources at the same time.

Batch operating systems are directed by control statements submitted at the beginning of each job in the form of one or more program instructions. These are known as *job control language (JCL)* instructions. The JCL statements give the computer the necessary instructions regarding data sets, output devices, and so on.

Batch operating systems are often found on small computers for which only a few input devices are used and no multitasking or multi-users are involved. Examples of batch processing are the preparation of payrolls and student grade reports.

Multi-user operating systems

Multi-user operating systems are designed to run several programs at one time. The process is called *multitasking* or *multiprogramming*. The operating system partitions its memory and shares it among several jobs or users. Once jobs are assigned priority, the computer allocates memory and I/O devices accordingly. Jobs are broken down into tasks and segments of the program are written into memory. By sharing memory and I/O devices, the computer can run several applications programs for different users concurrently.

Real-time operating systems

The *real-time operating system (RTOS)* is designed to respond to requests from many users as they occur and usually to execute several batch or interactive programs concurrently from on-line devices. For example, a real-time operating system is required when remote terminals are connected on-line to the computer. The system must be able to respond promptly to the requests of each terminal user.

This type of system processes jobs in a hierarchical order rather than in sequence; that is, jobs with higher priorities are executed before jobs with lower priorities. An RTOS is capable of beginning execution on one job, suspending operations on that job to execute a job with a higher priority, then resuming execution of the suspended job where it left off. An RTOS can also schedule jobs at a preset time. For example, it can schedule the preparation of an inventory report at the end of each working day.

Some operating systems are designed to handle batch and real-time tasks at the same time. The computer can process a stream of batch programs fed into a local batch terminal and at the same time respond to real-time terminals, such as remote automatic teller machines (ATMs).

Network operating systems

With the growth of telecommunications, more and more computers are being operated in a network environment. This calls for the implementation of operating systems designed to handle network computing. A *network operating system* coordinates the operation of numerous computers located at different geographic points, enabling them to function as an integrated whole. Network operating systems are equipped with security and access controls that allow certain users to access selected parts of a system or software. They also allow many users to share common resources, such as laser printers and high capacity disk storage drives.

Local area networks (LANs), discussed in an earlier chapter, require network operating systems. The operating system must not only coordinate the many workstations on the network, but it must handle resource and file *contention*. A resource conflict, or contention, occurs when two or more users seek to simultaneously use the same printer or file server, such as a disk drive. A file contention occurs when two or more users seek to simultaneously access the same file or record. Operating systems in this class provide *record lock* facilities. This means only one user can access or change the contents of a file or record at one time. Network operating systems avoid the possibility of two users changing the same record at the same instant.

These operating systems may also provide spooling capability. It sometimes happens that two or more users want to send their output to the same printer at the same time. In *spooling*, output is sent to an intermediate disk storage device and then transferred to a printer as it becomes available. By spooling, many users can share the same printer with no resource contention.

MICROCOMPUTER OPERATING SYSTEMS

Just as microcomputer hardware has evolved, so have operating systems. One of the first operating systems for microcomputers was the Control Program for Microcomputers (CP/M), developed by Digital Research Corporation. Microsoft Corporation's MS-DOS became widely used on the IBM Personal Computer and other compatibles. The UNIX operating system was developed by the Bell Labs and has become widely available on Digital Equipment Corporation's computers.

Here are some of the more important microcomputer operating systems, including those designed to run on IBM and Macintosh microcomputers.

MS-DOS

MS-DOS was developed by Microsoft Corporation. This operating system was widely implemented on IBM PCs and compatible computers in the early 1980s. Several versions of MS-DOS have evolved, and it remains the most popular operating system for desktop systems. MS-DOS can be used on many different computers including those equipped with 8088, 80286, 80386, and 80486 microprocessors.

OS/2

OS/2 was developed in the late 1980s for use on IBM's line of PS/2 computers. OS/2 supports multitasking capability, that is, it allows several applications programs to be operated at the same time. It also has a graphical user interface that features a window-like screen display that is easier to use than the single line commands users have to type in MS-DOS.

Microsoft Windows

In the late 1980s Microsoft introduced its Windows Graphic User Interface (GUI). With the introduction of Windows 3.1, this interface has become an important tool for computer users. By 1993 it is estimated that over twenty million computers worldwide were using this GUI.

The Windows GUI relies upon a basic "desktop" containing graphic symbols, called icons, that help users issue commands to the computer—mainly for selecting applications. Several windows can be displayed at one time on the screen, allowing multiple programs to be run at one time. Using a mouse, various options can be selected from the choices displayed on the screen. Windows avoids the need for entering complicated lines of command instructions and is suited to the novice as well as the advanced computer user.

DESQview

Quarterdeck Office Systems markets a Windows-like operating system known as DESQview. This software will run on the earlier 8088 and 80286 and the newer 80386 and 80486 microprocessors. It provides multitasking for desktop computers in a Windows environment.

Apple Macintosh

Apple Computers sought to implement a totally different approach to operating systems. The Apple Macintosh operating system has gained widespread acceptance because of its simplicity and use of icons. An *icon* is a small graphic image or symbol that stands for an operation. The user selects the symbol by pointing to it with a mouse and then clicking the mouse button. This action activates the operation.

The Apple Macintosh operating system also supports pull down menus. Users can pull down a menu of options from a bar at the top of the screen and make a choice by selecting it with the mouse. The icon-oriented user interface has gained widespread acceptance and has been copied by other software developers because of its user-friendly approach.

UNIX

A powerful and rapidly expanding operating system known as UNIX was pioneered by Bell Laboratories in the late 1960s. UNIX initially gained a following and has continued to expand as programmers have become familiar with its wide variety of commands and rich vocabulary.

UNIX is more difficult to use than operating systems such as MS-DOS or the Apple Macintosh system. It does not provide icon symbols but requires carefully constructed command lines. Because of its power UNIX is preferred by advanced computer users. UNIX runs on DEC and many other computer systems.

MAINFRAME OPERATING SYSTEMS

The demands of mainframe computers require controlling many peripheral devices and managing the resources of a large central processing unit. Several operating systems have been developed for mainframes including systems which provide virtual memory.

IBM virtual memory (VM)

Large IBM systems utilize the IBM VM operating system. VM is designed to be run on large mainframe computers and supports multi-users and multitasking, both of which place heavy memory demands on the computer. IBM VM resolves the problem by using a paging system that swaps parts of a program into main memory as required. For example, a large program containing 20KB would be broken down into five 4KB pages, which are then brought into memory as needed. When the section is no longer needed, the next page is written over it.

By bringing in sections of a program only as needed, the computer's physical memory is used more efficiently. This technique, known as *virtual memory*, in effect expands the computer's physical memory capacity, and allows lengthy complex programs to be reduced to small sections that are brought into primary memory for execution.

FAULT-TOLERANT OPERATING SYSTEMS

Since many operating systems were designed to do multiprocessing that links several computers together as a team, it soon became evident that there was a potential for greatly increasing the reliability of these systems. Operating systems have been developed that are based upon *parallel processing* and *fault-tolerant* computers.

Parallel processing relies upon two central processing units functioning together in parallel. Since these computers are designed with redundant components, they can back up each other. By including fault-tolerant software, it is possible to create systems that are able to process large amounts of data quickly and reliably.

If the operating system detects a hardware failure, it is able to substitute redundant facilities and continue processing without a hard failure. Fault-tolerant computer systems are marketed by Tandem Computers, Inc., and Stratus Computer, Inc. Future operating systems developed by other companies are expected to be built upon fault-tolerant parallel processing capabilities.

This chapter introduced our discussion of computer software, including operating systems. The next chapters will describe applications software used to solve local problems.

Operating system programs manage the resources of the computer, automate its operations, and facilitate programming, testing, and debugging. Among the tasks handled by operating systems are scheduling I/O operations, communicating with operators, handling interruptions, logging jobs, monitoring status, combining phases, handling multiprogramming, loading compilers and interpreters, maintaining the program library, and coordinating the activities of two or more computers.

The nucleus of the operating system is stored in primary memory and the balance on the resident storage device. Internal commands are those which may be executed immediately; external commands are processed by routines called into memory as needed. Operating systems include two types of programs. Control programs manage the operation of the system, and service programs perform frequently used routines.

A language translator converts program statements into commands the computer can execute. A compiler converts an entire program into machine instructions before the computer begins executing; an interpreter translates each line of code as it is executed. An assembler converts assembly language into machine language. Diagnostic programs facilitate the location of errors in a program.

The common types of operating systems are batch, multi-user, real-time, and network. Using spooling, output is sent to a disk storage device before being transferred to a printer. By bringing sections of a program into memory only as needed, virtual memory operating systems are able to expand the use of the computer's physical memory capacity.

Major microcomputer operating systems in use are MS-DOS, Apple Macintosh, UNIX, and OS/2. A major mainframe operating system is the IBM virtual memory (VM). Operating systems have been developed specifi-

cally for networks and are known as network operating systems. Microsoft Windows has become an important graphic user interface (GUI). Fault-tolerant operating systems take advantage of the computer hardware's redundancy and parallel processing features, increasing the system's reliability.

Selected Readings

Capron, H. L. *Essentials of Computing*, Benjamin Cummings (1992). Chapter 8.

Long, Larry. *Computers*, Prentice-Hall (1993). Chapter 9.

Mandell, Steven L. *Computers and Information Processing*, West Publishing Company (1992). Chapter 10.

Manes, Stephen. *Gates*, Doubleday (1993).

REVIEW QUESTIONS

True or False Questions

1. Operating systems are programs defined as solving local problems.
2. The function of an operating system is to control the overall system.
3. There is only one type of operating system in use.
4. Control programs and service programs differ in their function.
5. The function of a service programs is to save time and programming effort.
6. Language translators are not available for microcomputers.
7. Utility programs are available that merge, update, and sort files.
8. Operating systems provide software security measures.
9. The function of a resident storage device is to hold the operating system.
10. There are no differences between internal and external commands.
11. MS-DOS is a major microcomputer operating system.
12. Novell is a major network operating system.
13. Windows is a major mainframe operating system.
14. Few changes have taken place in the evolution of operating systems.
15. The function of a page swapping system is to provide system security.

Completion Questions

1. _____ is a GUI microcomputer operating system interface.
2. _____ operating system commands are resident within primary memory at all times.
3. _____ operating system commands are called into memory as needed.
4. High level languages require language _____ to convert statements.
5. A _____ microcomputer operating system is stored on disk.

ANSWER KEY

True or False Questions

1. F
2. T
3. F
4. T
5. T
6. F
7. T
8. T
9. T
10. F
11. T
12. T
13. F
14. F
15. F

Completion Questions

1. Windows
2. Internal
3. External
4. translators
5. MS-DOS

8

WORD PROCESSING SOFTWARE

*P*rior *to the introduction of applications packages, programmers spent countless hours writing and testing programs. However, it soon became obvious that many business, government, and educational institutions had the need to solve similar problems. This demand encouraged the development of applications packages.*

Software packages perform such varied tasks as assisting in the preparation and editing of a manuscript or the creation of statistical reports. Software packages are used by writers, teachers, accountants, secretaries, office workers, and others. For example, packages enable accountants to prepare income tax returns or other accounting documents. Payroll, inventory management and cost accounting packages are widely used by accountants.

In this chapter we will look at word processing software, one of the major applications packages. The next chapter will discuss desktop publishing software, and later chapters describe spreadsheets and graphics software, database management software, communications software, and integrated software packages.

SELECTING A SOFTWARE PACKAGE

*Applications package*s are fully developed programs that require little or no programming effort and can be loaded on a computer ready to run. Today there are thousands of applications packages on the market. Most computer users begin by assessing their software needs. For many, a ready-made package is desirable to avoid the complex and detailed steps in preparing a unique program.

After the user's needs have been determined, a review of available software products on the market is undertaken. Some software vendors provide demonstration programs, sample software, or tutorial programs to assist in making a selection. Once a specific applications program has been selected, it is installed on the computer.

Most applications software for microcomputers is provided on floppy disks, ready for installation, together with one or more instruction manuals. Installation involves copying one or more disks onto the computer and usually running an installation program. The *install program* tailors the applications software to the specific computer, monitor, and printer in use. Thus, with no programming effort, a highly sophisticated applications program can be placed on a computer and made ready to run in only a few minutes.

These programs run under the control of an operating system such as MS-DOS, widely used on desktop computers. The applications programs can produce color graphic images, print out reports, letters, and memos, create spreadsheets, and perform many other tasks. Let's begin our discussion with the most widely used applications packages, those designed for word processing.

WORD PROCESSING PACKAGES

Word processing software is designed to manipulate words, phrases, and sentences to create a letter or a report that can be printed out. This software is sometimes referred to as a *text editor* since its principal function is to create and edit text. Word processors are particularly valuable when extensive editing or revisions are needed, or for long, frequently used documents like legal contracts.

Some word processing programs have a thesaurus and built-in spelling checker, which checks spelling against a standard dictionary stored in the computer. Others are equipped with grammar checkers that review sentence structure and syntax. Word processing packages eliminate most or all of the retyping usually needed in revising a document. Some popular word processing packages on the market are WordPerfect, Microsoft Word, WordStar, and PC-Write.

OVERVIEW OF WORD PROCESSING

Text to be manipulated by the word processor is typed in without regard to line width or formatting. Errors are corrected by backspacing and retyping. The text as typed and corrected is stored in the computer's memory and may also be saved on a floppy disk. After all the text has been entered, a hard copy may be printed out.

As the user keyboards the document, words, phrases, or sentences can be replaced, rearranged, or deleted. The computer inserts the revisions into the stored text. At any time, the machine can be instructed to print out an updated draft. The operator can also instruct the computer to print out drafts with different formats, line widths, or page lengths. Word processing programs can automatically center lines, provide page numbers, or insert headers or footers.

After text editing is completed and the format decided upon, the operator instructs the computer to print out a finished copy. This version contains headings, page numbers, and other typographical elements and is evenly spaced and neatly typed.

LEARNING TO USE A WORD PROCESSOR

In order to illustrate how a word processor works and introduce the basic concepts of word processing, we will discuss *WordPerfect*, a widely used word processing package. WordPerfect is an example of a *menu-driven* word processor.

PREPARING A DOCUMENT

The preparation of a document using WordPerfect involves several distinct steps. We shall overview this process and then come back to each step and discuss it in greater detail. The steps include:

Entering WordPerfect
Keyboarding the document
Making changes, corrections, or alterations
Saving the document
Printing out the document

Before a document can be keyboarded or printed out, certain preparatory steps are usually followed.

Application example

Suppose you have been assigned the task of preparing a short essay for an English class, and you have decided to use WordPerfect as your word processor. We shall assume that you have turned on your computer and are ready to begin.

WordPerfect is usually stored on a hard disk or a floppy disk, ready for use. You start WordPerfect by typing:

`WP`

You have placed an empty formatted disk in the A drive to hold your personal files.

Whether you are using a floppy disk or hard drive, WordPerfect will respond by displaying the normal *editing screen* shown in Fig. 8.1. The screen contains a cursor and a status line at the bottom. The editing screen is like a fresh sheet of paper placed in a typewriter, ready for copy to be entered. The *cursor* points to the current position on the screen where the next data will be entered.

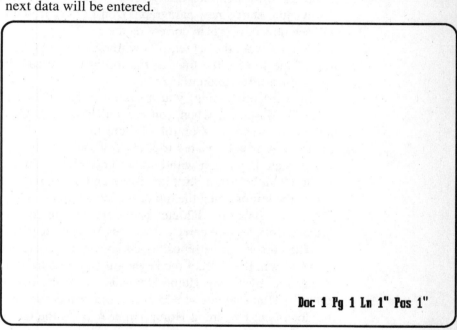

Fig. 8.1—Normal Editing Screen

The *status line* at the bottom of the screen tells you the document, page, line, and position numbers. Since the cursor is in the upper left corner, the status line will show Doc 1 Pg 1 Ln 1" Pos 1". The status line displays whether you are in document 1 or 2. WordPerfect allows you to move back and forth between two documents easily. Next you will see the page number, then the line and column positions.

WordPerfect begins with some initial default settings that automatically establish the margins, tab settings, and line spacing. These can be changed and modified throughout the document at any time. We will discuss these a bit later, after we have talked about how you keyboard a document into the computer.

KEYBOARDING THE DOCUMENT

After you have started WordPerfect, a cursor will appear at the top left of the screen and you are ready to enter text. All you need to do is type in whatever material you want. The margins, line spacing, page numbering, page justification, and other formatting elements are already set.

As you enter material, WordPerfect automatically handles your end of line carriage return. You do not strike the carriage return at the end of each line as you do when using a conventional typewriter. With WordPerfect's automatic *word wrap* feature, you only need to use the carriage return when you want to start a new paragraph. Don't worry if you make mistakes. You will see how easy it is to correct them.

As you type, the screen fills with characters. When you get to the bottom of the screen, the lines at the top of the screen disappear from view. These lines still remain in memory.

In word processing, you are often directed to strike several keys at once. For instance, when you want to press the Control and backspace keys, hold down the Control key and then strike the backspace key. The Control key is abbreviated to Ctrl. You may be directed to strike the Shift or Alternate key along with another key. The Alternate key is abbreviated to Alt. Hold the Alt or Shift key down and then strike the second key.

At the left or along the top of the keyboard are a group of *function keys*. These are labeled F1, F2, etc. These are used in conjunction with the Ctrl, Alt, and Shift keys to carry out various WordPerfect operations.

The cursor can be repositioned anywhere on the screen, using the four *arrow keys* at the right of the keyboard. You can move the cursor to the end of any line by typing Home Home ➤, or to the beginning of the line by typing a Home Home ◄. You can move the cursor to the beginning of the document by typing Home Home ▲ or to the end of the document by typing Home Home ▼.

You can also *scroll* up or down on a page by using the + or - keys at the extreme right of the keyboard. This causes the computer to move a screen window up or down. The *PgUp* and *PgDn keys* on the keypad can be used to move a full page up or down.

When you reach the end of a page, WordPerfect automatically inserts a dashed line across the page. This tells you that you have reached the bottom of the page.

Features

WordPerfect, as do most word processors, provides the user with many convenient typing features. For example, lines can be automatically centered, copy indented, or tabbed to line up on selected columns, and pages can be numbered in different places on the page.

Headers and *footers*, which are titles or descriptive lines, may be placed at the top or bottom of a page and run throughout a document. *Footnotes* may be added at the bottom of a page and automatically referenced to the text.

A word processing user can set copy in *boldface* (darker type), *underline*, or a different type style, depending upon his or her needs. WordPerfect makes it possible to *search* for the occurrence of a word or phrase and then direct the computer to automatically *replace* it with another word or phrase. For example, WordPerfect can search for every occurrence of "Smith" and replace it with "Smythe" wherever it occurs in the document.

MAKING CHANGES AND CORRECTIONS

As you keyboard your document, you will no doubt want to make changes and corrections. WordPerfect makes it easy to modify a document.

Deleting material

Use the *delete key* to correct or eliminate an unwanted letter or word. Position the cursor on the character and press the delete key until the material is erased. For example, let's say you misspell the word "the" as "thhe." To delete the extra "h," position the cursor on the second "h," and press the delete key. The "h" will be removed and you will be left with "the."

The *backspace key* is also used to delete characters. It differs from the delete key in that it erases the character to the left. To eliminate an entire word, place the cursor on the word and press the Ctrl and backspace keys. For example, take the sentence "This is my very first time using WordPerfect." Let's suppose you want to eliminate the word "very." Position the cursor on the word and press the Ctrl and backspace keys. The sentence will now read, "This is my first time using WordPerfect."

You can delete a sentence to the period by striking the Ctrl and F4 keys, and then selecting the 3 option. You can delete to the end of a line by striking the Ctrl and End keys. You may delete to the end of the page by striking the Ctrl and PgDn keys. WordPerfect has provisions for deleting an entire block. This is done by striking the Alt and F4 keys, and then selecting the delete option.

Inserting new material

If you want to *insert* a new word into material you have already typed, position the cursor at the point at which you wish to add text and then keyboard the material. For example, in the sentence "This is my first time using WordPerfect," let's insert the word "very" to make the sentence read "This is my very first time using WordPerfect." Position the cursor in the space between "my" and "first." Type in the word "very." If you wish to type over existing words, turn off the insert mode by striking the Insert key.

This places you in the type-over mode. To turn the insert mode back on, strike the *Insert key* once again.

Formatting

WordPerfect defaults to automatic *formatting*. This means that if you delete a word or phrase, the gap is automatically closed up. If you add words, the computer properly spaces all lines, giving paragraphs a neat finished look. As the machine formats, WordPerfect does not hyphenate words. If you wish to change this default and turn hyphenation on, type the Shift and F8 keys, select option 1, and then option 1 again.

Spell checker

WordPerfect has a built-in *spell checker*. This allows you to scan the document and automatically check it for misspelled words. To spell check a document, strike the Ctrl and F2 keys. The computer will then compare each word against a standard dictionary stored in memory.

The spell checker allows you to select from a group of correctly spelled choices, to change the spelling manually, or to ignore the spelling.

Thesaurus

WordPerfect also has a built-in *thesaurus*. This may be called in at any point in a document by striking the Alt and F1 keys. The thesaurus gives suggested substitutions and alternate words from a standard thesaurus with over 100,000 synonyms stored in the computer. Together with the automatic *outline generator* and a *grammar checker*, the spell checker and thesaurus provide powerful tools to generate correctly spelled and clearly written text.

DEFAULT SETTINGS

Default settings determine whether a document will be double or single spaced, the size of the page, whether pages will be numbered, etc. Default settings, already established by WordPerfect, can be changed as desired. For instance, you can specify:

whether the document is single or double spaced
whether it is right justified
the left or right margin settings (line width)
whether pages are to be numbered consecutively
other features as needed

This information is provided to the computer by selecting options from a menu screen. Let us see how each of these steps is handled in Word-Perfect.

Specifying line spacing

You can specify whether the document will be single or double spaced. This is done by striking the Shift and F8 keys. This will display the format screen. You can change *line spacing* from single to double spacing. WordPerfect defaults to single line spacing. Other choices on the format menu allow you to change left and right margin settings, justification, hyphenation, etc.

Right justification

Documents can be set right justified, if so desired. This means that both the left and right hand margins are neatly aligned. *Justification* is achieved when the computer inserts extra spaces into the lines to make them all come out even at the right-hand margin.

Justification is turned on or off, using the format menu discussed above. The computer automatically defaults to full right-hand justification. You can easily reverse the condition at any time by going back to the format screen and changing the justification settings. Choices include left-aligned, centered, right-aligned, or full justification.

Margin settings

The left and right *margins* are set to default at one inch. These are set from the format menu, Shift F8. Hold down the Shift key and strike F8. The computer will display the left- and right-hand margin settings. These can be changed if desired.

Page numbering

WordPerfect defaults to no page numbering. You can set *page numbering* if you desire. Strike the Shift and F8 keys to display the format menu. This menu gives you the option to set page numbering, to center a page top and bottom, etc. You can choose whether you want every page numbered, alternate pages numbered, or no pages numbered.

PRINTING THE DOCUMENT

The last step in the cycle is to *print* the document. This is done by typing the Shift and F7 keys (Print). This displays the Print menu (Fig. 8.2). The Print menu gives you several options. By selecting a 6, you can view the page on your monitor as it would appear if it were printed. If you select 1, the computer will print out the full multipage document. By choosing 2, you can print only selected pages of your document.

Some printers are equipped to print either letter- or draft-quality documents. If you select T from the Print menu, you will be given several text-quality choices. You may then select draft, medium, or high quality.

```
Print

        1 - Full Document
        2 - Page
        3 - Document on Disk
        4 - Control Printer
        5 - Multiple Pages
        6 - View Document
        7 - Initialize Printer


Options

        S - Select Printer                    HP LaserJet IIP
        B - Binding Offset                    0"
        N - Number of Copies                  1
        U - Multiple Copies Generated by      WordPerfect
        G - Graphics Quality                  Medium
        T - Text Quality                      Draft



Selection: 0
```

Fig. 8.2—WordPerfect Print Menu

DIRECTORY OF SAVED PROGRAMS

Once you have saved or printed a file, it is saved in a *directory*. You may later *retrieve* the file, delete it, move it, or make other changes. If you would like to see a directory of your programs, strike the F5 key. This will cause the computer to display the directory line. When you hit the Enter key, a directory of all your files is displayed.

The arrow keys are used to highlight a particular file. Once this is done, you may retrieve the file by striking a 1. This brings the document back onto the screen. You may delete the file by striking a 2. Other options allow you to print the file, copy it, or merely look at it without making any changes.

In this application example we have presented only a few of the many commands and features available in WordPerfect. As in any endeavor, a user becomes more productive as he or she gains skill and expertise. WordPerfect provides a comprehensive reference manual to assist in learning its software and its many features.

Many of the newer word processing packages have been expanded to provide desktop publishing features. These programs can prepare newsletters, bulletins, or other typeset-quality printed documents. They allow the computer user to lay out and design multipage publications on the screen and print them out on a laser printer. The next chapter describes desktop publishing software in detail.

*A*pplications programs are written to solve a specific user problem. They are sold as packages containing a disk and documentation. Users assess their software needs, review available software products, and then make a selection. Word processing packages are used to write, revise, and arrange textual matter such as correspondence and reports. Some have built-in spelling checkers. Text is entered, displayed on the screen, and revised, and a finished document is printed out.

WordPerfect is a menu-driven word processor. The editing screen displays a cursor and a status line. WordPerfect provides automatic word wrap. Control, Alt, Shift, and arrow keys are used to position the cursor on the screen. Among the features provided by WordPerfect are headers, footers, footnoting, boldface, underlining, and search and replace.

Text can be inserted or deleted. Paragraphs may be formatted to realign text. A spell checker, thesaurus, outline generator, and grammar checker are provided. Default settings control line spacing, justification, margin settings, and page numbering. Once composed, documents can be printed out. Some word processing programs perform desktop publishing functions and are used to prepare bulletins, brochures, and other documents.

Selected Readings

Hutchinson, Sarah E. *Computers*, Irwin (1992). Module B.

Parker, Charles S. *Understanding Computers and Information Processing*, Dryden Press (1992). Chapter 9.

Rochester, Jack B. *Computers*, Irwin (1993). Chapter 4.

REVIEW QUESTIONS

True or False Questions

1. Applications software is designed to solve local information problems.
2. Software selection does not involve evaluating a program's capabilities.
3. WordPerfect software is able to create, edit, and print out a document.
4. Documents can be created and edited using WordPerfect, but require separate software to be printed out.
5. The WordPerfect status line always shows the current date.
6. The status line appears at the upper left of the screen.
7. WordPerfect does not contain default settings.
8. Right justification is easily accomplished using WordPerfect.
9. Changes and corrections are made in WordPerfect using the delete and backspace keys.
10. WordPerfect can underline but not boldface words.
11. New material is inserted in a document by positioning the cursor and then keyboarding.

12. The formatting function creates neatly aligned paragraphs.
13. The function of the spell checker is to check correct grammar.
14. The function of a thesaurus is to find words with similar meanings.
15. WordPerfect has no file naming conventions.

Completion Questions

1. WordPerfect is an example of a _____ driven program.
2. _____ programs tailor software to a specific computer, monitor, or printer.
3. Word processing programs are sometimes known as _____ editors.
4. The _____ feature eliminates the need for typing a carriage return at the end of each line.
5. F1, F2, and F3 are examples of _____ keys.

ANSWER KEY

True or False Questions

1. T
2. F
3. T
4. F
5. F
6. F
7. F
8. T
9. T
10. F
11. T
12. T
13. F
14. T
15. F

Completion Questions

1. menu
2. Install
3. text
4. word wrap
5. function

9

Desktop Publishing Software

*D*emand is increasing for desktop publishing hardware, software, and related equipment. Both large and small businesses, schools, government agencies, and private individuals use computers, scanners, and other equipment to perform desktop publishing.

In this chapter we will study the principles of desktop publishing, review page makeup software, and describe some of the typical applications for desktop publishing. The chapter discusses desktop publishing hardware, software, and procedures.

DESKTOP PUBLISHING DEFINED

Desktop publishing is the application of the personal computer to the editing, composition, and layout of the printed word and the generation of artwork, pictures, and type for reproduction. Desktop publishing includes the production of newsletters, brocures, magazines, posters, reports, letters, memos, and other publications on a personal computer without the aid of professional printers or typesetters.

Desktop publishing is the manipulation of text, art, photographs, illustrations, lines, and other typographic elements in order to generate high quality output that can be copied on an ordinary photocopier or duplicated in volume by offset printing or other techniques. It is the result of an evolution in computer hardware and software and is a step beyond word processing.

Word processing is the manipulation of words, phrases, or textual matter to generate letters, memos, and reports. In word processing, a manuscript is keyboarded into a computer. The text is subsequently edited and revised and, after appropriate formatting, a finished draft is generated. Word processing focuses upon words and phrases. The domain of desktop publishing is the document, chapter, or even an entire book or other publication.

Because of advances in software, it is possible to create desktop published documents using sophisticated word processing software. It is also possible to generate text-oriented documents, such as memos and reports, using desktop publishing software exclusively. As a result, the areas of desktop publishing and word processing have begun to overlap.

DESKTOP PUBLISHING CYCLE

In desktop publishing, documents move through a series of steps from idea origination to finished document. Information, including both text and art, is input, positioned or pasted up on-screen, and output. During the *desktop publishing cycle*, information can be typed directly onto the on-screen document or imported into the system from the word processor in the form of files (Fig 9.1). Files may be either text or graphic, allowing both pictures and words to be integrated.

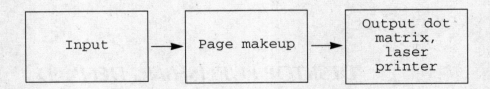

Fig. 9.1—Desktop Publishing Cycle

A powerful feature of desktop publishing software is its ability to use master pages and templates. A *template* is a predesigned page format that incorporates all of the typographic elements, type sizes and styles, rules, borders, and page margins into a form that serves as a basis for formatting the final page (Fig. 9.2). Templates are also known as *style sheets*. Various documents can be created using a template as a base, thus allowing numerous documents, all bearing similar design characteristics, to be generated.

HEAD 1

In se perpetuo Tempus as revolubile gyro Iam revocat Zephyros, vere tepente, novos. Induiturque brev Tellus reparata iuventam, Iamque soluta gelu dulce virescit humus. Fallor? an et nobis redeunt in carmina vires, Ingeniumque mihi munere veris adest? Munere veris adest, iterumque vigescit ab illo (Quis putet?) atque aliquod iam sibi poscit opus. Castalis ante osculos, bifid umque cacumen oberrat. Pyrenen somnia nocte ferunt. Concitaquq arcano fervent mihi pectora motu, Et furor, et sonitus.

HEAD 1

Me sacer intus agit. Delius ipse venit. Iam mihi mens liquidi raptatur in ardua caeli, Perque vagas nubes corpore liber eo. Perque umbras, perque antra feror, penetralia vatum; Et mihi fana patent interiora Deum. Intuiturque animus toto quic agatur Olympo, Nec fugiunt oculos Tartara caeca meos. Quid tam grande sonat distento spiritus ore? Quid parit haec rabies, quid sacer iste furor? Veris, io! rediere vices; celebremus honores Veris, et hoc subeat Musa perennis opus. Iam sol, Aethiopas fugiens Tithoniaque arva, Flectit ad Arctoas aurea lora plagas.

HEAD 1

Est breve noctis iter, brevis est mora noctis opacae, Horrida cum tenebris exulat illa suis. Iamque Lycaonius plaustrum caeleste Boötes Non longa sequirtur fessus ut ante via, Nunc etiam solitas circum Iovis atria toto Excubias agitant sidera rara polo. Nam dolus et caedes, et vis cum nocte recessit,

Name
Address
City, State Zip

Name
Address
City, State Zip

Company Name

Title
Placeholder

HEAD 1

Forte aliques scopuli recubans in vertice pastor, Roscida cum primo sole rubescit humus, "Hac," ait, "hac certe caruisti nocte puella, Phoebe, tua, celeres quae retineret equos." Laeta suas repetit silvas, pharet ramque resumit Cynthia. Luciferas ut videt alta rotas, Et tenues ponens, radios gaudere videtur Officium fieri tam penetralia vatum breve fratris ope. "Desere," Phoebus aid, "thalamos, Aurora seniles; Quid iuvat effoeto procubuisse toro? Te manet Aeolides viridi venator in herba; Surge."

Caption

HEAD 1

"Tuos ignes altus Hymettus habet." Flava verecundo dea crimen in ore fatetur, Et matutinos oscius urget equos. Exuit invisam Tellus rediviva senectam, Et cupit amplexus, Phoebe, subire tuos. Et cupit, et digna est; quid enim formosius illa, Pandit ut omniferos luxuriosa sinus, Atque Arabum spirat messes, et ab ore venusto Mitia cum Paphiis fundit amosma rosis? Ecce, coronatur sacro frons ardua luco, Cingit ut Idaeam pinea turris Pim; Et vario madidos intexit flore capillos, Floribus et visa est.

HEAD 1

Polsse placere suis, Floribus effusos et erat redimita capillos, Taenario placuit diva Sicana Deo penetralia vatum. Aspice,

Phoebe, tibi faciles hortantur amores, Mellitasque movent flamina verna preces. Cinnamea Zephyrus leve plaudit odorifer ala, Blanditiasque tibi ferre videntur aves. Nec sine dote tuos temeraria quaerit amores Terra, nec optato poscit egena toros; Alma salutiferum mediocos tibi gramen in usus Praebet.

Et hinc titulos adiuvat ipsa tuos. Polsse placere suis, Floribus effusos et erat redimita capillos, Taenario placuit diva Sicana Deo. Nec sine dote tuos temeraria quaerit amores Terra, nec optato poscit egena toros. Aspice, Phoebe, tibi faciles hortantur amores, Mellitasque movent flamina verna preces.

HEAD 1

In se perpetuo Tempus as revolubile gyro Iam revocat Zephyros, vere tepente, novos. Induiturque brev Tellus reparata iuventam, Iamque soluta gelu dulce virescit humus. Fallor? an et nobis redeunt in carmina vires,

Caption

Ingeniumque mihi munere veris adest? Munere veris adest, iterumque vigescit ab illo (Quis putet?) atque aliquod iam sibi poscit opus. Castalis ante osculos, bifidumque cacumen oberrat, Et mihi Pyrenen somnia nocte ferunt. Concitaquq arcano fervent mihi pectora motu, Et furor, et sonitus rae sacer intus agit. Delius ipse venit. Iam mihi mens

Caption

liquidi raptatur in ardua caeli, Perque vagas nubes corpore liber eo. Perque umbras, perque antra feror, penetralia vatum; Et mihi fana patent interiora Deum.

HEAD 1

Intuiturque animus toto quic agatur Olympo, Nec fugiunt oculos Tartara caeca meos. Quid tam grande sonat distento spiritus ore? Quid parit haec rabies, quid sacer iste furor? Veris, io! rediere vices; celebremus honores Veris, et hoc subeat Musa perennis opus. Iam sol, Aethiopas fugiens Tithoniaque arva, Flectit ad Arctoas aurea lora plagas penetralia vatum. In se perpetuo Tempus as revolubile gyro Iam revocat Zephyros, vere tepente, novos. Induiturque brev Tellus reparata iuventam, Iamque soluta gelu dulce virescit humus. Fallor? an et nobis redeunt in carmina vires, In dommus daemon ure veris adest?

Fig. 9.2—Templates and Style Sheets

After text and illustrations have been input, they can be arranged or rearranged on a page in a process known as page makeup. *Page makeup* involves positioning art or text, aligning elements along a margin, and adding rules, borders, or other typographic elements.

The last step in the cycle is the output of a finished document. This is done by printing pages on a letter-quality dot matrix or laser printer. Laser printers are preferred because they can output a wide variety of type styles and sizes closely resembling professional typeset quality. Short runs can be printed out on a laser printer or, if only a few copies are desired, on a dot matrix or other letter-quality printer. Production runs, usually 100 or more, are best reproduced either on an office copier or by the offset printing process.

ON-SCREEN AND MECHANICAL PASTEUP

Prior to the advent of desktop publishing, virtually all preparation for printing was done through the use of mechanical pasteups. Since books, articles, and advertisements are photographed for platemaking, a mechanical pasteup was required. This involved pasting down typeset paragraphs of text, artwork, drawings, and illustrations. Individual pieces of art were glued to a heavy piece of pasteboard using either rubber cement or a thin layer of wax applied to the back of the artwork. Individual elements could be moved about on the pasteboard, but this process required a degree of skill on the part of the designer. The procedure was time consuming and required a T-square to ensure that all elements on the pasteup were aligned.

Changes and revisions were difficult to make on mechanical pasteups. Individual pieces of art had to be removed, repositioned or substituted, and then repasted accurately to accommodate alterations. Once the final pasteup was approved, it was sent to the camera department where it was photographed and converted into plates for printing.

Page makeup software eliminates the need for rubber cement or wax coating. It is a more flexible means than mechanical pasteup and requires less manual skill, although design talent still comes in handy. Layouts are prepared using a computer with images displayed on a screen. This replaces the pasteboard. Text is typed directly on the monitor, or read in from word processing files stored on disk. The monitor displays the pasteup page showing the position of each element as it will appear on the final document. This type of display is known as *WYSIWYG* (What You See Is What You Get).

The computer automatically ensures that all elements are square and neatly positioned. Elements may be moved around or repositioned on the screen and paragraphs may be added or deleted easily, since rubber cement and wax are not used. Once the final pasteup is satisfactory, the operator directs the computer to print out a finished document. This may be done using either a dot matrix or laser printer, depending upon the quality requirements of the job. The finished document may then be photocopied or duplicated by offset printing. Page makeup software is quickly becoming the preferred method of preparing copy for reproduction because of its ease and convenience.

DESKTOP PUBLISHING APPLICATION EXAMPLE

Alice Summers operates a small import and export company and relies heavily upon her desktop publishing system. Alice's experience illustrates the way a desktop publishing system functions. Summers Trading Company publishes a catalog of imported jewelry. The catalog consists of a descriptive page on each of the more than 200 unique accessories sold by the company. Each of Summers's customers is provided with a three-ring binder and regularly receives updated catalog sheets.

Alice produces these catalog sheets in her own office, using her desktop publishing equipment. A basic *style sheet* has been developed for the catalog pages. The style sheet includes the company logo, descriptive text on the product, and a photograph. It defines the type sizes, margins, spacing, and position of artwork for all elements on the page. To produce each of the catalog pages, Alice Summers begins with the layout described in the style sheet.

When a new catalog page must be prepared, Alice loads a style sheet from computer memory. She calls in a text file, previously generated on a word processor, that includes a product description and other data. The illustration of the product is created by scanning a drawing or photograph that has been provided to Alice by her supplier. The finished catalog sheet, including text and illustrations, is then displayed on her monitor. After Alice has proofread and checked the design and contents of her new catalog sheets, she directs the computer to output them on a laser printer.

The laser printer outputs a high-quality piece of artwork that can then be copied on her office copier or reproduced in quantity by offset printing. Alice's desktop publishing equipment cost less than $8000 and is housed on a tabletop in one area of her office. The same system that produces her catalog sheets is used to generate sales brochures, letterheads, and other items. The system serves Alice Summers well, providing her with a closely controlled in-house means of setting type and preparing layouts for printing.

OTHER DESKTOP PUBLISHING APPLICATIONS

Let us take a look at other types of jobs that may be produced efficiently and economically using desktop publishing technology. The uses for this new technology will no doubt expand as more organizations become familiar with it.

1. Letters, memos, and other documents. Professional-looking office communications can be generated using desktop publishing equipment. Attractive type styles and typeset-quality composition, closely resembling professional printing, can be achieved. Many organizations prefer desktop publishing output to documents prepared manually or on a word processor.

2. Marketing literature. A wide variety of sales literature and promotional materials can be constructed using desktop publishing facilities. Employees can paste up text, photographs, drawings, and artwork on-screen. These elements can then be manipulated and output as attractive brochures at a minimal expense. Later, revisions and changes can be easily made.

3. Newsletters. Newsletters and company bulletins are another major use for desktop publishing. Multipage documents can be developed using text stored on disks. The finished newsletter may contain a variety of stories prepared on word processors and provided to the desktop publisher on floppy disk files. Once a format has been established, the next month's issue can be prepared easily by simply changing the text files and allowing new information to flow into the pages.

4. Posters and banners. Large posters and banners can be generated using desktop publishing. Many systems are able to set large size type with lettering sometimes ten or more inches high. This provides an inexpensive means of creating signs, pennants, and large graphics.

5. Transparency masters. Overhead transparency masters and colored thirty-five-millimeter slides can be generated using desktop publishing. This eliminates the need for sending material out for typesetting or preparing laboriously hand-lettered artwork.

6. Pamphlets, manuals, and books. Desktop publishing jobs are not limited to one- or two-page documents. In fact, desktop publishing is particularly suited to multipage jobs. Standard page layouts can be prepared and then long documents generated from text stored on disk. Desktop publishing software is capable of formatting, laying out, and automatically numbering pages for lengthy documents. It can also control hyphenation as well as "widows" and "orphans," typographic terms referring to dangling words or partial lines carried onto a new page, detracting from typographic quality.

BENEFITS OF DESKTOP PUBLISHING

Prior to the advent of desktop publishing, clients generally turned the task of laying out and designing a printed document over to a professional artist or designer. The designer created the finished pasteup board, selected appropriate typefaces, and prepared a piece with pleasing margins, type, and color. The basic responsibility for creating the design and specifying the type styles for the typesetter to follow was in the hands of the designer. Proofreading was, and still is, handled by the client.

Desktop publishing has shifted these tasks to the creator of the document, who now has the responsibility for all aspects of the publishing cycle. In some settings, the creator is a professional designer; in others, a manager, secretary, small business owner, or the like. The nonprofessional designer must now both specify typefaces and style the type, lay out pages, proofread, and perform various other tasks that were formerly delegated to a professional. However, this new technology has brought with it a number of advantages not possible under the traditional client-designer relationship.

Let us look at some of the benefits of desktop publishing.

1. Speed. Organizations which produce their own publications, reports, and documents on an in-house system can save a great deal of time. Important jobs need not be sent outside and can be given top priority in-house. Therefore, jobs that once took days or weeks can now be ready in hours or even minutes.

2. Closer control. Owners of desktop publishing systems can exercise a high degree of control over their work. They are not bound by the economic limitations or production restraints sometimes placed on documents that are sent to a commercial vendor. The desktop publisher is the one who sets production priorities, running some jobs ahead of others and working evenings or weekends when necessary. Changes, which might be logistically difficult if not impossible when a commercial vendor is doing the job, become considerably simpler when work is done in-house.

3. Cost savings. For many jobs it is substantially less expensive to prepare a publication in-house. A typesetter need not be paid to set type, and a printer need not be paid to prepare illustrations and duplicate documents in limited quantities. These tasks can be performed on an ordinary personal computer with the proper hardware and appropriate software. Many businesses and organizations own a computer and a number of them have laser printers. Thus there is little capital investment required because the equipment is already available in-house.

4. Security. A high degree of document security and confidentiality can be maintained when the entire production and reproduction process is kept within the originator's grasp. Documents containing financial information, patent data, proprietary formulas, marketing strategies, competitive reports,

and other sensitive material can be designed, proofread, and output without using outside sources.

5. Integration into overall corporate strategy. Through the use of desktop publishing, managers are able to integrate their printing and publishing requirements into overall strategies and plans. Uniform type styles, logos, and layouts can be established and utilized. For instance, a standard report design may be developed for use throughout an organization. If all departments of an organization use similar software and hardware, they can produce uniform documents more easily than in the past. Tying together a corporate image in this way is essential for many large organizations.

DESKTOP PUBLISHING CONSTRAINTS

Although desktop publishing has many advantages for large and small businesses, government agencies, and other organizations, it is not without its limitations. Before considering an investment in a desktop publishing facility, the following points should be evaluated.

1. Training costs. To get the most out of computer hardware and software, users must gain a degree of skill in their use. While some desktop publishing programs are easy to learn in less than an hour or so, others are more complex and require a substantially greater investment of time and effort to master.

2. Technical limitations. It is not reasonable to expect that a desktop publishing system costing only a few hundred dollars can replace a full-service printing plant or equal phototypeset quality. Commercial printers who are equipped with high-quality facilities are able to produce professionally screened photographs and color pictures. Some also have bindery equipment to produce multipage booklets. Some shops employ creative printing designers who have years of experience in layout and design. If this level of quality and skill is required, then a document generated on an in-house system may not suffice.

3. Capital investment costs. A desktop publishing system that meets a user's requirements may cost upwards of several thousand dollars. To obtain the look of true typeset quality, a very high-resolution laser printer is a necessity. A microcomputer with hard disk storage is also needed. A full capability system requires a mouse, scanner, and specialized software.

HARDWARE CONFIGURATIONS

The capabilities of a desktop publishing system are largely dependent upon the hardware and software components that make up the system. A minimum desktop publishing *configuration* can be constructed from an inexpensive microcomputer equipped with a dot matrix printer and a single desktop publishing program. A system with maximum capability will include a high-powered computer, a laser printer, scanner, mouse, and several specialized desktop publishing programs. The systems described below illustrate a range of hardware and software configurations.

Basic system

Practical desktop publishing can be performed on an inexpensive desktop computer such as an IBM PC or compatible, Apple, or Macintosh. A minimal computer system is useful for word processing or other general-purpose computing and is suitable for simple desktop publishing tasks, such as newsletters, reports, and manuals. Let us go over the basic hardware components.

PERSONAL COMPUTER

A personal computer equipped with keyboard and monitor is a necessity. These systems are usually equipped with at least an *80286 microprocessor chip*. The minimum requirement is 640K memory on a system with a hard disk drive. Additional memory increases the system's capability and speed.

MONITOR

A standard *monochrome monitor* is suitable for minimal desktop publishing tasks. However, the small screen on an inexpensive monitor limits the size of page that can be displayed on the screen. Since only part of a page can be seen at once, the user must scroll in order to see different parts of the page. Large screen and color monitors with high resolution are preferred for more extensive desktop publishing projects, especially where graphics are involved.

PRINTER

Documents of minimal quality can be generated using a *dot matrix printer*. These output devices form images composed of small dots. They are not suitable where high-quality or letter-perfect images are required.

A system such as the one just described is not able to scan pictures or drawings into memory. It cannot display an entire 8-1/2-by-11-inch page on the screen except in a reduced view that doesn't show details. All pointing and input must be done from the keyboard. Color images cannot be manipulated, and output does not meet typeset-quality standards. Nevertheless, a monochrome system is adequate for clubs, schools, small businesses, and many personal uses.

Full-capability system

A more sophisticated computer system is required if high-quality pages are to be generated, color is needed, or photographs or artwork are to be scanned. A fully featured system makes up a fast, full-range desktop publishing system.

HIGH PERFORMANCE COMPUTER

A computer with a high speed CPU chip, such as an *80386* or *80486*, is generally required for desktop publishing systems with maximum capability (Fig. 9.3). The computer should include a hard disk with upwards of eighty megabytes of secondary storage. The system should also have at least four megabytes of primary memory. These greater memory requirements are needed because desktop publishing files can often occupy more than one megabyte. This is especially true when artwork, drawings, and figures are to be scanned.

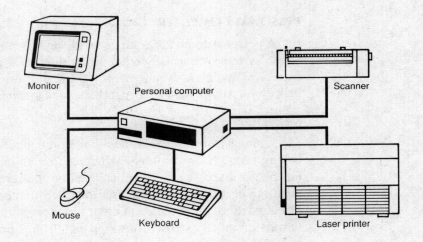

Fig. 9.3—Full-Feature System

HIGH-RESOLUTION MONITOR

High-resolution monitors are preferred because they display images with fine details. Large screen monitors are also used because they can display a full 8-1/2-by-11-inch page vertically. Some monitors can also display two facing pages. These monitors facilitate page makeup and design, since several pages can be displayed at the same time.

MOUSE

A *mouse* is a pointing device that is moved about on a tabletop and positions a cursor on a screen. It can supplement or replace a keyboard as a means of information entry. Using a mouse does not require keyboarding skills and the user can point to areas on a screen easily with this device. A mouse helps designers move and place design elements and artwork precisely on a page.

SCANNER

A *scanner* is an input device that converts text or images into files that can be manipulated by the computer. The scanner allows text, line drawings, and photographs to be read from a page, displayed on a screen, or stored in memory.

LASER PRINTER

A *laser printer* is an output device that can image a page with typewritten letters or printed fonts, line drawings, pictures, or illustrations. These devices generate output consisting of 300 dots or more per inch. They create words and pictures with higher resolution than is possible on a dot matrix printer.

DESKTOP PUBLISHING SOFTWARE

Many different desktop publishing programs have come on the market in the last several years. Some desktop publishing software does little more than format and output single-page newsletters. Others are fully featured and can generate multipage documents with pictures, drawings, and good-quality typesetting. They can insert rules, borders, and boxes, position artwork, generate reverses and tint screen areas, and provide WYSIWYG page display.

Desktop publishing software can be grouped into several categories:

1. Basic desktop publishing software. A variety of desktop publishing software, priced at several hundred dollars or less, is on the market. These programs prepare newsletters, brochures, leaflets, and other documents. They are referred to as low end software because their price range and capabilities are below those of the more elaborate products costing $500 or more. These programs produce good results for uncomplicated documents.

Basic programs provide WYSIWYG on-screen editing capability. This allows the page to be seen as it will appear in the final printout. Low end software can produce multicolumn documents, output various typefaces and sizes, and import text files which can be formatted into columns. This software is not suited for complex multipage documents or those involving extensive artwork, figures, and illustrations. Most low-end software is unable to handle lengthy documents that require changing formats for each page in the document.

2. Full-feature software. These sophisticated software packages can be used to make up and compose multichapter books and manuals. They can import text files generated by word processors or receive input directly from the keyboard.

Full-feature software offers the widest range of typographic options. These packages allow the user to format pages of varying sizes, including text, in a variety of typefaces. Boxes, vertical and horizontal rules, and figures and illustrations can be integrated into the pages. Initial letters, hanging indented paragraphs, and various line spacing can also be included. Leading full-feature products are Ventura Publisher and Aldus PageMaker.

Software in this category features full WYSIWYG display. This enables the operator to lay out and design full size pages as they will appear in the finished document while observing size and spatial relationships. When output on a laser printer, the finished documents closely resemble those generated on conventional typesetting equipment.

TURNKEY SYSTEMS

The task of integrating computer hardware and software can sometimes be complex. An efficient and functional desktop publishing system requires the selection of the proper microcomputer, monitor, and printer. In addition, appropriate software must be purchased and properly installed. If any element in the system is incompatible or not properly installed, satisfactory results cannot be obtained.

Sometimes users of desktop publishing systems experience difficulty in getting all parts of a system to work together. Although a degree of industry standardization has taken place, not all printers, scanners, and computer software are fully compatible. Software written for one computer, such as an IBM or Macintosh system, may not function on another computer from a different manufacturer. Special cables may be required to link printers with a computer, and many programs are designed to work with specific types of monitors.

As a result of these start-up problems, a number of firms have put together microcomputer-based desktop publishing systems. These packaged systems, known as *turnkey systems*, are fully integrated. A number of desktop publishers follow this approach to hardware and software selection. Many vendors provide instructions, courses, user manuals, and sample programs to help the purchaser learn desktop publishing with a minimum of effort.

We have overviewed several different types of desktop publishing systems in this chapter. We have also discussed page makeup software, as well as the advantages and limitations of desktop publishing. All indications are that desktop publishing will continue to grow into one of the major applications of computer usage in the office. In the next two chapters we will look at other applications for the computer in business and industry.

Desktop publishing applies the personal computer to the task of editing, composing, and laying out documents. While word processing manipulates words, desktop publishing concerns itself with the production and layout of overall documents. A basic desktop publishing system uses a desktop computer equipped with keyboard, monitor, printer, mouse, and possibly a scanner.

A basic desktop publishing configuration can produce utilitarian documents. A full-capability system will include a high-performance computer, high-resolution monitor, mouse, scanner, and laser printer. Laser printers are preferred because they can output high-resolution images consisting of both text and illustrations. A template is a predesigned page format that incorporates all the elements in a page and serves as a basis for formatting the final page. Page makeup involves positioning of art and the alignment of all elements into the finished page.

A benefit of page makeup software is the flexibility and ease with which text and illustrations can be manipulated. It is replacing mechanical pasteup techniques, which involve cutting and pasting paper documents. A WYSIWYG display shows the appearance of the final printout on a monitor.

Desktop publishing brings the convenience of the print shop to the business office. Its benefits include cost savings, speed, control, security, and integration of publishing into an organization's overall strategy.

Desktop publishing software can be grouped into categories. Basic desktop publishing software can generate multicolumn documents in a variety of typefaces and sizes and can import text files. Full-feature software can produce complex multichapter books and manuals. Vendors market complete systems known as turnkey systems.

Selected Readings

Parker, Charles S. *Understanding Computers and Information Processing*, Dryden Press (1992). Chapter 9.

Silver, Gerald A. *Introduction to Desktop Publishing*, W. C. Brown (1990). Chapter 1.

Silver, Gerald A. *Layout, Design, and Typography for the Desktop Publisher*, W. C. Brown (1991). Chapter 1.

REVIEW QUESTIONS

True or False Questions

1. The steps in the desktop publishing cycle begin with input.
2. The function of templates is to allow different printers to operate on one system.
3. A minimum configuration desktop publishing system usually includes a scanner.
4. The requirements of a full-capability desktop publishing system include a scanner, laser printer, and mouse.
5. The function of the mouse is to scan documents.
6. The function of the scanner is to input text and drawings.
7. Desktop publishing is defined as high-speed word processing.
8. The advantage of page makeup software is it eliminates manual pasteup.
9. Speed is an advantage of desktop publishing.
10. High equipment cost is a limitation of desktop publishing.
11. A newsletter is an example of a desktop publishing application.
12. A WYSIWYG display does not show the finished page.
13. Desktop publishing cannot be integrated into an overall corporate strategy.
14. Type can be set on desktop publishing equipment.
15. A turnkey system usually does not include a computer.

Completion Questions

1. The desktop publishing cycle ends with _____.
2. There is a wide variety of desktop publishing _____ available for sale.
3. A _____ desktop publishing system includes hardware, software, and integration.
4. PageMaker is an example of _____ software.
5. A _____ is often used to create a standard design newsletter.

ANSWER KEY

True or False Questions

1. T		9. T	
2. F		10. T	
3. F		11. T	
4. T		12. F	
5. F		13. F	
6. T		14. T	
7. F		15. F	
8. T			

Completion Questions

1. output
2. software
3. turnkey
4. full feature
5. template, style sheet

10

Spreadsheets and Graphics Software

Spreadsheet software packages are extremely useful in allowing computer users, particularly in business and scientific endeavors, to arrange data in columns, perform mathematical operations, and print out results. Spreadsheets are like electronic ledger sheets that enable data to be displayed and revised quickly and easily. They are essentially electronic versions of a pencil, columnar pad, and calculator.

One of the most powerful features of spreadsheet software is its ability to perform computations. Formulas can be entered into the spreadsheet. The computer then executes the formula and displays the answer. Formulas may be simple, such as adding the value of two cells, or they may be complex, performing multiplication and division, extracting square roots, computing interest or the present value of the dollar.

WHAT-IF ANALYSIS

Spreadsheets are ideal mechanisms for preparing reports that are to be revised based upon changing assumptions. *What-if analysis* describes a procedure in which one value is changed in a spreadsheet and all subsequent computations are modified accordingly. What-if analysis can be used to experiment with increasing or decreasing costs, sales figures, or changing commission rates. In what-if analysis one or more values can be adjusted and the software recalculates all dependent values.

For example, a manager may wish to know how much money is available each month if a department budget is increased by ten percent. A budget for the coming year can be constructed using a spreadsheet. This consists of rows and columns of numbers for each month in the coming year. The spreadsheet automatically totals all expenses for the month and then adds up all monthly expenses for an annual total. The manager may change one or two expense items in a given month, and the software will automatically recalculate all monthly totals and the annual total.

SPREADSHEET SOFTWARE

Spreadsheet software packages were developed to facilitate the manipulation of data in an electronic worksheet. An early spreadsheet program, VisiCalc, was developed by Dan Bricklin. Today, spreadsheets are used by accountants, managers, office personnel, researchers—virtually anyone who needs to perform computations on data which can be placed in tables.

Some popular spreadsheet packages are Lotus 1-2-3, SuperCalc5, and Multiplan. These ready-to-use packages allow business and personal computer users to manipulate complex tables of values and to prepare reports with columnar or tabular material quickly and easily. Spreadsheet packages are especially useful in preparing business forecasts, budgets, and projections.

Overview of operation

A spreadsheet is an electronic ledger sheet into which data can be entered. The information is displayed in rows and columns and can be changed, revised, or updated by keyboarding in new data.

Spreadsheets allow the user to scan any section on the electronic page quickly and conveniently. The page can be *scrolled* up or down, the display window can be positioned horizontally or vertically, or the screen can be split. With the *split screen*, different types of information can be displayed simultaneously. For instance, a table of numbers can be exhibited on one half of the screen and a visual graph on the other half of the screen.

The information displayed on a spreadsheet is arranged in rows and columns (Fig. 10.1). A *row* is a horizontal division on the worksheet, usually identified by a number. A *column* is a vertical division on the worksheet, usually identified by a letter. The rows and columns together make up a *matrix*. The entire matrix is called a *grid sheet* or simply a *grid*.

Each intersecting point or coordinate is called a *cell* or *entry position*. A cell can contain numeric or alphabetic data or a formula in any position

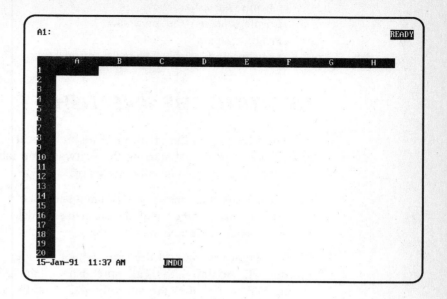

Fig. 10.1—Lotus 1-2-3 Blank Grid

on the grid. The actual information located in a cell is called an *entry*. A particular entry position can be selected by highlighting it. The user can then change or modify the contents of the cell.

Perhaps the most important feature of a spreadsheet is its ability to store a *formula* in a cell. The computer executes the formula, placing the result of the calculation in the cell. A change in the contents of one cell automatically causes the computer to search its memory and revise all related information that is dependent on that cell.

Spreadsheet packages also allow users to copy formulas easily. Once a formula has been entered in one cell, it can be copied to one or more cells.

Sometimes information stored in a given cell must be protected from change. The software provides *cell protection*. This feature allows information to be locked in so that it cannot be changed.

STEPS IN USING A SPREADSHEET

We have chosen to discuss *Lotus 1-2-3* because it is broadly representative of spreadsheet software. Lotus 1-2-3 is an ideal program for creating budgets, expense lists, or other documents containing numeric values.

The creation and manipulation of a spreadsheet using Lotus 1-2-3 involves four distinct steps. These include:

Creating the spreadsheet
Loading data into the spreadsheet
Printing reports
Updating and revising data in the spreadsheet

CREATING THE SPREADSHEET

The first step in the creation of a spreadsheet is its setup. Setting up a spreadsheet consists of starting the software and labeling various columns to hold data. The spreadsheet consists of:

Worksheet area consisting of columns and rows
Control panel at the top of the screen to enter data
Status line at the bottom of the screen

The eight columns in the spreadsheet are identified with the letters A through H. Actually, the full spreadsheet has 256 columns, labeled A through IV, though they are not fully visible on the screen.

Twenty rows are displayed. The rows are numbered from 1 to 20. The full spreadsheet consists of 8,192 rows, numbered 1 through 8,192. A column is identified by its column letter and a row by its row number.

The open display window is a space consisting of a grid of individual cells. The intersection of every column and row creates a cell. Each cell has an address identifying it by column and row number. For instance, the intersection of column A and row 1 creates the cell A1. This cell is nine characters in width and can hold either numeric or alphabetic data.

As we shall see later, it is possible to place a formula in a cell. That formula, for example, can direct the computer to add up all of the cells in a given column and place the total in the cell at the bottom of the column.

The active cell is highlighted. It is the cell in which the next data will be entered. Any cell can be selected by using the arrow keys on the keypad at the right of the keyboard. Let us look at the Lotus 1-2-3 screen more carefully.

CONTROL PANEL

The *control panel* displays information about Lotus 1-2-3 and its operations. It contains three lines. The first line shows the current cell address, the cell format, protection status, column width, and, once entered, the data in the current cell.

On the right of the first line is a mode indicator. It is always visible and tells you what mode you are in, such as READY, EDIT or HELP.

A second line is displayed when creating and editing an entry. This occurs when the / (slash symbol) is typed. This line also prompts for information needed to complete a command.

The third line shows information about a highlighted command. It lists a submenu of choices available for each command selected.

THE WORKSHEET AREA

The *worksheet area* contains up to 256 columns, each containing a maximum of 8,192 rows of data. The current cell, the one in which data will be entered next, is identified by the *cell pointer*. The cell pointer is the highlighted cell.

THE STATUS LINE

The *status line* consists of a date and time indicator, the UNDO indicator, the CIRC indicator, and an indicator which tells whether the NUM (Num Lock), CAPS (Caps Lock), INS, or other key is in effect. The status line also provides the current time and day, and tells whether the operator can undo a command and whether a formula needs to be recalculated.

SLASH COMMANDS

Lotus 1-2-3 contains a group of commands that are called in by a slash. The *slash commands* perform such functions as inserting, deleting, copying, or editing data, loading files, or outputting information. Slash commands are accessed by typing a slash, causing the computer to display a menu on the second line of the control panel.

SPREADSHEET APPLICATION EXAMPLE

Suppose you have been assigned the task of preparing a simple spreadsheet, such as the income statement shown in Fig. 10.2. Let us review the steps followed in setting up and printing out the spreadsheet.

Enter Lotus 1-2-3 and display the spreadsheet window and
    worksheet area
Type in spreadsheet title
Type in column heads
Type in row heads
Enter data
Enter formulas
Save the spreadsheet
Print report

Let us build a spreadsheet step by step. Our spreadsheet consists of an income statement for a four year period. We will want to show net sales,

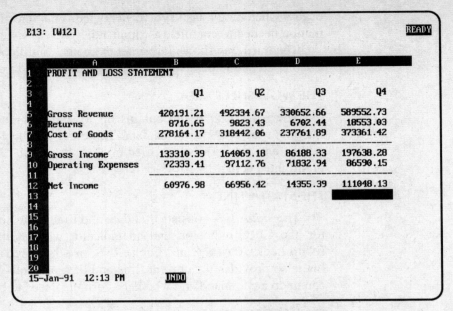

Fig. 10.2—Income Statement Example

cost of goods, and other items for the four years. A study of this example will help you understand how columns and rows of information are entered, computations performed, and other spreadsheet features are carried out.

We begin by entering the directory containing Lotus 1-2-3 and starting the software running:

```
123
```

This will cause a blank worksheet area to be displayed on the screen. The columns are identified by letters of the alphabet and the rows by numbers. Lotus 1-2-3 defaults to a standard column width of nine characters.

We will next title the spreadsheet and then place column headings in the appropriate cells. We position the cursor to cell A1. This is done by using the arrow keys. Once we have highlighted the A1 cell, we may then load data into it. The title INCOME STATEMENT is typed and appears at the top of the screen in the second line of the control panel. Pressing the Enter key transfers the contents of the line into cell A1.

You can edit the line before you press the Enter key by backspacing and typing over. Characters can be inserted or deleted using the Insert or Delete keys. We need not be concerned about the length of the title, since Lotus 1-2-3 allows text to occupy as many spaces as necessary across the columns.

If you detect an error after the data is loaded into the cell, you can still make changes. Highlight the cell to be corrected using the arrow keys, retype the data correctly on the entry line, and press the Enter key.

Lotus 1-2-3 defaults to a standard column width of nine characters. For many purposes, especially for the beginner, it is easier to work with the columns widened to twelve characters. In the example below, a standard column width of twelve characters is used. To widen the columns, enter the following command:

```
/Worksheet,Global,Column-Width,12
```

You need only type in the first letter of each word and then the number, as:

```
/WGC12
```

Next we must widen the first column to fifteen characters. We select the following commands: /Worksheet,Column,Set-Width,15. This can be entered as:

```
/WCS15
```

This command allows us to widen only the first column, whereas the previous command applied globally, that is, to all other columns in the worksheet.

The column headings will be entered next. Using the arrow keys, highlight the position of the first column head. This will be in location B3. The heading Q1 is typed on the entry line and the return key is pressed, transferring it to the proper cell. The cursor is then positioned to cell C3 and the column titled Q2. Cells D3 and E3 are titled accordingly.

We next label the rows. The cursor is positioned in cell A5. This allows you to type in the row head Net Sales. The arrow key is used to place the cursor in cell A6. The heading Cost of Goods is entered into this cell. We next draw a horizontal line from cells B7 to E7. This could be done by highlighting each cell and typing in an apostrophe and twelve hyphens to form a line. The apostrophe is needed to denote that a string of alphabetic characters rather than numeric data is to be entered.

But there is a shortcut. We can copy the contents of cell B7 to cells C7 through E7 using the copy command. To copy a cell, enter:

```
/C
```

The /Copy command causes Lotus 1-2-3 to ask you for a range to copy from. Enter B7. It then asks for a range to copy to. Enter C7..E7. This will cause the horizontal line to extend to the right through all cells on the page. Next, the heads are typed in for rows 8 and 9. Another horizontal line is drawn from B10 to E10, using the same technique as discussed above. Finally, Net Income is typed in as the heading for row 11.

This completes the first step in the creation of the spreadsheet. Data and formulas have not been entered yet. We will next want to load information into the various cells that have been created by the intersection of the columns and rows.

LOADING THE DATA INTO THE SPREADSHEET

Data can be loaded into a cell in a manner similar to that used for typing in headings. Use the arrow keys to highlight cell B5. Type in the numeric data 610000 that is to appear in the cell. As you type, the data appears on the entry line. Check to make sure the proper data has been entered. You may use the backspace or delete key to correct the entry. When you are finished, press the appropriate arrow key. The right arrow key moves the cursor to the cell in the next column, while the down arrow key moves it to the next row. At the same time, the data is moved from the entry line to the chosen cell position.

Continue entering data to complete the cells in rows 5 and 6. If you have made an error, you may go back and highlight a cell, using the arrow keys. The new data is then entered into the cell.

After you have loaded rows 5 and 6, load in the expense items on row 9. As you have probably guessed, we are going to have the computer perform the computations to find gross income for us. We will need to direct the computer to subtract Cost of Goods from Net Sales to find Gross Income. We will also have the computer subtract Expenses from Gross Income to find Net Income.

Loading formulas

A formula, rather than numeric or alphabetic information, may be loaded into a cell. If a formula is used, the computer will execute the formula and place the results in the cell. Formulas must be enclosed in parentheses. In constructing formulas the following mathematical operators are used:

```
+ addition
- subtraction
* multiplication
/ division
```

The next step involves placing specific formulas into cells to perform the necessary calculations. Highlight cell B8. Then enter the following formula:

```
(B5-B6)
```

Press the Enter key to transfer the formula to the cell and the computer immediately executes the formula, placing the result, 95000, in cell B8.

The cursor is positioned in cell C8. The formula (C5-C6) is then entered. We move across each column, entering the correct formula, always subtracting Cost of Goods from Net Sales.

Lotus 1-2-3 has a high degree of intelligence and can assist you in copying formulas from one location to another. Let us see how this is done in the computation of Net Income to save us time. Position the cursor on B11. We now wish to subtract expenses from gross income. Therefore, we enter the formula (B8-B9) into the cell. The computer performs the computation and places the result, 42000, in B11.

We next position the cursor in C11, only this time we will direct the computer to copy the formula from B11. This is done by using the /Copy command. When Lotus 1-2-3 asks for the range to copy from, enter B11. When it asks you for the range to copy to, enter C11..E11. This causes the computer to copy the formula in B11 to all cells in the range that we have specified. The double periods between C11 and E11 mean that a range is specified. The moment the Copy command is issued, the computer copies the formulas into the range and then executes each formula. The finished result should look like the figure.

Saving the spreadsheet

To save a spreadsheet, enter /File,Save. The /FS commands prompts you to type in the name of the file you wish the data to be stored under. Enter a file name such as:

```
INCOME
```

The computer then saves the file, appending a .WK1 as the default extension. If you again save the file later, the computer asks you if you want to cancel, replace, or create a new backup file.

File names should consist of eight letters or less, and they should help identify the contents of the file. The extension WK1 is automatically appended to Lotus 1-2-3 worksheet files. By using this extension, you can quickly identify Lotus 1-2-3 worksheet files. Examples of acceptable file names are:

```
JUNE.WK1
EXPENSES.WK1
SMITH.WK1
```

Printing reports

After all data have been entered into the spreadsheet and the file saved, you will want to generate a hard copy report. Be sure your printer is turned on and loaded with paper. The standard printer default is eighty characters wide and sixty-six lines deep. Since our spreadsheet is smaller than this size, we will not need to adjust our defaults. Enter the following command to print the report:

```
/PPRG
```

Selecting /Print begins the process and displays a menu of options. Choosing Printer directs the output to the printer. Selecting Range asks you to specify the range. You can print out a single entry, row, or column, depending upon your needs. Choosing Go causes the printer to output your report.

Exiting Lotus 1-2-3

After you have printed out the report, you may leave the print mode using the /Quit command. Type:

```
/Q
```

This brings you back to your spreadsheet and you may then terminate operations with another /Q.

Templates

A useful feature of spreadsheets is their ability to use templates. A *template* contains labeled column heads and rows and includes formulas but no data. It provides a useful structure that is readily available for many purposes.

A template may be used in preparing standard order forms, invoices, part requisitions, or other documents. The user need only call in the template and enter relevant data. As the information is entered, the spreadsheet template performs all the calculations. A finished report, containing both the standard data and the new information, is easily printed out. Templates save much time and effort and ensure that information and computations are handled in a consistent manner.

SPREADSHEET GRAPHICS

Lotus 1-2-3 and other spreadsheet software provide excellent graphics capability. This feature enables bar graphs, line charts, pie charts, or other graphics to be created easily. To use the graphics feature, the operator creates a spreadsheet and loads data into the cells in the usual manner. Then the /Graph mode is entered by typing:

```
/G
```

Lotus 1-2-3 provides a group of options, including bar, line, pie, stacked bar, and XY (scatter) charts. The operator selects the type of chart and then specifies the range of values that are to be used in creating the chart. Lotus 1-2-3 automatically generates a graphic (Fig 10.3). The chart may contain a title and other identifying text.

The chart can be printed out using the /Graph Save command. This saves a graph file that can be printed out using the PrintGraph program.

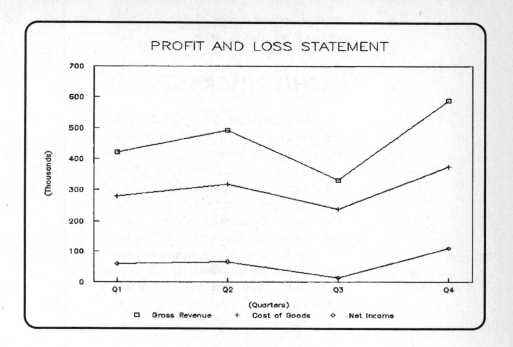

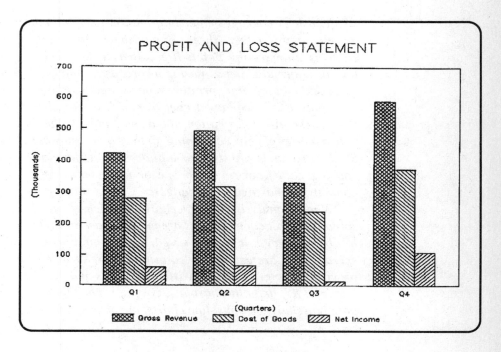

Fig. 10.3—Lotus 1-2-3 Graphs

Depending upon the type of printer, graphs may be printed out in monochrome or in various colors.

GRAPHICS PACKAGES

Graphics software is designed to prepare various types of graphic images. This type of software can generate graphics, including charts and tables, from data provided by Lotus 1-2-3 or any spreadsheet or other software, such as word processors or database managers. The advantage of this type of program is that charts and graphs may be printed out from data generated by programs that do not have graphic capability.

Other graphics software, such as Applause, is designed to create graphics and visuals from spreadsheets that may be converted into slides or overhead transparencies. These programs create multicolor graphics for use in presentations or for broadcast over television.

In the next chapter we will look at database, communications, and integrated software packages, rounding out our discussion of ready-made software.

Spreadsheet packages enter information for manipulation and display on an electronic ledger sheet. Spreadsheets are composed of rows and columns. Intersecting points are called cells. A cell may hold a number, text, or a formula. Steps in using a spreadsheet include creating the spreadsheet and loading data, printing reports, and updating or revising data.

Lotus 1-2-3 displays a control panel, a worksheet area, and a status line. These give information about the status of the spreadsheet and provide a matrix of cells containing up to 256 columns and 8,192 rows of data. Slash commands are used to initiate such actions as widening a column, copying data from a cell to one or more other cells, deleting rows and columns, or making other changes.

What-if analysis is a procedure in which if one value is changed in a spreadsheet all computations are modified accordingly. Once a spreadsheet has been created, it may be saved, revised, and printed out. In Lotus 1-2-3 spreadsheets are usually saved using the .WK1 extension. Lotus 1-2-3 has provisions for generating a variety of charts and graphs. These include bar, line, pie, XY, and other formats. Graphics packages are used to easily prepare bar charts, graphs, line charts, pie charts, and other visual displays.

Selected Readings

Capron, H. L. *Essentials of Computing*, Benjamin Cummings (1992). Chapter 13.
Grupe, Fritz H. *Microcomputer Applications,* W. C. Brown (1992). Part III.
Parker, Charles S. *Understanding Computers and Information Processing*, Dryden Press (1992). Chapter 10.

REVIEW QUESTIONS

True or False Questions

1. What-if analysis cannot be easily performed using a spreadsheet.
2. Rows, columns, and cells are part of the status line.
3. A formula may be placed in any spreadsheet cell.
4. The function of cell protection is to keep data from being accidentally erased.
5. The first step followed in starting Lotus is to type 123.
6. The worksheet area is composed of rows and columns.
7. The contents of the control panel include three lines.
8. The contents of the status line display date and time.
9. The function of the slash command is to delete character by character.
10. Data or formulas cannot be copied from one cell to another.
11. A spreadsheet is saved using the status line command.
12. A spreadsheet report is prepared using the /PPRG command.
13. The function of a template is to erase data.
14. The function of graph programs is to display paragraphs of text.
15. The function of the /Q command is to start the program.

Completion Questions

1. Spreadsheet software can easily prepare a _____ of automobile expenses for three years.
2. The _____ command is used to print out a report.
3. Columns can be widened using the _____ command.
4. A _____ may be used to prepare a standard order form.
5. The _____ command is used to copy the contents of a cell.

ANSWER KEY

True or False Questions

1. F
2. F
3. T
4. T
5. T
6. T
7. T
8. T
9. F
10. F

11. F
12. T
13. F
14. F
15. F

Completion Questions

1. budget
2. /PPRG
3. /WCS
4. template
5. /C

11

Database Management Software

Word processing, desktop publishing, and spreadsheet software provide enough power to meet most organizations' information processing needs, but several major capabilities need to be addressed. Many organizations maintain lengthy files on employees, goods in manufacture, customer addresses, or price and parts lists.

Others manage complex projects that involve tracking the beginning and ending dates and other details of many subprojects. Many organizations need computers that can communicate with one another. Database management systems meet all these needs.

In this chapter we discuss database management system (DBMS) programs, project management, communications software, and integrated packages. In conjunction with word processing and spreadsheet software, these programs provide computer users with a powerful ready-made set of programs that handle a broad range of financial, production, management, marketing, and distribution applications.

DATABASE MANAGEMENT SYSTEM (DBMS) SOFTWARE

A large portion of the work performed on many computers involves the updating, querying, or retrieval of information stored in files known as databases. A *database* is a collection of files and records containing fields of numeric, alphabetic, or other information that can be accessed and manipulated.

Applications programs called *database management systems (DBMS)* facilitate the processing and manipulation of information in a database. Among the more popular database management packages are dBase IV and FoxPro.

A database management system manages large files of records. It permits users to locate individual records, search for data, and display information quickly and easily. An electronic DBMS replaces filing card systems or other manual methods and allows thousands of records to be searched in only a few seconds.

OVERVIEW OF OPERATION

There are several basic steps followed in using database management software. First a *structure* is created to hold data. The structure consists of specific fields, their widths, and the type of information to be entered into each field. Then data are loaded into the structure. This involves keyboarding alphabetic or numeric data into the fields, generating a file of records. The process is similar in concept to setting up a manual file of records, such as a card catalog containing separate records on each book in the file.

After entering the data, the records may be rearranged. This is done by sorting or indexing them to place each record in a particular sequence.

In a *sorting* system, records are physically rearranged to create a new sequence. For example, a list of records may be sorted alphabetically.

In the *indexing* method, the contents of records are not physically moved about. Instead, *pointers* direct the computer from record to record. Records may be displayed or entire files printed out. The database may be revised or updated by *appending* (adding) and deleting records or changing their contents.

A variety of *reports* may be generated using DBMS software. In its simplest form, the data in the file may be listed on a printer according to a sequence (for example, alphabetically) organized by an index file. More elaborate reports, including column headings, subheadings, and page numbering, may be created using a *report generator*. The operator specifies the page width, number and placement of columns, report title, and other information. The computer then prints out a neatly organized report generated from the contents of the database.

LEARNING TO USE DATABASE SOFTWARE

Database management programs allow an operator to enter files of data containing names, addresses, telephone numbers, part numbers, etc. Once entered, the data can be rearranged, sorted, or organized in many different ways. For example, a list of employee names entered at random can be sorted alphabetically. The resulting list can then be printed out.

This section describes the fundamentals of *dBase*, a powerful program used for generating tabular reports or for maintaining files with hundreds or even thousands of records. dBase is representative of other database applications packages and contains many powerful features that allow records to be searched, sorted, categorized, and sequenced.

STEPS IN USING DBASE

The creation and maintenance of a database using dBase involves five distinct steps. We shall overview this process and then come back to each step and discuss it in greater detail. The five steps include:

Creating the structure
Loading records into the structure
Sorting and rearranging records
Displaying information and printing out reports
Updating and revising files

DBASE VERSIONS

Over the past decade several versions of dBase have evolved. These were known as dBase II, dBase III, dBase III Plus, and dBase IV. They differ in the way commands are given as well as in their features. Depending upon the version of dBase available on your computer, you will find three different forms of commands:

Dot prompt	All dBase versions
Assist menu selections	dBase III Plus
Control center commands	dBase IV

Dot prompt

The *dot prompt system* is available on all versions of dBase. The dot prompt appears immediately after starting dBase. If the dot prompt method is selected, all directions will be given to the computer on a line that begins with a dot (period). This method is fast and is preferred by skilled dBase users. It will work on all versions of dBase.

DATABASE APPLICATION EXAMPLE

Suppose you have been given the task of setting up a file of employees and preparing a printed report. Let us review the steps in creating the database and printing out the report.

CREATING THE STRUCTURE

The first step in developing and managing a database is to *create a structure* to hold the data. Creating a structure consists of several steps. Begin by naming the file that will hold the database. In creating the file, you will need to specify:

> Name of field
> Field type
> Width of field
> Placement of decimal point in field

This information must be provided to the computer before entering information into the database. Let's see how these preliminary steps are handled in dBase.

Creating a database file

Once the dot prompt is displayed, the operator may proceed to create a database file. Do this by typing:

```
. CREATE STAFF
```

All commands are entered after the dot prompt appears and are followed by pressing the Enter key. The word CREATE begins the process of setting up the file called STAFF. File names should contain eight letters or less. dBase will automatically append the extension .DBF to all database files unless you use a different extension.

As soon as the create command has been entered, a file setup screen will be displayed (Fig. 11.1). The screen describes how to use the cursor keys, how to insert or delete characters and words, etc. Our task will be to enter the name of the fields, their type, width, and placement of the decimal point.

We will need a field for each employee's name and others for address, city, state, zip, etc. We have selected a field width of twenty characters for the name, twenty for the address, thirteen for the city, two for the state, and five for the zip code. The phone field is thirteen characters wide.

dBase requires that you specify the type of information to be stored in the field. *Alphabetic fields* are known as character fields. Fields containing numbers are called numeric. You must also specify the field width. *Numeric fields* may contain decimal places. Since our only numeric field is

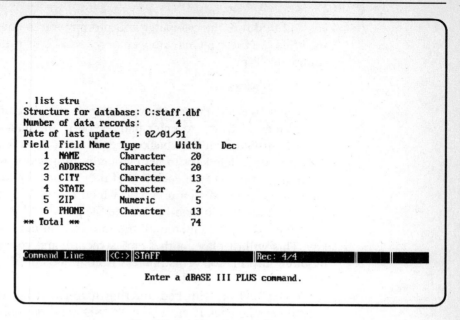

```
. list stru
Structure for database: C:staff.dbf
Number of data records:        4
Date of last update    : 02/01/91
Field  Field Name  Type      Width    Dec
    1  NAME        Character    20
    2  ADDRESS     Character    20
    3  CITY        Character    13
    4  STATE       Character     2
    5  ZIP         Numeric       5
    6  PHONE       Character    13
** Total **                    74
```
Command Line |<C:>||STAFF |Rec: 4/4 | | |

Enter a dBASE III PLUS command.

Fig. 11.1—Database Structure

the zip code and it does not have decimal places, we enter a zero. This will allow us later to sort our file numerically on the zip code field.

You may go back and change or correct the field name, type, etc. This is done by positioning the cursor using the arrow keys. When you are finished, enter Ctrl End. dBase will ask you to confirm, strike Enter. You will then be asked whether you wish to enter data records now. At this point, let us strike N since all we are doing is setting up the structure.

You can always go back and *modify a structure*, putting in fields, deleting fields, etc. This is done using the MODIFY STRUCTURE command.

If you would like a permanent printout of your structure for your files, type:

. LIST STRUCTURE TO PRINT

It is always a good idea to keep a listing of your structure handy so you will be able to check on the field names, widths, etc. easily.

LOADING RECORDS INTO THE STRUCTURE

In order to *load records* into the structure, we must begin by telling dBase which file we plan to use. Do this by typing:

. USE STAFF

You must always specify the name of the file you intend to work on. If you fail to do so, the computer will prompt you to enter it. Once you have specified the file, you may now enter records. This is done with the *append* command. Type:

. APPEND

This will cause the computer to display the structure on the screen with blank areas in which to enter data. Type in the data as requested. If you make a mistake, you can backspace, erase, and retype. You may also use the Insert or Delete keys to help you edit information on the screen. Hit the Enter key after you type each line of information. Note that the status bar at the bottom of the screen tells you which record is being entered, the total number of records in the file, and the file name.

When you have entered all the information necessary, strike the PgDn key. This will display another empty record, and you need only type in the required information. This process is continued until all records have been entered.

When you are finished entering records, strike the Escape key. You may always go back later, type APPEND, and add more records as desired.

If you would like to *list* the records you have entered so far, type:

. LIST

This will list all of the records on the screen. Notice that each record has been assigned a record number. If you would like a hard copy printout of your records, type:

. LIST TO PRINT

If you detect an error, you may want to go back and *edit* or modify a specific record. This is done with the edit command. The edit command is followed by the record number you wish to change. Suppose you wish to modify record 10. Type:

. EDIT 10

This will cause the computer to *display* record number 10. You may then delete, change, or insert data as necessary. By typing the up and down arrow keys, you may move up or down in the record while still in the edit mode. This allows you to make changes in other records. Always terminate the edit mode when you are finished. This is done by typing Ctrl End.

Deleting a record is a two-step process. First go into the edit mode, and display the record you wish to delete on the screen. Mark it for deletion with Ctrl U. The status of the record will change on the screen. Go through the file and mark all records that are to be deleted. When this is done, leave the edit mode, using Ctrl End. The last step is to *pack* the records. This is done by typing:

. PACK

This will cause the computer to physically delete the unwanted records from the file. All remaining records are automatically renumbered sequentially.

Browse command

A somewhat faster method of looking at or editing records is with the *browse command* (Fig. 11.2). While the edit command displays only one record at a time on the screen, the browse command displays several. To enter the browse mode, type:

. BROWSE

This displays several records at once. You may then move about the file, using the arrow keys. Additions, deletions, or corrections can be permanently entered into the file. You may delete an entire record by positioning the highlighted bar on the record and entering Ctrl U. When you are finished, you must leave the browse mode by typing Ctrl End. If you have marked records for deletion while in the browse mode, you must enter the pack command to physically remove them from the file.

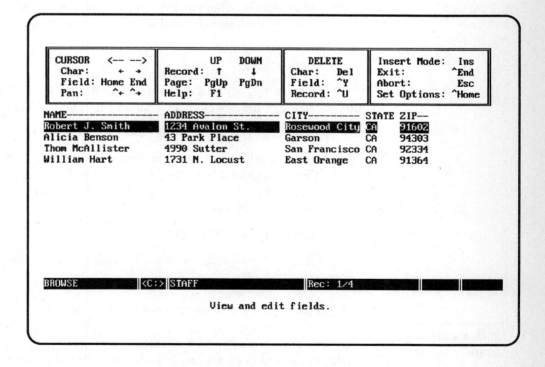

Fig. 11.2—Browse Command

SORTING AND REARRANGING RECORDS

One of the most powerful features of dBase is its ability to quickly sort and rearrange records, which allows you to take records that have been entered in no specific order and rearrange them numerically or alphabetically. This is useful in alphabetizing a list of employee names, preparing a mailing list sorted by zip code, or generating a list of employees sequenced by ID number.

As we will see below, the sorting process may be done by either of two methods. One involves physically resequencing a group of records and creating a new sorted file, using the sort command. The second involves preparing an *index file* that contains a group of pointers that rearranges the file without physically resequencing each record. The latter method is faster, uses less storage space, and is the most common for sorting records. Let us look at both of these methods. Suppose we have an unalphabetized list of employees and we wish to generate an alphabetized listing. Let us see how this is done using each method.

Sort command

dBase is able to sort a file based on one or more fields. This is done using the *sort command*. Suppose we wish to sort an unalphabetized file of employee names into an alphabetized list. First we must bring the unsorted file into use:

```
. USE STAFF
```

Next we issue the command to sort on a specific field. We must also identify the name of the newly created sorted file. This is done as follows:

```
. SORT ON NAME TO STAFF.SRT
```

This command will cause the computer to sequence all records stored under STAFF into a second file called STAFF.SRT. This will be done using the sort field NAME. Had we wished to sort on the zip code, we could have issued the command this way:

```
. SORT ON ZIP TO STAFF.SRT
```

Once a file has been sorted, we can then call in the new file:

```
. USE STAFF.SRT
```

and list the file on the screen or print it out on the printer.

**Index com-
mand**

For large files it is often best to create a sort using the *index command*. The index command does not create a second sorted file. Instead, it creates an index file that must be used in conjunction with the unsorted file. Suppose we wish to sort the same list of names discussed above, this time using the index procedure. We would begin by calling in the unsorted file:

```
. USE STAFF
```

We would then set up a separate index file. This is done as follows:

```
. INDEX ON NAME TO STAFF.NDX
```

This sets up the index file. In all future reference to the index file we would call it in with the following command:

```
. USE STAFF INDEX STAFF.NDX
```

From this point on we could list the sorted file on the screen by simply typing:

```
. LIST
```

or we could send it to the printer using:

```
. LIST TO PRINT
```

By the way, if we do not wish to list record numbers, we could issue the following command:

```
. LIST OFF TO PRINT
```

Notice that the size of the index file is substantially smaller than the main file. This illustrates the saving of memory over generating a second sorted file. In all future use of the sorted file we will always want to call it in together with the index file. If we fail to do so and only modify the main file without the index file, we will not generate an accurate sorted list.

DISPLAYING INFORMATION AND PRINTING REPORTS

Now that we have been able to sort and rearrange records, we will want to look at their new order. We have already discussed several means of looking at records. We can display the newly organized records on the screen, using the list command. You can easily send the list to the printer by typing:

```
. LIST TO PRINT
```

This will give us a hard copy of each record with its record number. We can delete the record number from the listing by typing:

```
. LIST OFF TO PRINT
```

These procedures generate relatively simple *reports*. Reports exceeding one page in length print as lengthy uninterrupted lists. Fortunately, dBase has a mechanism for creating neatly spaced reports, including column heading, totals, etc. This is done using the create report command and the report form command.

UPDATING AND REVISING FILES

Periodically, you may wish to update or revise a file. We have already discussed some of these mechanisms. For instance, you can change the contents of a record by first calling in the database with the use command and then use either the edit or browse commands. A single record may be changed by typing:

```
. EDIT 10
```

This displays the tenth record and allows you to edit it. Typing:

```
. BROWSE
```

allows you to display several records on the screen at once, all of which may be edited. Use the Ctrl End keys to terminate these modes.

You may purge all records from a file with the zap command. But be careful, because all records will be removed. Type:

```
. ZAP
```

This leaves your structure intact, allowing you to load in new data. You can delete a record by typing:

```
. DELETE 10
```

Typing:

```
. PACK
```

will remove the record from the file.

It is possible to erase an entire database with all of its records and its structure. This is done with the *erase command*. If you type:

```
. ERASE STAFF
```

you will permanently remove the file. This command should be used with caution.

TERMINATING A SESSION

It is extremely important that you terminate a session in dBase properly. You should never restart your computer or exit dBase without the quit command. To terminate a session, type:

```
. QUIT
```

The *quit command* closes your files and saves the data. It must always be issued before going back to DOS or turning off your computer.

Now that we have discussed dBase, let us look at several other important software packages.

COMMUNICATIONS SOFTWARE

Today many computers are connected to others that may be located hundreds or even thousands of miles away. They are linked by telephone lines, satellite relay stations, fiber optic cables, or microwave circuits. More than elaborate hardware is needed to allow communication between two computers; the appropriate software is also necessary. Some popular *communications software* packages for computers are Smartcom III, Crosstalk XVI, and Procomm Plus.

Communications software allows computers to originate transmissions and answer messages. It establishes the switching routine needed to set up contact between distant computers and ensures that data will be sent in the proper format and at the proper speed.

A computer equipped with a software package may emulate a terminal or upload or download a file. *Terminal emulation* is provided by the software and allows a microcomputer to function as if it were a particular remote terminal to a mainframe computer. *Downloading* is the process by which a computer receives a data file over a communications line. *Uploading* is the process by which a computer transmits a file to a remote computer. These and other features are provided by software packages available for microcomputer systems.

Large mainframe computers are equipped with software that detects transmission speeds and codes and routes information to appropriate hardware. This is usually done through a *front end communications computer* and *front end software*. Communications software also checks for errors in transmission and handles interruptions or transmission priorities.

Communications software is essential if the computer is operated as part of a network. The software package manages the flow of data throughout the network, balances system loads, and performs file security and access protection.

PROJECT MANAGEMENT SOFTWARE

Programs have evolved that assist in the management of large complex projects. *Project management software* allows the user to create Gantt charts, network charts, target date schedules, and hard copy printouts showing beginning and ending dates of individual elements within a project, as well as lists of all resources. These programs have become indispensable tools in managing such large projects as a satellite launch, building construction, and installation of complex plants involving machines, equipment, and personnel.

INTEGRATED PACKAGES

Some software publishers are integrating several programs into a single package. *Integrated software* packages can generate spreadsheets with from two to four windows and allow the user to edit material while it is on the screen. They include database management functions. They prepare bar, line, pie, and other graphs. They also have word processing capability.

Integrated packages perform more functions than any one individual software package, but as yet none provides the full range of capabilities provided by separate, individual pieces of software.

In the previous chapters we have reviewed the most common uses for applications software: word processing, desktop publishing, spreadsheets, and database management. We have described in detail three of the major software applications programs on the market, and more are on the way. Thousands of hours and millions of dollars go into developing sophisticated and powerful software packages that greatly expand the computer's usefulness. Computers equipped with word processing, graphics, communications, and database management system software serve a broad range of uses and make the computer a more valuable tool.

Database management system (DBMS) software is used to manage large files of records and data. A structure is created containing the name of a field, its type, width, and decimal places. Data are loaded into the structure and may be viewed, sorted, or resequenced. Finished reports may be printed out.

Files may either be sorted or indexed. An indexed file uses pointers to direct the computer from record to record. Records may be appended or deleted from a file. A variety of reports may be generated using DBMS software. More elaborate reports may be generated using a report generator.

dBase is a widely used program for maintaining files and generating reports. The five steps in using dBase software include creating the structure, loading records into the structure, sorting and rearranging records, displaying information and printing out reports, and updating and revising files.

Different versions of dBase are available. Some provide an assist menu, and all versions provide the dot prompt. Once records have been loaded into a file, they may be displayed using the list or browse command. Records are deleted using the pack command. A dBase session is terminated with the quit command.

Communications software handles communication between computers, detects transmission errors, and routes signals through a network. These packages may emulate a terminal or assist in uploading or downloading a file. A group of project management software programs have been developed to assist in the management of large projects. These programs create charts, schedules, and reports. Integrated software packages combine the functions of individual software packages.

Selected Readings

Alter, Steven. *Information Systems*, Addison-Wesley (1992). Chapter 8.

Grupe, Fritz H. *Microcomputer Applications*, W. C. Brown (1992). Part IV.

Parker, Charles S. *Understanding Computers and Information Processing*, Dryden Press (1992). Chapter 11.

REVIEW QUESTIONS

True or False Questions

1. A database must be created before data are loaded into it.
2. Reports are easily generated using dBase.
3. The function of the dot prompt is to avoid pull down menus.
4. The function of the assist menu is to utilize the dot prompt.
5. There are several versions of dBase in use.
6. The purpose of changing a logged drive is to create a structure.
7. Records are sorted by using the index command.
8. An index file is created using the sort command.
9. Once a file is created, records can be appended later.
10. Records are deleted from a file using the pack command.
11. The function of the list command is to enter records.
12. The list command does not differ from the browse command.
13. The function of communications software is to link computers together.
14. Project management software is usually not needed on complex projects.
15. There are few advantages to integrated software packages over individual programs.

Completion Questions

1. An upcoming calendar of events could be managed using _____ software.
2. The _____ command can be used to print out a report.
3. A database consisting of a personnel file could be _____ by employee's name.
4. Records are added to a database using the _____ command.
5. Records may be revised using the _____ command.

ANSWER KEY

True or False Questions

1. T
2. T
3. T
4. F
5. T
6. F
7. F
8. F
9. T
10. T
11. F
12. F
13. T
14. F
15. F

Completion Questions

1. database
2. list
3. sorted, indexed
4. append
5. edit

12

Analysis and Design of Computer Information Systems

Prompt and effective decision making is vital to the success of any business enterprise. Sometimes only a few dollars rest upon making the correct business decision, but at other times these decision involve thousands of dollars and affects hundreds of people. Systems analysis is a useful tool for solving general business problems. It can also be applied to making more specific judgments about computer equipment and procedures and ensuring that they are used efficiently in business.

In this chapter we look at the business enterprise as a total system and review the role of the business systems department, problem solving methodology, and the means by which computer and information systems are planned, evaluated, and implemented. We also look at specific details that must be assessed when installing information processing systems.

WHAT ARE BUSINESS SYSTEMS?

A *business system* is a collection of hardware, personnel, procedures, and techniques that function as an organized whole. A business system is the organizational structure within a firm that enables the company to achieve its goals. Business systems include policies, methods, personnel, information processing software and hardware, and communications procedures.

Systems are composed of subsystems. These smaller units have individual functions, but they act in accord with the goals of the overall system. The total system is greater than the sum of the parts. Figure 12.1 diagrams a simplified business system.

Information in business systems

In all organizations, whether in business, government, or education, decisions are made by administrators. Administration in a business system usually consists of a board of directors and management. An essential function of the board of directors is to determine long- and short-range goals. Establishing objectives requires a careful analysis of business conditions, customer needs and buying patterns, production capacity, staff, and finances. To assess these elements accurately, the administration must have data acquired, processed, and reported in its most useful form.

Once the organization's directors select certain objectives, it is management's job to direct the subsystems of the firm toward these goals and to measure progress toward them.

Because different levels of management need various types of information at different times from all divisions of the firm, the firm's facilities for recording, manipulating, and reporting data can be one of its major assets. Good management decisions rest upon the availability of data and many other factors. To be of most value to a firm, data should be:

Ready when needed
Ready where needed

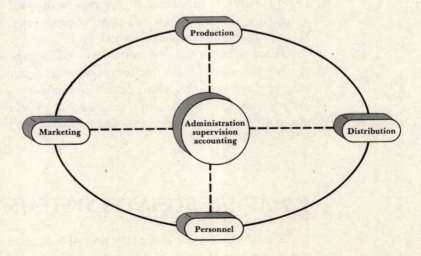

Fig. 12.1—Simplified Business System

Appropriate to the problem in terms of relevance and completeness
Accurate
Gathered, processed, and reported at a reasonable cost

Need for business systems

Business firms cannot afford to solve data flow problems in a disorganized, unsystematic way. Mistakes are expensive; time is limited. A planned and organized strategy for processing information is essential to:

Gain maximum cost savings in processing and handling data
Gain maximum time savings in outputting results
Establish an orderly procedure for growth
Develop a uniform method of operation
Avoid costly errors
Improve the quality of decisions
Improve organization responsiveness to customers' needs
Improve allocation of physical resources
Produce the best product at the lowest cost
Eliminate duplication of effort

Evolution of business systems

At the beginning of this century, when most firms were small and material and labor costs were low, information processing needs were minimal. Few firms used systematic business methods to plan their activities and carry out their goals. When a problem came up, it was solved on the spot. The solution chosen was usually the easiest one to implement. The result was a patchwork of policies and procedures. Careful analysis of problems and attention to strategy were frequently ignored in favor of finding immediate answers. This approach is sometimes called "brush fire" problem solving. To this day some firms use these methods.

As firms grew, capital investment increased, costs of labor and materials rose, and management turned to more orderly means of solving problems. One or two employees were assigned the task of using quantitative means to examine business procedures. They became known as *business systems analysts* or *business systems engineers*. Eventually, many firms established a separate *business systems department*. This department is responsible for applying measurable and quantifiable approaches to data flow problems.

FUNCTION OF BUSINESS SYSTEMS DEPARTMENTS

Since World War II business systems departments have continued to grow in importance. Teams of business systems engineers, analysts, and

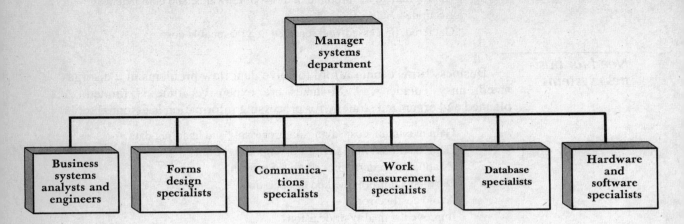

Fig. 12.2—Business Systems Department Organization Chart

information processing specialists are indispensable to many business firms. Figure 12.2 diagrams the organization of a typical systems department. The systems experts make critical studies of the departments of the firm and make recommendations regarding their operations.

A major responsibility of the business systems department is to improve the flow of data. In studying a system, analysts review its current forms, procedures, policies, and methods. The personnel, machines, space requirements, and office layout are looked at to see if and how the system could be improved or whether a new system should be developed. Analysts ask six basic questions in investigating each element in the study:

1. What is done?
2. How is it done?
3. Why is it done?
4. Who does it?
5. When is it done?
6. Where is it done?

Systems analysts conduct many types of surveys to evaluate a system. Data flow and word processing studies point out bottlenecks and problem areas. Time and motion studies further define problems and even point to solutions.

When solving business systems problems, systems analysts generally move through five basic phases: (1) preliminary study and planning, (2) systems analysis, (3) systems design, (4) systems development, and (5) systems implementation and evaluation. Let us review each of these major phases in detail.

PRELIMINARY STUDY AND PLANNING

The object of the *preliminary study* is to answer the question "Does a new or revamped system appear to be sufficiently practical and economical to warrant further study and investigation?" The preliminary study looks at the fundamental needs of a business and reviews broad plans for making needed improvements. It defines the problem, states ultimate objectives, and offers some tentative plans.

An important part of the preliminary study is selecting the people who will conduct the study and defining their responsibilities. In the *task force* approach management forms a committee of knowledgeable employees from various departments. After the committee has completed its study and made recommendations, it disbands.

Another approach is to appoint an *ongoing committee* with members from operating units, information processing and business systems departments, and managers. This type of committee does a preliminary investigative study, makes recommendations to management, and has the continuing responsibilities of implementing recommendations and monitoring the need for future modifications or changes.

Still another approach is to give one individual, with the title of *project director*, the necessary funds and authority to carry out the study. He or she may also be responsible for implementing changes and recommendations.

The preliminary study should provide a clear definition of the goals of the new system. The outcomes desired from a new system must be stated in measurable terms, with specific times and dates defined. The study should begin to answer such questions as: How many dollars will be saved? When? What specific problems will be solved by the new system? How much faster, more accurate, and more precise will the results be? What existing machines can be eliminated? When? What new machines need to be purchased? When?

During this phase, the business systems analyst discusses the firm's needs with people inside and outside the organization; employees, managers, division heads, customers, vendors, other firms, and consultants are among those whose views whose views should be heard.

The preliminary phase of the study is essential to avoid making unnecessary changes or changes that do not justify the costs involved. It is also essential for planning because a successful new system cannot be designed until its goals are defined, and there would be no way of evaluating its success without a measure for comparison.

SYSTEMS ANALYSIS

In the second phase of solving business problems, the analyst reviews the existing system in greater detail, gathers more data, and analyzes information. This step involves systematically collecting all pertinent information that will later be used to design the new or improved system.

During the systems analysis phase, a number of people, from inside and outside the firm, are called upon for help and cooperation. Outside consultants may be hired. Department and branch managers are interviewed to determine their data needs. Personnel, hardware, and software are evaluated in terms of their usefulness in meeting the firm's needs and their cost to do so.

Work measurement

A variety of study techniques are used in the analysis phase. The systems analyst observes machines in operation and employees at work.

One tool the analyst may use is a *work sampling study* to determine the content of each job. In work sampling, a measure is made of such quantities as the number and types of calculations performed and the number and types of forms handled.

Work measurement enables the analyst to compare the output of employees before and after a new system is in place. It allows the quantity as well as the quality of clerical work to be measured.

Logs, run books, histories, and records may be reviewed to gain some idea of the quantity of information processed by the firm. Special detailed records may be kept for a short period of time to learn more about the nature of a given information processing problem.

Time studies are often used to determine how long it takes to perform a task. This is usually done by observing and timing employees as they go about their assigned responsibilities.

Cost

The analyst must thoroughly examine all aspects of the proposed system to determine whether it is worth the expenditure. Some of the questions asked are:

Should equipment be leased or purchased?
What will maintenance costs be?
Which outside supplier will provide maintenance service at the lowest
  cost?
What one-time costs are involved?
What recurrent costs are involved? What would it cost to change or
  expand the new system at a later date?
What training and implementation costs are involved?
How much will physical plant alterations cost?

How do the costs of the new system compare to the cost of operation of the old system?

Hardware

The analysis of any system that requires the purchase of new equipment will entail some study of the performance, speed, and capacity of key pieces of equipment. The issue of whether to purchase microcomputers or whether to use mainframes must be resolved. Suppose a large computer is being evaluated. Here are some specific questions analysts ask regarding the equipment.

What size CPU and amount of primary storage are required for present needs?

What peripheral equipment should be purchased for present needs? Can the selected equipment be expanded to meet growth needs? Which brand of computer is best in terms of present and anticipated needs?

Should equipment be centralized or decentralized?

Should one large computer or several small ones be purchased?

How difficult is it to program the computer?

Who will be in charge of the new equipment?

Software

The programming and software of a new system must also be studied. The following questions are often asked:

Should programs be written or purchased?

Are appropriate applications software packages available?

What training is needed to use a software package?

How long will it take to write, test, and debug new programs?

What skills will the staff need to write the new software?

What software is available from equipment vendors at no cost?

Can existing programs be converted to the new system? Can the new programs be run on machines that may be purchased later?

Personnel

Implementing a new system affects the individual employees of a firm as well as the organization as a whole. The analyst studies the personnel area and needs to determine:

Will new people be needed? How many?

Will people be laid off? How many?

How many jobs will be upgraded?

How many employees will have to be relocated?

Will retraining be necessary?

How will salaries be affected?

Are there people now in the firm who already have the new skills that will be needed?

What will the effect be on employee morale?

Who should supervise the changes to the new system?

Time

A new system must be feasible from a time as well as cost standpoint. It is necessary to know:

What would be the best point in the business cycle to install the new system?

How long will the installation take?

Should the old system be operated alongside the new? For how long? For how long should consultants be employed to monitor the new system?

How long will it be before the new system can be expected to run smoothly?

These are typical of the questions asked by analysts. There are many more questions that may be asked, depending upon the specific problem and the facilities being considered. A study team report may now be prepared summarizing the progress made and describing the proposed system.

SYSTEMS DESIGN

Once the relevant information has been gathered and analyzed, a system must be designed. The analyst, working with equipment suppliers, consultants, and other knowledgeable people, actually designs the system in this phase. Plans, drawings, and layouts are prepared. Specifications are written for the purchase of equipment, forms are designed, and policies established. Specific pieces of hardware and particular computer programs or other software are selected. In this phase the analyst concentrates on the following elements.

Office layout and equipment

The analyst recommends the most efficient office layout to facilitate data flow. He or she is concerned with shortening processing time and reducing labor and equipment costs.

The analyst may also be responsible for the purchase of any new equipment required by a system and for arranging for the most efficient use of the equipment after it has been installed.

Establishing procedures and policies

A new system must be documented to help employees learn how to use the equipment efficiently. The systems analyst often devises procedure and policy manuals for this purpose. Manuals help to ensure uniform practices and policies. They specify such things as which forms to use, when to use them, how to handle exceptions, and where forms are to be routed.

Well-written policy manuals help both the employee and the organization. They not only provide the employee with a clear statement of company policy and methods, but ensure that each branch or division in the company will acquire, report, and process information in the most efficient way.

Forms design

Data forms are essential to almost all business systems. In some cases hundreds of different forms are used within a firm. The success of a new system often depends on whether adequate forms and source documents have been developed.

The systems analyst must specify content, layout, distribution, and routing of the forms. He or she is also responsible for designing source documents and reports. All documents designed must comply with existing hardware requirements.

Forms design includes the physical characteristics of the form as well as its content. Consideration must be given to size, paper, type size, number of copies required, printing process, and cost. The analyst must also determine the quantity to be ordered, the system of inventory to be used, and the methods of packing and dispensing the forms. Forms must be reviewed periodically to see that they are adequate, necessary, and up-to-date.

Information retrieval and file design

The job of the analyst also includes designing data files for information storage and retrieval systems. Modern business depends heavily on data files to store a firm's records. The analyst should design files that will yield accurate and complete data and will be easy to correct and update. In some organizations this task is delegated to the DBMS administrator.

Selecting personnel

The systems analyst may also write job descriptions and job orders. Job descriptions outline the duties and functions of each job. Job orders specify the number of employees needed for each job classification.

In writing a job description, the analyst indicates the level of skill and training required to perform the job. This information guides the personnel department in hiring new employees.

The duties of the systems analyst may also include planning programs for job orientation or in-service training. He or she may arrange classroom training or instruction from vendors and prepare, revise, and order training manuals, teaching aids, slide films, video cassettes, and other media.

SYSTEMS DEVELOPMENT

Once a system has been designed, the next step is to build it. In the development phase the analyst begins assembling the system now on paper.

Equipment is ordered, forms printed, and programs written, tested, and debugged.

The development and physical construction of a system may take months or even years. In some instances building specifications must be drawn up, bids let out, or teams of programmers assigned to write and develop software. An effort is made to schedule specific dates when new equipment is to arrive and personnel are to be shifted to the new system. Recruitment of employees may begin.

Hardware installation

Sophisticated hardware, such as computers, word processing machines, copiers, or facsimile equipment, is installed and tested. It may take many weeks of on-site testing before a piece of equipment is certified ready for use. It is particularly important that hardware be thoroughly checked out and broken in. Careful attention to hardware at this stage can reduce costly breakdowns and interruption of service after the full system is in operation.

Software preparation

If a system uses a computer or involves electronic information processing, programs must be written, debugged, tested, and maintained. Often, the analyst specifies the function and purpose of a proposed program, flowcharts the preferred algorithm, and indicates the input/output requirements. These specifications are then given to a programmer who actually writes the program. When the program is running satisfactorily, documentation is prepared explaining such things as the program logic, how data are input, and program options.

An important piece of software written by programmers is the benchmark program. A *benchmark program* includes various options and functions to be run on a computer in order to test its capability and compare its performance against others. Accurate time records are kept to see which computer is able to perform the benchmark program the fastest, thus giving an indication of the overall efficiency of the equipment.

Communications

The systems analyst contracts for equipment to meet the communications requirements of a system. Microwave links or coaxial cable may be installed. Data entry machines may be put in place and data concentrators and leased lines acquired.

Vendor capability

A *vendor* is an individual or organization that supplies goods or services to another individual or organization. The systems analyst should look at a vendor's abilities in many areas before selecting a particular make of equipment. Several key factors are evaluated: reputation and past performance, thoroughness and attitude in responding to proposals, capabilities, size of maintenance staff, and extent of support services.

Two major considerations in selecting vendors are their experience in their field and their ability to handle the specific needs of a particular firm. Some vendors specialize in computers, communications equipment, office machines, or software. A number of manufacturers have been in business for many years and employ an experienced staff of systems engineers, machinists, technicians, and consultants.

The support services provided by vendors vary greatly. Some include full installation, maintenance, and repair services in their purchase or lease fee. Some have large branches located in major cities and provide training courses, operating manuals, and extensive help in adapting to a new system.

SYSTEMS IMPLEMENTATION AND EVALUATION

Once a new system has been developed, the systems department must implement it properly. Systems implementation requires careful planning to see that the transition is made without waste, errors, or excessive costs. Employee morale is a factor in maximizing productivity. The systems analyst must have the cooperation of both employees and management. Personnel must be shown the advantages of the new system and how it will affect each individual.

A new system may be implemented in several ways. It can begin all at once or progress step by step. Sometimes a new system is set up to operate in parallel alongside the old. When the new system is running smoothly, the old system is dropped. The systems analyst must observe the new system in operation to make sure that there is no backsliding into the old, less efficient method.

The final step in the process is measuring results. Were the results expected? Did costs go down? By how much? Are results more accurate? In what way? If the benefits did not materialize, why not? How can the system be improved?

As output of the new procedure is evaluated, the systems analyst may decide to modify the plan. Then this revised plan is implemented and the output once again evaluated. This procedure is repeated until the most efficient arrangement of staff, equipment, office layout, and information processing methods is reached.

SYSTEM CONTROL

In many instances the systems analyst is involved in the analysis and design of a system, but then loses control once it is implemented. There are instances where a well-conceived business system has gone awry after it is installed. This was due to the lack of follow-up by the analyst, or in some cases the system was installed in a location distant from the analyst's office. Some cases of system failure are traced to poor system management or follow-up rather than ill-conceived plans. Ideally, the analyst tries to conceive and implement a system that will correct its own errors or bring failures or omissions to the attention of management before they create losses of data, erroneous results, or serious financial problems.

The real test of a system is its ultimate performance. Systems analysts must carefully assess whether or not the equipment that has been installed in fact meets the test benchmark standards and the needs of the enterprise. Business needs are continually changing, and a piece of equipment or system that was suitable at one time may not be at another. The challenge faced by the systems analyst is to see that the business system remains responsive and competitive in a rapidly changing world.

A business system is a collection of hardware, software, personnel, procedures, and techniques that functions as an organized whole to accomplish the goals of the firm. For information to be of greatest value, it must be available when and where needed, be at the right level of accuracy, be of the necessary kind and quality, and be processed at a reasonable cost.

Business problem solving strategies evolved from "brush fire," nonsystematic approaches to orderly methods. Business systems departments involve experts who study the flow of data in organizations. They analyze what is done, how and why an operation is performed, and ask who performs it, when, and where.

Systems analysis moves through several phases. First a preliminary study is done to define goals. In the systems analysis phase, information is gathered and analyzed, interviews are conducted, and time study, work sampling, and other measurement techniques are used. Factors related to cost, hardware, software, personnel, and time are investigated.

In the systems design phase, the analyst cooperates with consultants, vendors, and others to write specifications and establish policies. Office layout, procedures, forms design, information retrieval and file design, and personnel are considered. In the systems development phase, equipment is installed; forms are printed; programs are written, tested, and debugged; communications links are installed; and vendors are evaluated and selected. The final phase is systems implementation and evaluation. Outcomes are measured and compared to anticipated goals. A system may be modified to produce the most efficient arrangement of personnel, equipment, and methods.

Selected Readings

Burch, John G. *Systems Analysis, Design, and Implementation*, Boyd & Fraser (1992). Chapter 1.

Shelly, Gary B. *Systems Analysis and Design*, Boyd & Fraser (1991). Chapter 1.

Silver, Gerald A. *Systems Analysis and Design*, Addison-Wesley (1989). Chapter 5.

REVIEW QUESTIONS

True or False Questions

1. Business systems should be viewed as a collection of independent parts.
2. Early methods of solving business problems have not changed because of the computer age.
3. The guess, hunch, or chance method is not an effective way to solve business problems.
4. A major responsibility of the modern business systems department is forms design.
5. Organizations use the systems approach because it saves time and money.
6. The duties of the systems analyst include preliminary study and planning.
7. There are four basic questions frequently asked when investigating a problem.
8. A preliminary study and planning effort is usually conducted after systems development.
9. Many vendors provide support when a firm plans a new computer system.
10. It is not important to measure system performance when a careful plan has been followed.
11. The task force is one approach to selecting study personnel.
12. Work sampling is not conducted in any phase of a systems study.
13. Numerous hardware questions are asked when evaluating a new system.
14. Few software questions are asked when evaluating a new system.
15. Personnel questions are often asked when evaluating a new system.

Completion Questions

1. There are _____ steps in the analytical approach to problem solving.
2. There are _____ questions often asked by business systems analysts investigating an improved system.
3. _____ analysts often prepare a set of policies and procedures for use by an organization.
4. A _____ program is run to test a computer's capability and performance.
5. A time study and work sampling effort is usually part of the _____ phase.

ANSWER KEY

**True or False
Questions**

1. F
2. F
3. T
4. T
5. T
6. T
7. F
8. F
9. T
10. F
11. T
12. F
13. T
14. F
15. T

**Completion
Questions**

1. five
2. six
3. Systems
4. benchmark
5. systems analysis

13

Database Management Systems

Information is at the heart of most business enterprises. For information to be useful to businesses in problem solving and decision making, complete and accurate data must be available at the right time and place. They must also be processed at a reasonable cost.

A database is the total collection of information accumulated by an organization and structured in a systematic way to eliminate duplication and to facilitate access by several users for different applications. A database management system (DBMS) is the most efficient way to process information in a database.

In this chapter we look at the procedures and techniques for collecting, storing, and reporting data in a systematic manner. We will review database principles and software and commercial database vendors.

EVOLUTION OF INFORMATION SYSTEMS

One logical way to organize data is simply to put them in a file. A file, in general terms, is a collection of related information. For example, you may maintain a file on the courses you take at school. This file might include grade cards, course titles, course descriptions, schedules, and other records related to your schoolwork.

For years businesses have maintained files that are organized to serve the needs of particular departments. For example, an accounting department keeps accounts receivable and accounts payable files; a personnel department, employee roster and hourly wage files; and a production department, files of finished goods in inventory and raw materials in inventory. Information can be retrieved from these files and from the files of other departments by physically checking the records.

The technique of looking up information in a file, making use of it (reading or changing it), and returning it to the file is called *file processing*. When the computer came on the scene, it was logical to use it to process information in ways that had already proved reliable. In effect, the computer was used like a giant electronic filing cabinet.

However, the computer added a new element of speed and convenience to processing. Electronics replaced the physical files and physical checking. A user could rapidly search a file, update its contents, and print out records electronically. The needs of organizations with large volumes of data led to the development of *database processing*.

The early database management systems were designed to serve a single user (Fig. 13.1). Later systems allowed a group of users to share a common database. They could revise, update, or query information in the common database. Soon organizations began installing databases that could be shared by dozens of users with different types of terminals and varied applications

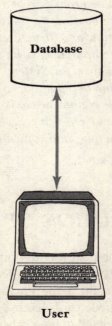

Fig. 13.1—Single-User Database

As data communications technology improved, business organizations turned to *distributed database processing* in which a common database is geographically distributed throughout the system and users share data through a data communications network (Fig. 13.2).

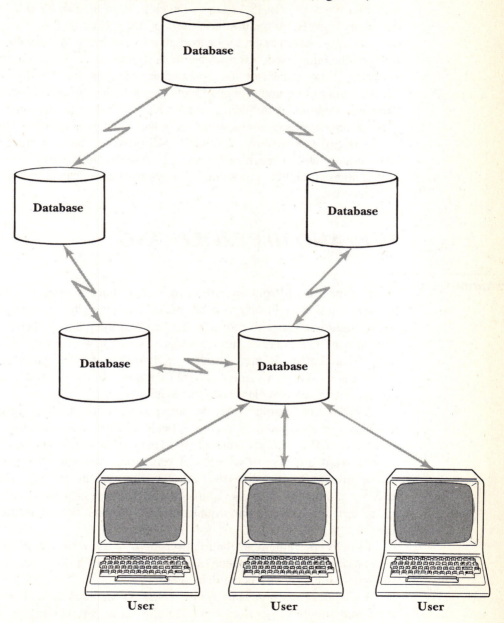

Fig. 13.2—Distributed Database

At first businesses built database management systems for their own use. However, it soon became clear that the vast collections of data built up by some companies, for example, Dow Jones, Reader's Digest, and the New York Times, could be extremely useful for many other firms and individuals; thus two types of DBMS began to develop. A *proprietary DBMS* is maintained exclusively for the in-house users of one company. Proprietary DBMS are generally not accessed by or available to outsiders. A *commercial database*, on the other hand, offers access to its resources through communications networks. Such databases are operated by vendors such as CompuServe, Mead Corporation, and Control Data. Anyone who wishes to access these databases may do so by paying usage charges. Today, many companies use commercial databases as well as maintain their own proprietary systems.

Low-cost microcomputers and DBMS programs have brought information systems within reach of home and small business users. Now anyone with a microcomputer, a modem, and a telephone line can access a commercial database.

FILES AND FILE PROCESSING

Terminology

You may recall from an earlier discussion that the smallest unit of data is a *bit*, and that eight bits together make up a character or *byte*. In a database, a *field* is a group of related bytes, such as the name of a customer or a part number. Fields are combined to form a *record*. A record may be a hard copy document or an area on tape or disk that stores a group of related fields. For example, a student record may contain a name field, identification number field, and class enrollment field.

A *file* is a collection of two or more records in the same category. A file in business may contain such data as personnel lists, accounts payable lists, parts lists, and inventory. Related files make up a *library*. An organization may maintain a library in several different cities, with each place containing files pertinent to that location. All the libraries in an organization are referred to collectively as its *database*. The database is the total collection of all information related to an organization. It may be located at one or more sites.

To help you remember the relationship of these terms, think of them as a hierarchy. The smallest piece of information is a bit; the most global and encompassing structure is the database.

A *database management system (DBMS)* includes the software, hardware, and structures necessary to maintain and manipulate files of information so they can be accessed by one or more users.

**File-based
processing
limitations**

There are several problems associated with an information system based on files, even if they are maintained by computers, as compared to one that is structured around the entire database. If different parts of an organization each maintain their own files, there is likely to be a lot of duplication. There is also likely to be little standardization of the format or content of information stored in files. These inconsistencies lead to errors and inaccurate output and, worse, prevent departments from sharing data.

Many file-based systems are program dependent; that is, the files are structured in such a way that they can be used only by a given computer program. Some systems are hardware dependent; that is, they can be accessed only by a specific piece of hardware, such as a selected terminal or disk drive.

**Advantages
of database
management
systems**

Database management systems are program and hardware independent. The information in the files is organized in a way that allows for general access. This means sets of data can be reached by various programs, even those written in different computer languages. The same database can also be accessed through a simple language called a query language, similar to spoken English, in which no program need be written. Finally, file updating and maintenance is simplified since information is routinely collected, managed, updated, or purged.

Organizations that use database management systems have experienced many benefits. Cost saving is a major benefit of DBMS. It is more economical to maintain a large database in which there is little or no redundancy of records or duplication of equipment. Access is available to many, but the integrity of confidential information can still be preserved through a security system. Collections of information can be expanded, be kept up-to-date in a logical and systematic way, and be routinely eliminated according to the needs of the organization.

DBMS do have limitations associated with personnel and equipment. DBMS installations require a high level of information processing sophistication in the personnel who manage them. Some firms find it necessary to employ special DBMS administrators and programmers to oversee and control the growth of their databases, although some companies manage to reduce the personnel demands by buying ready-made DBMS software. There are operating costs associated with maintaining large files. Another limitation is that distributed DBMS are subject to problems of network and communication failures.

STRUCTURE OF DATABASES

Let us now take a look at how databases are set up and the various types of files and means of accessing them.

One of the first tasks of an administrator assigned to establish and maintain a database is to structure the database system. Part of this task involves setting standards so that data will be collected, stored, and maintained in a consistent and logical manner. Setting these standards involves developing a plan or schema. The database administrator must then coordinate data collection efforts and see that use of the system is monitored and controlled.

For example, suppose an organization decides to set up an inventory file of goods purchased from various suppliers. Item names may be spelled differently by different vendors. Some suppliers might use metrics, while others might use U.S. standard sizes and weights. The same color may be called by different names by various suppliers. It is the administrator's responsibility to establish uniform nomenclature for each item and to describe a common weight and measuring system. In the absence of standardization, errors in handling data, duplications, and shortages could occur.

Schemas

A *schema* is the logical structure, plan, or method by which data are organized in a system. Schemas include a model of the basic data elements or attributes. The *data model* defines all data elements. It spells out precisely what information is contained in a field, how many characters it will hold, and whether alphabetic or numeric information will be entered. The data plan assigns the standard numbers or identifiers used to reference individual pieces of data.

A major factor in planning the data model is its use. Data models begin with an assessment of the needs of the organization and its users. Some schemas are structured for only local processing, that is, only local users are allowed access to the data within the structures. Other schemas provide for a distributed database in which data are maintained at many different locations. Still others involve both local and remote users within one company. In such a schema the database manager must decide what information can be accessed locally and what information can be accessed by all users. A schema could make available to all users on the system, regardless of location, names and addresses of all employees. These would be defined as *global data elements*. Information about employees' salaries could be restricted to access from selected terminals. This information would be defined as *restricted local data elements*.

The design of database structures is a complex task. There are many different approaches to organizing data in files so that information can be accessed from the database quickly and easily. Large files containing thousands of records cannot be easily sequenced. Imagine if a file with 10,000 names in alphabetical order had to be completely redone every time a name was added or deleted! In order to get around this, a plan or schema is set up that allows records in a file to be located when they are not numerically or alphabetically in order. Provision must also be made to add, modify, and delete records from a file.

Let us look at four common database schemas.

List structure

One frequently used schema is the *list structure*. The list structure enables out-of-sequence records to be treated as though they were in sequential order. Records can be added or deleted at any point without file reorganization. This is done by a system of numeric *pointers* that directs the computer to the next record, even though it is not in sequence. However, all records in the file must be stored in serial form on a direct access disk so they can be located at random.

Suppose a programmer wishes to print out alphabetically a group of names stored in a list structure file, such as that shown in Fig. 13.3. For

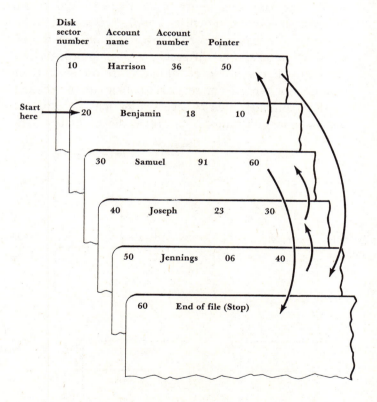

Fig. 13.3—List Structure

various reasons the records are not in alphabetical order. Each record is stored on a different area of the disk and includes the account name and number and, most important, a pointer or *linkage address*. This address is automatically assigned by the system. To begin, the computer goes to the entry point in the file, in this instance disk sector 20, and prints out the first alphabetical name, Benjamin. Then it follows the pointer to the next alphabetical record in the file. In this instance it is physically the first record on the disk, but logically the second. After printing out the name Harrison, the computer moves to the name Jennings, then to Joseph, and then Samuel. At Samuel's record, the pointer finally directs the computer to the end-of-file record, where it stops.

This basic arrangement allows the computer to hop and skip through an unsequenced file using the pointer to produce a neatly alphabetized list.

Tree or hierarchical structure

The *tree* or *hierarchical structure* contains a group of master records, sometimes known as *parents* or *owners*, and a group of subordinate records, sometimes known as *children*. Each subordinate record has only one owner or master record. There are times when it is necessary to locate information on several different physical records that are related to one logical entity. Each master record may therefore have to direct the computer to a number of subordinate records to obtain all the needed information.

The computer always accesses the master record first and then goes to one or more subordinates to obtain the necessary data. Figure 13.4 illus-

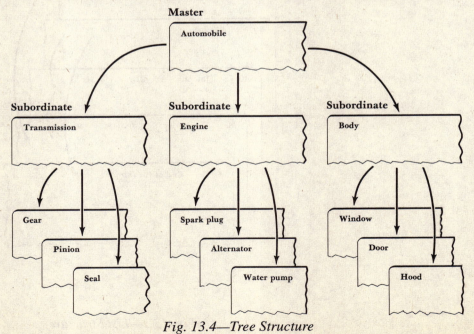

Fig. 13.4—Tree Structure

trates this concept. Suppose a user wishes to obtain data on a specific automobile, engine, and water pump. This information, related to one logical entity, is actually stored on one master and two subordinate records. Using a hierarchical database, the computer first seeks the master record "automobile." It then branches to the subcategory "engine" and finally moves down the hierarchy to the detail record "water pump." Thus, all related information is brought together, even though it is stored on different physical records.

Network structure

The *network structure* provides still another mechanism by which records in a database can be accessed. The network file is composed of both master and subordinate records. A master record may have several subordinate records, and a subordinate record may be linked to more than one master record. Thus the network differs from the tree, in which all subordinates are linked to only one master record.

Figure 13.5 is a simplified illustration of computing order charges using a network structure. Two master records direct the computer to seek information from five subordinate records. Some charges are common to

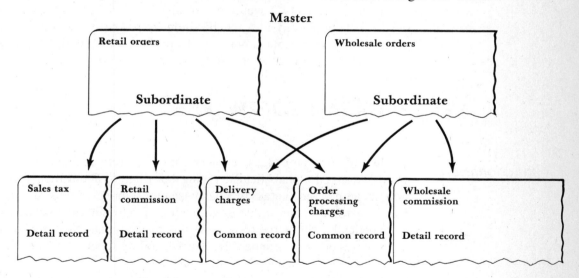

Fig. 13.5—Network Structure

both retail and wholesale orders, while others are related to one or the other. If a retail order is being processed, sales tax and retail commission are obtained from two detail records and delivery and order processing charges from two common records. If a wholesale order is being processed, wholesale commission is pulled from one detail record and delivery and order processing charges from the two common records. The network structure enables records to be linked to one or more master records without the one-to-one constraint of the tree structure.

Relational structure

The *relational structure* is the most flexible database schema. The elements to be searched need not be defined before the database is constructed. Pointers are not used. Instead, the schema uses a group of tables to show relationships. Once the table or file is constructed, any relationships can be searched out.

Figure 13.6 shows four files. The first file lists accounts by type of store. It relates customers and the type of store they operate. A second table lists customers and type of goods they purchase. The third table relates customers and the monthly volume of goods they purchase. The fourth keys the customer to the sales representative. There are so many types of relationships between customers and aspects of their business that it would be impractical to keep all the information in one file. By using the relational schema, the user can locate all customers who buy a given type of goods or all those who purchase a given volume of goods. It is easy to isolate customers by type of store, salesperson, territory, or any other attributes stored in the database. Thus, it would be possible to locate the customer who buys only a certain quantity of a specific item from a particular salesperson in a given area. The computer branches from the customer file to the type-of-goods file to other files to obtain the necessary information.

DATABASE SOFTWARE

Data dictionaries

In ordinary languages, a dictionary is a reference book containing words arranged alphabetically, giving information about their form, function, meaning, and syntax. In a database management system, a *data dictionary* is a comprehensive list or collection of information, usually arranged alphabetically, giving the form, function, meaning, and syntax of data. Data dictionaries describe standard field sizes, coding schemas, and the kind and type of data to be managed by the system.

Data dictionaries are a prerequisite to setting up a functioning system. They establish consistency and eliminate repetitions and omissions. They may also contain a security function; that is, they may define which files or fields may be accessed by specific users and which may be changed or modified. Once the database dictionary has been prepared, the DBMS administrator can set about the task of actually setting up the files, entering data, and implementing the system.

The value of a data dictionary is illustrated by the following example. Suppose two managers in the same company, located in different cities,

Type of store

Acct. #	Name	Type of store
16	Jones	Gen mdse

Type of goods

Acct. #	Name	Type of goods ordered
16	Jones	Chairs, tables

Volume

Acct. #	Name	Volume purchased
16	Jones	$200,000

Sales representative

Acct. #	Name	Sales rep.
16	Jones	Diaz

Composite

Acct. #	Name	Sales rep.	Type of store	Volume	Type of goods
10	Smith	McDonald	Retail furn.	$100,000	Couches
16	Jones	Diaz	Gen mdse	$200,000	Chairs, tables
23	Ellis	Slade	Disct. furn.	$83,000	Lamps, chairs, tables

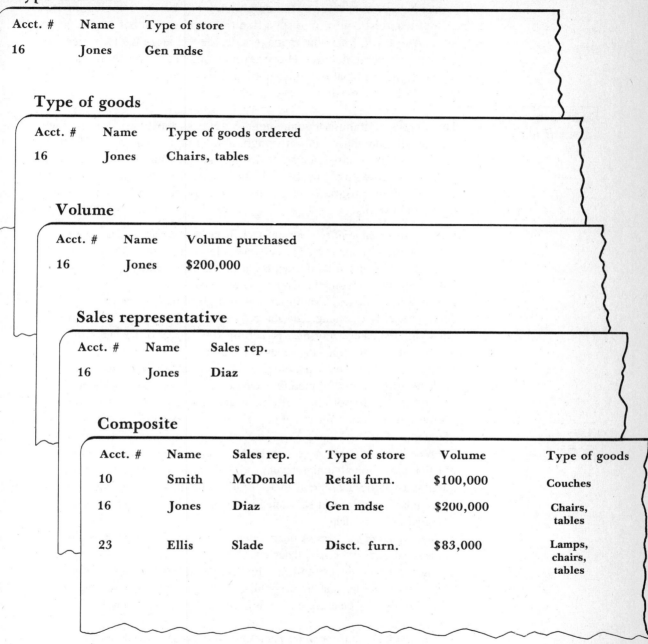

Fig. 13.6—Relational Structure

wish to establish address files on their local accounts. According to company policy they must refer to the data dictionary before establishing new files. The files must conform to specified field width, number of characters, format, and so forth. Later the managers decide to merge the two files, giving both a broader database. Had they not consulted the dictionary, the managers might not be able to merge their files because the formats or field widths might be inconsistent.

Database capabilities

The simplest database management systems support only one user who can access the database only through a language such as COBOL or BASIC. The more sophisticated DBMS may support hundreds of users in a distributed system with a variety of means of accessing the database.

The following programs or capabilities may be written into database management systems:

1. *Single-user capability*. The most elementary database management systems support one user. The software allows one terminal to access, change, or modify the information in the database. Software such as this is available for small microcomputer systems.

2. *Multiuser capability*. Multiuser software gives many terminals concurrent access to a single database. Users may be restricted to only querying the database or may be permitted to update or change information, depending upon the needs of the users.

3. *Distributed database capability*. Using special software, users are able to access, query, or modify databases distributed over a wide geographic area. The software must allow concurrent use of the database. It must also provide for system recovery in the event of transmission failure.

4. *Procedural language access*. A DBMS may provide access to information only through a high level procedural language. This means the user must write a program in COBOL, FORTRAN, or BASIC, for example. The user must be trained in the use of a high-level language in order to access data.

5. *Query language access*. A query language allows an untrained user to access information in the database. A program does not need to be written. Instead, an easy-to-learn, English-like query language is used. Other software may enable unsophisticated users to prepare reports or print out data by entering only a few simple commands from the keyboard.

6. *Relational database management*. One of the most flexible means of accessing databases is through relational files. Relational files allow users to structure different data paths without the necessity of restructuring the files. Special software is necessary to process relational files in place of ordinary list files using pointers.

7. *Security facilities*. Security programs allow only selected users to access the database. Some files, records, or fields are restricted to selected users by means of passwords or user numbers. Only qualified users may change the contents of the database, while all may access it. For instance, a department supervisor may be permitted to change prices from a restricted terminal, using a special password, while line employees can only display prices in the database.

Querying the database

The value of a database lies in its ability to be accessed in many different ways. Experienced programmers may prefer to access the contents of a database using a program written in a procedural language such as COBOL or BASIC. However, this requires adherence to strict programming rules and the skills of a trained programmer. Query languages were developed to eliminate the need for using a procedural language to access a database.

In the mid 1970s, IBM developed the *Structured Query Language (SQL)*. This language has become the model for accessing databases in both microcomputers and mainframe computers. Rather than needing to learn a complex language such as COBOL, a user need only learn thirty or so SQL language statements.

For instance, in SQL language, the SELECT command retrieves data from the Inventory table for all parts for which the stock on hand is greater than fifty. The computer will retrieve from the database the rows and columns specified that satisfy the condition of On_hand that is greater than fifty.

Generating reports

Much of the power of a DBMS lies in the simplicity with which a report may be generated from the contents of a database. Prior to the introduction of *report generators* it was necessary for the user to write a complex set of instructions in order to obtain a formatted report from information stored in a database. The user had to lay out the report, carefully positioning column headings, establishing margins, structuring the number of lines on a page, etc. This required programming effort. By using a report generator, the user can easily create a neatly formatted report with virtually no programming effort.

COMMERCIAL DATABASE SERVICES

During the past decade millions of pieces of information have been assembled into databases readily accessible to business, industrial, educational, and domestic users. This growing industry is sometimes referred to as *database publishing* or *electronic publishing*. It has expanded into a multibillion dollar a year industry which is growing at the rate of nearly thirty percent per year. Let us look at some of these services.

The New York Times maintains a database of over two million abstracts of newspaper articles. Dow Jones has a subscriber base of 310,000 customers who rely upon its general news and corporate data. The Dow Jones corporate profiles include income and balance sheet statements for major industrial companies and extensive reports on their financial operations, officers, directors, and ownership of subsidiaries. LEXIS, offered by Mead Corp., and a competing database called WestLaw, offered by West Publishing Company, contain citations on thousands of Supreme Court and appellate decisions. CompuServe Information Service, owned by H & R Block Company, has 489,000 subscribers. Knight-Ridder's Dialogue and Equifax's Financial Control Services collectively contain files ranging from general news and air line schedules to credit reports, medical bibliographies, and stock prices.

Access to commercial databases

To access a commercial database, a user must go through a common carrier (a telephone or telecommunications system), such as AT&T, GTE, or MCI. GTE, for example, offers its Telenet service to users. Telenet is a common carrier that enables users to access the network from hundreds of cities across the country or from over forty foreign countries. Telenet can be accessed by terminals having many different speeds, formats, or data codes. Another company in the field is Tymshare, Inc., which offers its Tymnet service. These firms provide access to commercial databases, and some even operate databases of their own.

The cost to the user depends on the communications network's access charge and a database usage fee based on how long a terminal is connected to the network, the amount of central computer time taken, or the amount of information accessed.

Once the user is connected to the database, a list of options appears. This list is called a *menu*. The user selects an option from the menu. The computer may then display *submenus*, narrowing down the selection. Through a system of menus and submenus, a user with no programming skills can easily access complex databases.

Commercial database examples

We will conclude with a description of how two different kinds of databases are used. The discussion should help you grasp the depth and scope of database applications.

The entire content of Grolier's Academic American Encyclopedia has been entered into a computer database. This electronic encyclopedia consists of approximately nine million words that fill twenty-one printed volumes and 28,000 articles. Customers of CompuServe gain access through computers connected to the database by coaxial cable or telephone wires. The fee for the service is under $1 per minute, with a monthly access charge. Several hundred schools and libraries are among the thousands of subscribers to the service.

The computer allows different levels of coverage to be presented. A rather simple and untechnical discussion of various topics is available for the elementary school student. A more advanced user can direct the computer to print out or display a more complex discussion.

American Banker News Service's Innerline is an example of a database of information designed for bankers and financial institutions. When a banker or investor wishes to use Innerline, he or she first accesses a menu. The computer displays the options, including the day's banking news, morning market comments, bank stock prices, and even legislation pending before Congress or lawsuits before the courts. The user selects one of the options and receives a display. Innerline charges users by the minute to access the system and has a small additional report charge. This service allows bankers and financial managers to make important decisions based upon current information readily available through the Innerline database.

A database is a collection of common records structured in a systematic way to serve one or more users. File processing involves updating records and returning them to the file. In database processing records are searched electronically and updated by computer. In a distributed database arrangement many users share information dispersed geographically throughout the system.

A library is a collection of files. A file is made up of records. A record is composed of fields that are made up of bytes. A database is constructed from a collection of libraries. The advantages of database management systems (DBMS) are cost savings, elimination of duplication, and access by many users to information that can be controlled and secured.

A schema is a logical plan or structure around which data are organized. It includes a data model that defines all data elements. Database structures in use include the list, tree, network, and relational structures. These structures use pointers, linkage addresses, or other means of locating records.

A data dictionary is a comprehensive list of information describing the field size, coding schema, and other details related to files and records. Database software includes programs for single-user, multiuser, and distributed database capabilities. Some provide for access by high-level languages, such as COBOL or FORTRAN, while others use an English-like query language. Using a Structured Query Language (SQL), the user may access a database, selecting information according to a condition that must be satisfied.

A report generator simplifies the process of creating formatted reports that are properly spaced and include data totaled and subtotaled in columns. Commercial databases are available from electronic publishing systems. They first display to the user menus and submenus that describe various services or areas of data from which the user chooses.

Selected Readings

Hutchinson, Sarah E. *Computers*, Irwin (1992). Chapter 11.

Mandell, Steven L. *Computers and Information Processing*, West Publishing Company (1992). Chapter 15.

Stair, Ralph M. *Principles of Information Systems*, Boyd & Fraser (1992). Chapter 5.

REVIEW QUESTIONS

True or False Questions

1. The term database refers to traditional file processing techniques.
2. File-based processing is the same as database processing.
3. The terms field and record are used in describing files.
4. A file is a collection of records.
5. An advantage of database management systems is ease of file upating.
6. The term schema means a bit made up of bytes.
7. Pointers are used in the list structure.
8. Syntax information is contained in a data dictionary.
9. The purpose of a query language is to ease the burden on the database user.
10. Only government agencies may access commercial databases.
11. Commercial databases are accessed through common carriers.
12. A single-user database management system supports many users.
13. A multiuser database management system is limited to one user.
14. Distributed database management systems allow concurrent use of databases.
15. The function of a report generator is to provide information security.

Completion Questions

1. Any group of records is called a _____.
2. The _____ language is used to query a database.
3. _____ DBMS services are available for a fee.
4. Files are groups of _____ .
5. A data _____ defines the form, function, and meaning of data.

ANSWER KEY

True or False Questions

1. F
2. F
3. T
4. T
5. T
6. F
7. T
8. T
9. T
10. F
11. T
12. F
13. F
14. T
15. F

Completion Questions

1. file
2. SQL
3. Commercial
4. records
5. dictionary

14

Management and Decision Support Systems

The vitality of a business enterprise depends on the efficient flow of information, both internally and externally. Accurate, prompt, complete information is essential to the decision making process. Business executives must have adequate information to properly direct the operations of a business enterprise. The manufacturing, marketing, and distribution of goods are all dependent upon the availability of the right kind of information available at the right time and place in the business cycle.

Up to this point we have studied the computer and its hardware and software. We have seen how business systems are put together. We now take a look at management information systems (MIS). We will explore how the computer is used to enhance a manager's ability to plan, control, organize, and direct organizations. The chapter also discusses artificial intelligence and how an MIS is structured, and contrasts management information systems with decision support systems (DSS).

WHAT ARE MANAGEMENT INFORMATION SYSTEMS (MIS)?

A *management information system (MIS)* is a form of database management system. It is designed to provide information to managers for the effective control and decision making necessary to operate an organization. These systems manage and manipulate information.

Information is knowledge which is useful in the operation, control, planning, or management of organizations. Managers rely upon accurate information to make good decisions. Good decisions make good management and good management leads an organization toward its goals or increased profit.

Management information systems are an outgrowth of file processing systems. They generate reports, printouts, and documents that help managers at all levels in an organization make better decisions. Virtually any kind of information can be managed by an MIS, ranging from engineering, manufacturing, or raw material costs to labor, promotion, advertising, or transportation data. For example, reports can be generated for such matters as cash flow, trends in accounts payable and receivable, earnings ratios, and turnover ratios.

The MIS can give management data concerning distribution functions. These reports can provide information on finished goods in stock or in transit, goods in production, or backlogged orders. It can prepare shipping schedules, routing data, and shipping cost tables. This type of information may help to remedy late deliveries, misrouted goods, and over- or under-production of goods.

Investment planning and management of capital assets can be included in a management information system. For example, managers can receive reports on capital outlays, returns on investment, cost centers, depreciation schedules, and equipment maintenance and installation costs. This facilitates planning for the acquisition of new capital goods or the sale of outdated or unproductive equipment.

INFORMATION FLOW IN ORGANIZATIONS

To appreciate the need for an MIS in an organization one need only look at the vast amount of data that flows within an organization and outside to its customers, suppliers, governmental agencies, etc. Information flow may be either external or internal.

External information flow is information that moves between an organization and an outside agency (Fig. 14.1). The figure illustrates a firm at the center, surrounded by groups with which it interacts. Information flows back and forth between the center—the firm—and the peripheral elements—the suppliers, the customers, the federal and local governments, and the public. Some examples of external information flow are reports to the government on employee withholding and unemployment tax, earnings reports to shareholders, specifications to suppliers, and sales information to potential customers.

Internal information flow takes place within an organization and can be

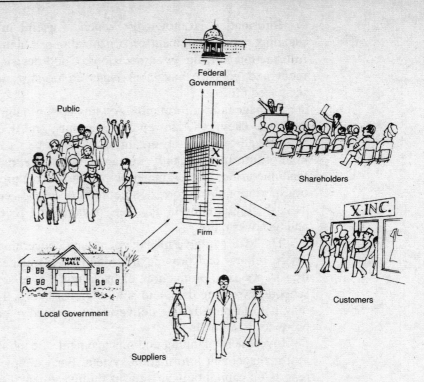

Fig. 14.1—External Information Flow

either horizontal or vertical. An example of vertical information flow is the data passing from a supervisor to line employees, or from a president to branch managers. Information may also flow from employees in lower echelons to their supervisor or to the president of the company. Horizontal information flow refers to the data passing between personnel on the same level of the organization. For example, the head of manufacturing may supply salary information to the head of the payroll department, or an employee in the shipping department may sign for goods and supply information to a clerk in the purchasing department.

THE TASK OF MANAGEMENT

Management is the coordinating process by which an organization achieves its goals. Management involves molding into common action the resources of an organization, including human, financial, production, and distribution elements. It is the process of achieving predetermined objectives.

Modern organizations can be viewed as pyramids. The pyramid is called the organizational *hierarchy*. The hierarchy defines the position of each person in the structure. At the top of the pyramid is the president, board of directors, or any individual or group with ultimate responsibility for the organization. At the bottom of the pyramid are the workers who must carry out the orders. At varying levels in the hierarchy are *managers*, who must direct subordinates. A *subordinate* is anyone who is directly responsible to someone at a higher level in the organizational structure.

LEVELS OF MANAGEMENT

In most organizations, it is possible to categorize three levels of management. The definitions that follow are somewhat general. The dividing line between levels is not clearly delineated in many organizations.

Top-level management (executives). This group includes the top executives and decision makers in an organization. *Top-level managers* are generally those who wield the maximum authority and power. They establish the major long-range goals and plans and make the key decisions. They select key personnel to staff the middle and upper levels of the organizational hierarchy. These managers are highly paid individuals with major responsibilities. They may have only a limited number of subordinates with whom they work directly, such as mid-level managers, but they are responsible for the overall performance of all subordinates in the organization. Up-to-date and accurate information is vital to managers in this group.

Mid-level management (managers). This group is subordinate to the top-level managers. *Mid-level managers* are charged with the task of carrying out the major decisions made at higher levels. Typical of this group are plant managers, division managers, and heads of major sections or departments. Mid-level managers often have several subordinate managers reporting to them. This level of manager is concerned with shorter-range plans and goals than is the top level. Managers at this level also rely heavily upon data to perform their functions.

Operational-level management (supervisors). At the lowest level of the hierarchy is the *operational-level management*. These are the supervisors, and information is vital to the performance of their jobs. These managers are located closest to the people on the line who actually carry out the work load. They are sometimes called first-line management. They are responsible to the mid-level manager and are charged with implementing short-range plans and policies established by mid- and upper-level managers. They are usually responsible for several subordinates, from a small group of two or three to a larger group of twenty, thirty, or more.

Information requirements

Top-level managers need data so they can frame long-range plans regarding the direction of the organization. They must have financial data and asset information and must have a complete picture of the available capital in the firm.

Mid-level managers need current data so they can frame strategies to implement the goals, policies, and directions established by top-level management. Once their strategies have been developed, then line-level managers must have information regarding the day-to-day activities of the firm. They must know what raw materials are on order, when goods are to be shipped, and have addresses and credit information on customers. Let us look at the specific functions performed by managers, and then we will explore the major elements of an MIS.

MANAGEMENT FUNCTIONS

Many authorities have attempted to define the specific functions that managers perform in their day-to-day activities. A function is a group of related activities contributing to a larger action. Most authorities agree that these functions include planning, organizing, staffing, directing, and controlling.

Planning

Planning involves setting goals and objectives. The planning function also includes devising a design, scheme, or program for the orderly achievement of an objective. Planning is always the beginning point of a sequence of activities and efforts designed to reach a specific goal. Planning may include either long-range or short-range plans. By definition, it is always oriented to the future.

Organizing

The *organizing* function involves developing a structure by bringing together many parts into a structured whole. Thus, organizing seeks to pull together many related activities into a united effort. For example, organizing consists of assembling the human resources, equipment, money, and raw materials necessary to reach an objective. Using charts to show the relationship of various individuals in the organization, the manager gathers and maintains the needed staff and trains people to work as part of the united whole.

Staffing

Managers often have the responsibility of *staffing* positions in the organization. They interview prospective employees, assess their qualifications, and place people where they can do the most good. The manager may be the one who introduces the new employee to the job or trains the employee for the position.

Directing

The *directing* function involves leading people by showing or pointing the way to the desired outcome and charting a course that others may follow. The key to this function is leadership. The manager points out the type and amount of effort needed to reach an objective. Part of the directing function involves motivating subordinates to reach the specified goals. A major part of directing consists in communicating with subordinates and conveying, by example, illustration, and explanation, how an objective is to be reached.

Controlling

Controlling is the measurement of progress against standards and the redirection of activities to achieve objectives. It involves monitoring the progress of the organization against standards established during the planning stage. If progress is not in the anticipated direction and of the expected magnitude, the manager must redirect efforts. Control can be exercised in many ways. A major form of control is in the allocation of funds. By giving more funds to one activity and less to another, the manager can redirect the progress of the organization. The control function stresses measurement and comparison of progress against predetermined benchmarks.

ACTIVITIES OF MANAGERS

In order to appreciate the need for an MIS, let us review the tasks performed by managers as they carry out their functions. Although the specific activities performed by managers in their day-to-day work vary with the type of organization, all are dependent upon the availability of accurate data. Here are some major management activities:

Policy making. The manager often must define specific courses of action. The establishment of policies is a prime executive activity. Managers set the operating policies that subordinates are expected to follow. Policy making looks toward the future and is therefore a planning function.

Decision making. A principal activity of the manager is decision making. Managers are continually assessing alternative courses of action and then selecting from among them. This decision-making process is a fundamental management task and is also a planning function.

Evaluating personnel. Managers periodically review personnel performance to ensure that employee performance is consistent with company objectives. If not, employees' efforts must be redirected. Managers often retrain employees or provide in-service training to update skills. This is both an organizing and a controlling task.

Evaluating overall organization performance. Managers assess the total effectiveness and performance of all facets of the organization. To do this, they study financial statements, personnel reports, sales data, warehouse records, and performance ratios. If performance is not what it should be, the manager must redirect efforts of individuals or whole departments. This is a control function.

Establishing short- and long-range plans. Managers and executives make plans and chart courses of action for the organization. Short-range plans may specify what will be done for a period of a few weeks or months. Long-range plans may chart a direction that will be followed for many years. This is a planning function.

Communicating. Both written and oral communication are part of the manager's job. The manager must devote time to communicating plans and policies. This involves talking to subordinates on a one-to-one basis and speaking to groups. Written communications include letters, memos, reports, and bulletins.

Leading. A manager must often set examples for others to follow, and must instruct, train, and guide subordinates. The manager may use a variety of leadership techniques to motivate employees, and must lead the way in coping with the changes facing the firm. Leading employees in accepting and adapting to new technology and methods is a directing function.

Coordinating. An especially important activity of managers is coordination, in which the manager attempts to make all parts of the organization work together.

MANAGEMENT INFORMATION SYSTEM (MIS) DEPARTMENT

Many organizations have delegated MIS functions to a single department. These departments are charged with the responsibility of coordinating and managing the information flow in the organization. Each department is usually headed by a manager or vice president of management information systems. Figure 14.2 illustrates a hierarchy that includes managers, database administrators, and analysts. This crucial group is a supporting function for other departments in the organization.

MAJOR ELEMENTS OF AN MIS

An MIS can be configured in many different ways to serve the needs of an organization. Figure 14.3 illustrates a typical MIS. It includes a database

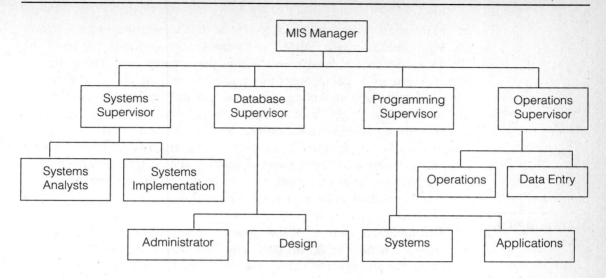

Fig. 14.2—MIS Department Hierarchy

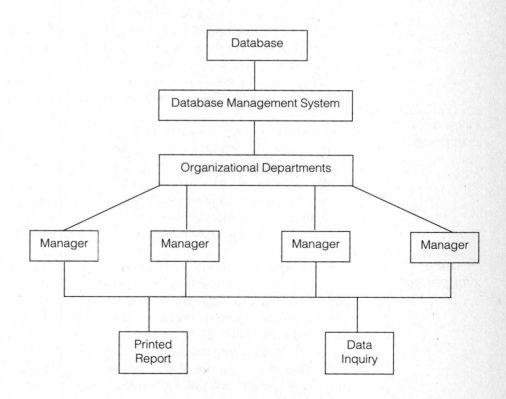

Fig. 14.3—MIS Example

of information which is serviced by a database management system (DBMS). We discussed DBMS software in the previous chapter. The DBMS serves major departments within the organization. These are the MIS subsystems or components that make up the total system. Subsystem components include marketing, personnel, finance, and manufacturing elements; they form major departments in an organization. Managers in these departments are able to access information via a local terminal, or they can generate hard copy reports. The queries and reports provide managers with information needed for their strategic planning and decision making.

The MIS serves as the foundation for the major departments in an organization. Let us look at the major MIS subsystems.

Marketing component

The marketing element of the system is designed to serve the needs of the sales and marketing department. The MIS can be used to prepare sales forecasts, manage inventory, process marketing information, and assist in planning and budgeting. The system can keep track of current sales, project future trends, and forecast changing demand. Using MIS terminals, marketing executives can plan advertising programs, project dealer inventories, and identify the best market for their product.

The MIS can perform order-point calculations. It can list the supply of goods on hand at any time and the date when replacements should be ordered to meet demand. The system can compute the most economical and efficient quantity of goods to order at one time, give minimum amounts that should be kept in stock, and indicate when reorders should be placed.

Personnel component

This element of the system is used to process payroll and maintain data on employees. It computes commissions, schedules work loads, and processes employment applications, promotions, and terminations. The MIS provides management with data on the composition of its workforce. It can print out information on job classifications and personnel capabilities. It can list employees by department, salary schedule, or seniority. The system prepares vacation schedules, overtime allotments, and health plan reports.

Finance component

This element serves the organization's financial planning and management needs. It maintains ledgers, journals, depreciation and inventory records, profit and loss statements, and balance sheets. The MIS is able to prepare a variety of reports for financial analysis. It maintains journals and ledgers and prints out bills, tax reports, profit and loss statements, and balance sheets. It also computes ratios and indexes.

The finance component also incorporates payroll accounting. It maintains payroll records, calculates earnings, computes withholding taxes, and other deductions, figures commissions, and can print out paychecks.

Manufacturing component

The MIS serves many applications in manufacturing and production. It is a valuable tool in cost accounting and in scheduling manufacturing operations. The MIS produces reports for management on raw materials, warehousing, inventory, shipping, and plant operation and maintenance.

Cost accounting systems are able to analyze production costs and compute budgeted hourly costs for individual machines or entire departments. They are able to track jobs in production and determine their cost according to the amount of time and materials needed. They also calculate return on investment and profit, and establish wholesale and retail selling prices.

The MIS provides ordering, warehousing, and cost data, listed by part numbers or bills of lading. It schedules work for an assembly line based on labor available by shift. It can print out a list of equipment and material needs for the assembly line for a given day. It can predict output, report the number of units produced, and provide follow-up cost data.

STRUCTURING THE MIS

The structure of the MIS should be based upon the needs of the organization. It must be designed to store and access information and prepare reports as needed. These reports may be generated at local or remote terminals. The on-line aspect of these systems allows the database to be queried and results displayed immediately.

The steps involved in developing and implementing an MIS include:

Defining the data to be stored in the database
Structuring files and specifying input media
Structuring query procedures and defining output media
Inputting raw data into the database
Opening the system to users
Updating and revising the database and inputting new information

The information managed by the system can come from many sources including:

Sales information
Order backlog
Customer buying patterns
Current selling prices
Shipping information and costs
Supply of raw materials
Cost of materials
Equipment and plant capacity
Financial data

Personnel data

Engineering costs

Accounts receivable

Fixed-asset inventory

Accounts payable

Budgets

DECISION SUPPORT SYSTEMS (DSS)

As MIS became more prevalent in business organizations, it was inevitable that managers who were not computer programmers would turn to these systems for their decision-making tasks. They needed to obtain vital information quickly and easily without writing programs or having to understand the inner workings of the computer. These managers preferred to work in an unstructured decision-making environment, one that did more than merely rely on historical reports or information generated by computers. They needed systems that emphasized long-range goals and future orientation.

This need led to the development of *decision support systems (DSS)*, an outgrowth of file processing and management information systems. Decision support systems are a form of database management that emphasizes decision making. They are generally implemented using color graphics terminals that access a database in real time and display information for the manager. Instead of simply generating printed reports for decision makers, DSS allow the manager to query the system, structure relationships, and then display the results. It is not necessary to learn formal programming rules or complicated system details.

A feature of decision support systems is their ability to deal in relationships. Organizations are represented as mathematical models that can be manipulated, tested, and experimented with. In implementing a DSS, pertinent data are gathered in a database and the relationships of business variables are defined. Reports can be generated that aid in decision making, and relationships can be altered and new information displayed instantaneously. With a DSS, the manager does not rely on just printed reports, but instead, on a real-time assessment of a model that shows future trends and graphically displays key data.

The differences between MIS and DSS are illustrated as follows:

MIS	*DSS*
Relatively structured procedures	Unstructured procedures
Emphasizes reports, printouts	Emphasizes decision making
Focuses on collection of data	Future oriented
Historical reporting	Real-time reporting
Bound by system constraints	User-friendly, visual display

ARTIFICIAL INTELLIGENCE

A step beyond DSS are management systems that simulate the thought processes of the human mind. These systems are known as *expert systems*. An expert system is one that is programmed to apply human logic and knowledge to solve a problem. Expert systems are able to learn through repetition and can solve practical business problems by applying the same intuitive thought processes followed by human managers.

Expert systems solve problems by following a set of rules. Computers with artificial intelligence apply each rule to a base of knowledge and reach conclusions without requiring a detailed set of programming instructions. These systems are programmed using English-like commands rather than structured computer languages.

ISSUES RELATED TO MANAGEMENT INFORMATION SYSTEMS

We have already touched upon how the MIS is used to help manage organizations. Management information systems simplify the manager's task but are not without their problems and limitations. The following are major issues related to the use of MIS and DSS:

Misuse of information. There is always a potential for misuse whenever information is stored. The improper use of such vital information as a firm's customer list, personnel list, wholesale prices or internal security procedures could be ruinous to an organization. Protection against these eventualities could involve costly and time consuming procedures.

Accessibility. An MIS extends across many organization and division lines. This raises the issue regarding who shall access and control the system. What security measures should be instituted? What kinds of information should be stored in the system? Which system users should be given the highest priority? Who shall have database query terminals and who shall be assigned passwords for their use?

MIS personnel. In the early days of information systems it was not uncommon for computer users to have hands-on contact with the hardware and software. Because of the risk of information loss, today only a few computer installations allow hands on use of the computer and permit access only through carefully controlled terminals. Only a limited number of people are permitted in the secure area around the computer. Procedures must be established to screen personnel who will set up and operate the MIS.

Physical security. The computer on which the MIS is run is subject to both internal and external hazards. Earthquakes, fires, floods, and other natural disasters are external threats. Theft, vandalism, fraud, and unauthorized use of information constitute internal dangers to the DBMS. Physical plant protection may include the use of burglar alarms, key card door locks, security police, closed circuit television, and other controls.

The threat of a virus is always present. A *virus* is an unauthorized program that finds its way into the computer and can destroy vital data in the MIS. Viruses attach themselves to programs and, much like human viruses, spread from one system to another. Some viruses are benign; that is, they simply display an unexpected graphic or written message on the screen in the middle of a program run. Others are more vicious and may actually erase an entire database. Viruses can infiltrate a program or database and blend into it, unknown to the user. Some find their way into operating systems and have been known to wipe out the contents of an entire hard drive.

Another destructive piece of software is known as a Trojan Horse. It finds its way into a program and may remain dormant for a long period of time. It then becomes active and destroys the contents of a database. A true virus program is able to reproduce itself and can infect one program or database after another, whereas a Trojan Horse does its damage and then is erased.

This raises the issue of data security and information handling procedures. Many organizations require all programs to be screened through viral diagnostic software. No program can be run until it is properly screened. These programs, known as anti-viral software, detect viruses and remove them from infected programs.

If security controls are too restrictive, individuals cannot make full use of the MIS. If procedures are too lax, irretrievable data can be destroyed, with disastrous consequences for the organization. A corporate security program is expensive in terms of time and money. Policies need to be established and individuals charged with the responsibility of implementing programs. End users must be given training in security procedures and provided with appropriate software and controls.

In this chapter we have outlined management fundamentals and how the MIS supports the major management functions. This chapter concludes our discussion of systems.

A management information system (MIS) is designed to provide information to managers for effective control and decision making. An MIS generates reports, printouts, and other documents. Information flow in organizations can be internal or external, and may flow vertically or horizontally. Management is the coordinating process by which an organization achieves its goals.

Top-level managers are those who wield the maximum authority and power in setting organizational goals and objectives. Mid-level management is charged with the task of carrying out decisions made at higher levels. Operational-level management is located closest to people on the line who carry out the workload. The major management functions include planning, organizing, staffing, directing, and controlling. Major management activities are policy making, decision making, evaluating, establishing plans, communicating, leading, and coordinating.

An MIS includes marketing, personnel, finance, and manufacturing components. Both hard copy reports and on-line access may be provided to these components. An MIS can keep track of current sales, project future trends, and manage inventories. It can assist with order-point calculations and handle numerous personnel management and workforce tasks. It can help schedule assembly line work, make output projections, and provide cost accounting data.

A decision support system (DSS) is a form of unstructured information system designed to serve managers. The expert system is a step beyond DSS and is programmed to simulate human logic and knowledge to solve a problem. It applies a set of rules to a base of knowledge in reaching conclusions. Issues related to MIS include misuse of information, accessibility, physical security, and screening of MIS personnel.

Viruses may infect programs or databases and erase their contents. Viral detection programs and security procedures may be put in place to prevent the unauthorized destruction of data.

Selected Readings

Hutchinson, Sarah E. *Computers*, Irwin (1992). Chapter 11.

Mandell, Steven L. *Computers and Information Processing*, West Publishing Company (1992). Chapter 15.

Stair, Ralph M. *Principles of Information Systems*, Boyd & Fraser (1992). Chapter 10.

REVIEW QUESTIONS

True or False Questions

1. The task of management is to achieve organizational goals.
2. Internal and external information flow relies upon information systems.
3. Vertical and horizontal information flow are synonymous.
4. There are three levels of management.
5. To date no major management functions have been defined.
6. Policy making is an activity performed by managers.
7. The elements of an MIS include its subsystems.
8. An MIS does not have a structure.

9. A DSS provides the same function as an MIS.
10. Policy making is a management activity.
11. Short- and long-range plans are developed by managers.
12. The function of the manufacturing component in an organization is to finance new construction.
13. The function of the personnel component in an organization is to acquire staff.
14. The function of the finance component in an organization is to raise capital.
15. The function of the marketing component in an organization is to sell goods.

Completion Questions

1. An _____ system is programmed to apply human logic.
2. Misuse, access, and security are issues related to _____.
3. A _____ describes a management hierarchy.
4. _____ the data to be stored is the first step in developing an MIS.
5. From organization to customers is an example of _____ information flow in a business.

ANSWER KEY

True or False Questions

1. T
2. T
3. F
4. T
5. F
6. T
7. T
8. F
9. F
10. T
11. T
12. F
13. T
14. T
15. T

Completion Questions

1. expert
2. MIS
3. pyramid
4. Defining
5. external

15

Critical Issues

We *have reviewed the technical and applied aspects of computers, and how they are integrated into business systems. A study of computers would not be complete without a look at some of the broader issues and the ethical questions raised by this powerful electronic tool.*

The computer has entered not only our businesses but our homes and schools and has had a profound effect on education and even domestic family life. It is a major hobby and recreational tool. The diverse applications of computers require people to be knowledgeable in the selection and purchase of these electronic marvels, as well as in their use.

In this chapter we discuss ethical issues, abuses of databases and information networks, legal considerations, and the need for industry standards. We also look at some of the philosophical and psychological questions raised by the use of computers.

LEGAL, ETHICAL, AND SOCIAL ISSUES

Certainly the computer has created new problems for our institutions: our schools, our legal system, and our technological society. Let us look at some of the major ethical issues that must be dealt with in the computer age.

Privacy questions

Used properly, the computer is a benefit to society, but it also bears a potential for misuse. A fine line exists between searching a credit file to approve Mr. Smith's purchase on a credit card and using the same file to discover that Mr. Smith possesses certain "high-risk" credit propensities.

Before the computer, manual *dragnet searches* of records could take hundreds of hours of time and were costly. Thus, most file searches were carried out only to locate a specific piece of information. However, with the aid of the computer, fishing and dragnet searches of huge files can be done with ease and at low cost. Thousands of records may be searched in a few seconds in hope of finding one or two dubious individuals or subjects.

Used together with *electronic surveillance* devices, such as hidden cameras, phone taps, videotape equipment, and remote transmitters, the computer can become a powerful weapon against all of us. The threat of "big brother" watching, spying, snooping into our private lives, and forgetting nothing becomes a reality because of the computer.

Here are some of the ethical questions that must be answered:

1. Who shall guard and protect information stored by private firms and government agencies?
2. Who shall be allowed to access files? Some government files contain data on a citizen's sexual, drinking, arrest, and mental health history.
3. Should the social security number or other identifiers be used to scan files and construct composite dossiers on citizens?
4. How long should information that is no longer timely or accurate remain in a file?
5. Should subjects have an opportunity to view their own files for completeness and accuracy? How should conflicts be handled when a subject disagrees with the contents of a file?
6. Is it ethical to search a file dragnet style looking for a "statistical stereotype" who possesses high-risk factors, rather than looking for a specific fact or piece of data?
7. Should information collected on a subject for one purpose be transferred to another unrelated file and perhaps the data later sold to commercial firms who in turn prepare or sell mailing lists?

Some organizations have adopted a practice of surreptitiously monitoring employees who use a computer in the office. Managers secretly *monitor* all information stored or handled by each computer or data communications device. These managers are quietly able to look over the shoulders of employees from distant locations and determine what data are being processed, what information is handled, and how much work is being produced by specific employees. Software is available that can provide a statistical profile of an employee, his or her work habits, speed, error rate, etc.

Employees complain that supervisors monitor transactions unnecessarily and have used the information to the detriment of the employee. Raises and promotions have been withheld. In some instances reprimands and outright dismissals of employees have occurred, based upon information derived from the computer.

It is a long established principle that a manager or an employer has a right to monitor the workload and performance of a subordinate. However, the speed and thoroughness of the computer raise many ethical questions. To what extent should an employer be permitted to electronically eavesdrop on an employee? Should this practice be permitted without telling the employee? Should it provide grounds for dismissal or reprimands? Clearly, these issues will need to be answered.

Medical and health concerns

The widespread use of computers has raised many health concerns. Questions that need to be addressed involve the effects of electromagnetic radiation, especially on women of childbearing age. Health concerns arise when operators must spend long periods of time in front of a monitor or must keyboard large amounts of data. Workers complain of eyestrain, back fatigue, difficulty with wrist movement, and muscle strain. Much more money and research must go into identifying health risks and methods of preventing or reducing health-related problems brought about because of the computer.

Code of ethics

The Data Processing Management Association (DPMA) has promulgated a *code of ethics* to foster responsibility amongst its members (Fig. 15.1). The code states that members have an obligation to uphold the privacy and confidentiality of information, and to refrain from using confiden-

Code of Ethics

I acknowledge:

That I have an obligation to management, therefore, I shall promote the understanding of information processing methods and procedures to management using every resource at my command.

That I have an obligation to my fellow members, therefore, I shall uphold the high ideals of DPMA as outlined in its Association Bylaws. Further, I shall cooperate with my fellow members and shall treat them with honesty and respect at all times.

That I have an obligation to society and will participate to the best of my ability in the dissemination of knowledge pertaining to the general development and understanding of information processing. Further, I shall not use knowledge of a confidential nature to further my personal interest, nor shall I violate the privacy and confidentiality of information entrusted to me or to which I may gain access.

That I have an obligation to my employer whose trust I hold, therefore, I shall endeavor to discharge this obligation to the best of my ability, to guard my employer's interests, and to advise him or her wisely and honestly.

That I have an obligation to my country, therefore, in my personal, business and social contacts, I shall uphold my nation and shall honor the chosen way of life of my fellow citizens.

I accept these obligations as a personal responsibility and as a member of this Association. I shall actively discharge these obligations and I dedicate myself to that end.

Fig. 15.1—Code of Ethics

tial information for personal gain. However, the code of ethics does not address all of the ethical issues and abuses that have arisen with the advent of the computer.

The proliferation of databases

One of the most significant attributes of the computer is its ability to store and retrieve vast amounts of data. Business and government institutions gather enormous amounts of data on millions of people or organizations and assemble this data into files that are electronically accessed, searched, revised, or printed out.

The National Driver Registration files, for example, contain entries on the driving records of people in every state in the union. TRW Credit Data, TransUnion, and other credit reporting agencies maintain records on over 150 million people. The Reuben H. Donnelley Corporation has mailing lists containing tens of millions of households. These lists are sold commercially. The Veterans Administration, Social Security Administration, Department of Commerce, and numerous other public and private agencies maintain millions of records on virtually everyone in the country. These lists are available to many agencies, but are generally not sold.

Perhaps information gathering and reporting systems such as these are necessary, but they also create potential problems. The dissemination of information about a person without that person's knowledge and consent is a serious invasion of privacy. A mistake in entering data into a computer can be detrimental to a person's ability to obtain credit, to be accepted at a school, or to be hired for a job. Computer errors have denied individuals loans or the right to purchase a home or automobile.

UNIVERSAL IDENTIFIER NUMBERS

Some information system professionals have proposed that the government issue a *standard universal identifier* number to every American citizen. The number would remain with that individual from birth until death. The experts propose the number be used as the basis for maintaining and preparing files, posting to accounts, and keying all vital information to each person. Some members of Congress have suggested that a secure, counterfeit-resistant identification card be required for all U.S. workers.

But there has been opposition to this idea, and Congress has regularly debated and resisted issuing universal identifier numbers because of the many problems such a system would create. Government agencies and businesses could access a vast variety of information on an individual using one key number. This number might be used to spy and maintain surveillance files or dossiers on people.

However, in the absence of a standard universal identifier, many business firms, schools, and government agencies have begun to use social security numbers to index files. The Social Security Administration never intended the social security number to be used as a standard universal identifier. It was designed exclusively to aid in cataloging social security files.

One of the main problems with using the social security number is that it does not meet the criteria for a successful standard universal identifier. First, duplicate social security numbers have been inadvertently issued by the Social Security Administration. Second, the number does not include an error-checking digit to eliminate the transposition or loss of digits.

Unless Congress enforces the limited use of the social security number, more and more private and commercial firms and nonfederal agencies will use it; it will become a de facto standard universal identifier.

LEGISLATION TO CONTROL THE USE OF DATABASES

Several pieces of legislation have been passed at the state and national levels to control the misuse of databases and credit information.

Freedom of Information Act

Passed in 1970, the Freedom of Information Act gives citizens and other agencies the right of access to many kinds of data kept in government files. This act represented an attempt by Congress to provide for the open flow of information in government and to protect the public's right to know about government activities. The act does allow government agencies to withhold certain information of a personal nature from the public, but with this major exception it is a formal declaration of the availability of the records and information of all government agencies.

Fair Credit Reporting Act

In 1971, Congress passed the Fair Credit Reporting Act in an attempt to eliminate abuses found in the consumer credit reporting industry. The act requires agencies to follow reasonable procedures to safeguard credit information. It requires that a subject be informed when a credit investigation is being conducted. It gives the responsibility for enforcement to the Federal Trade Commission.

Privacy Act of 1974

The Privacy Act requires that every federal agency identify every system of records that it maintains and regularly review the contents of its files to be sure that the information in them is necessary and relevant. The act specifically forbids maintaining data files on citizens' religious or political affiliations or activities. It also requires every federal agency to publish a list of the systems of records it maintains. This list must include the name and location of the data system and the category of individual on whom records are maintained. This information must be made accessible and available to citizens.

Right to Financial Privacy Act of 1979

By the end of the 1970s, many government agencies were still collecting and misusing data. The Right to Financial Privacy Act sought to limit the government's right to obtain information from financial institutions. The law forces government agencies to seek a subpoena before they can ask a bank to turn over records. They must show that there is a bona fide law enforcement reason for requesting such data. In the event data are released, the individual is to be notified that personal information has been released.

Federal Reports Act

The Federal Reports Act, revised in 1980, was designed to reduce the federal paperwork burden for individuals, small businesses, state and local governments, and others. Its goal was to minimize the cost to the federal government of collecting, maintaining, using, and disseminating information. The act has been instrumental in coordinating and integrating federal information gathering policies and practices and ensuring that confidentiality is kept, consonant with other federal laws.

ELECTRONIC CRIME

Although old-fashioned acts of fraud, theft, breaking and entering, and embezzlement are still prevalent, new versions of these *electronic crimes*, executed on or assisted by a computer, are occurring with increasing frequency. These crimes may be so subtle in nature that they are extremely difficult to detect. It is estimated that electronic crimes such as computer fraud or embezzlement exceed $100 million annually.

Electronic breaking and entering can be perpetrated on a computer file quickly and quietly. There are no jimmied locks or fingerprints but valuable information, programs, or services can be stolen. Fraudulent data can be entered to change a program to print out unauthorized checks or release funds. Records can be altered to cover up cash thefts. Computer processing time itself, a new valuable resource in our society, can be stolen.

The new criminal is not an unsophisticated clerk who sees the opportunity to pocket a few dollars from the till, but a person with skills in computer technology, programming, and communications science through which he or she can steal millions of dollars and cover up virtually every trace of the crime.

Businesses and law enforcement agencies are taking action against the growing number of electronic crimes. The FBI has given hundreds of its special agents courses in detecting computer crimes. Many local police departments have implemented special training programs in computer crime investigation techniques. Many states have passed laws to combat computer-related crimes, and more are considering new legislation each year.

Software piracy

Some software manufacturers invest millions of dollars developing new programs. These efforts may involve thousands of hours in programming, testing, and debugging. The finished product is then placed on the market for sale. Much to the chagrin of these developers, they soon discover that their efforts are being pirated by others. *Software piracy* is the theft of a proprietary product that is then sold to others or distributed free.

Software pirates make unjust profits by stealing the work of others. The speed and accuracy with which a modern computer can duplicate a file complicates the problem. With a minimum of effort, a software pirate can make thousands of duplicates of a piece of software for only the cost of the floppy disks used.

Lotus Development Corporation has led the fight to protect against copyright infringement. They have sued other companies for copying the *look and feel* of their software. At the heart of the issue is what constitutes piracy. Is the theft of a screen image, but not the coding and programming which created it, considered piracy? To what extent should a software developer be able to copyright and protect the look and feel of a given piece of software? Overly stringent copyright controls could mean the stifling of creativity in developing new programs.

Further complicating the issue is the question of profit motive. To what extent should an individual be held liable for making unauthorized copies of software for his or her own personal use, when there is no intent to resell it or make a profit? Undoubtedly, these and other ethical issues relating to software development and copying need to be resolved.

VDT risks

Much research and study is going into the question of the biological and health effects of video display terminals (VDTs). In offices and homes across the country, millions of people spend countless hours sitting in front of glowing computer screens. There is some evidence that continued exposure to VDT radiation may cause certain health problems. It may take many years of carefully controlled studies to determine what health risks, if any, are present due to VDT exposure.

In addition, problems have surfaced involving the fingers, wrists, hands, back, and neck of individuals who spend prolonged periods at a keyboard. These and other reported problems, including those of the eyes, raise many questions about the safety of extended periods in front of a computer.

To what extent should individuals be exposed to VDTs in the absence of long term medical studies? Who is responsible if an employee exhibits medical problems that may be related to extended use of VDTs or computers? Who should bear the ultimate costs for the medical care or therapy required to correct these problems?

LIABILITY FOR COMPUTER FAILURES

The issue of legal liability for serious computer failure has yet to be fully resolved. There is an increasing dependency upon computers as more businesses and government agencies install them. There is also a greater likelihood that a catastrophic computer error or failure will occur. For instance, a programming error in the nation's Federal Reserve accounting system could cost many dollars if it went undetected. A programming error in the missile guidance system of a military warhead could destroy an entire city.

Who is responsible for the loss of lives or property when a computer system fails? People are billed, credited, arrested, graded, selected, rejected, and promoted based upon computer processing. Others are given medical treatment, legal advice, or therapy as a result of computer analysis or diagnosis.

Suppose that because of a computer failure many lives are lost and millions of dollars of property damage occurs. Should the computer manufacturer be held liable? Or should the computer installer, programmer, or operator be held responsible? Should the systems analyst who designed the system or the clerk or technician who helped gather, transmit, or report the data be responsible? Are all equally at fault?

Some have suggested that such computer failures should be borne by society as a whole, rather than by those who are parties to it or who were the victims of the error. Society has long recognized that certain calamities are unavoidable and that the costs should be borne by the society as a whole. The roots of the workers' compensation laws and no-fault auto insurance laws are founded on this philosophy. Perhaps significant losses due to computer errors should be treated in a similar way.

Society will need to carefully define fault and responsibility in terms of computers and data communications. The old common law concepts may need revision in light of new technology. Perhaps a form of "computer malpractice" insurance is needed to cover anyone working with computers or data where significant losses could occur.

ETHICAL AND HUMANISTIC CONSIDERATIONS

Feelings of self-worth and the sense of being needed and wanted derive in large part from our work. In years past workers felt a kinship to their work and derived deep psychological satisfaction from it. Employees could see the results of their labor and derive from them a sense of pride that could be transferred to other areas of life.

As a result of the computer, many new jobs are fragmented. They are only a part of a more complex operation that is little understood by the individual employee. Workers may feel no personal relationship to this type of job; they may feel like cogs in a machine and as if their work has no beginning and no end. They often don't see the results of their efforts and rarely receive a pat on the back.

How will society ensure worker acceptance when the computer takes a person's job satisfaction away? What compensating psychological rewards or status can society offer workers so that they will feel part of the system, rather than in opposition to it? The computer has brought these issues into focus.

Before the introduction of computers, all judgments about people were made by people. Judges, teachers, doctors, friends, employers, and neighbors formed opinions. Raises, promotions, loan approvals, and so on were the result of a human thought process. Consider, for example, how the computer has affected the process of granting credit.

Previously, the client went to the bank, filled out some forms, and had a personal interview. The applicant's forms were reviewed by a loan officer, but the personal interview was critical. During the interview the client was evaluated by another human being on subtle human attributes, not the least of which were personal appearance, attitude, and trust. In short, the loan officer "sized up" the prospect's honesty, making judgments on character and ability to repay the loan. Many years of business and personal experience were brought into the transaction.

Today many loan and credit decisions are made not by people, but by computer. The computer analyzes factual data and provides the loan officer with a "go-no go" decision. The interaction between people is replaced by a mechanical exchange in which electronic input and machine output are substituted for human judgments.

The role of computers

A major ethical issue is to what extent society wants to turn over judgments to machines. The challenge will be to find ways to preserve human responses in an increasingly mechanized society.

There are no rules that tell us how much automation we can or should accept. We can control both the rate at which new inventions are integrated into society and the amount that will be spent on developing new technology. We can set limits on the expansion of automation to allow time for society to adjust to the shock waves.

If the balance between computers and people is allowed to be made wholly on economic considerations, we may discover an overabundance of technology in business and government and a critical shortage of social and humanistic considerations.

What could happen if computer judgments dominate in designing our machines, planning our destiny, and monitoring our progress? What could happen to our security if a computer takes over the role of decision maker and historian? What could happen to us if a machine became the primary force in society in which most judgments were made by machine, recorded by machine, and executed by machine?

Technology has brought air pollution, crowded cities, and depletion of natural resources in addition to its benefits. Yet we step into a jet airplane and are able to fly around the world in a matter of hours. We press a button and on our television screen see and hear a man at the moment he is speaking halfway around the world. A computer is programmed to search fifty million records in little more time than it takes for us to reach for a pencil and paper.

People need time to adjust and understand this new, faster way of life. They need places where they can be free of the modern computer society, where they can think, contemplate, and allow their minds to move at their own speed. The real challenge lies in defining the rightful role of the computer in society.

NEED FOR INDUSTRY STANDARDS

At present there are few *industry standards* governing the development of computer hardware, software, or systems. As a result, new computer languages, systems, and programs are being developed that are incompatible with one another. This represents an enormous loss of time and money in duplicated effort. For example, some computer peripheral equipment, such as disk storage devices and memory modules, cannot be used interchangeably from one computer to another. This may be to the advantage of certain computer manufacturers, but it works to the detriment of the user.

The computer industry is in a position much like that of other industries before the turn of the century. Chaos existed because there were few national standards. For example, electric power was available in alternating and direct current and in many different voltages and frequencies. There were few agreed-upon standards for wire sizes, fasteners, pipe, threads, drills, tools, and so on. The lack of standards threatened many industries and brought about the development of the National Bureau of Standards and the American Standards Association, later known as the American National Standards Institute (ANSI). These organizations and the International Standards Organization (ISO) have brought a degree of order out of this chaos.

If society is to make the most of computers, much needs to be done in establishing standards for computer hardware, software, and databases.

Efforts have already been made by ANSI, which publishes standards for certain languages, but much more needs to be done. For example, hundreds of computer manufacturers market computers that have similar but still different instruction sets, physical architecture, input/output design, operating systems, data exchange rates, and data transfer circuits. Data format, file processing, data gathering, processing, and reporting techniques also need to be standardized. Even the basic element of computer construction, the integrated circuit (IC), is not standardized. Hundreds of manufacturers produce IC chips that have little in common, save their supply voltage and pin design.

Another area that greatly needs standardization is computer logic and algorithms for problem solving. Presently a programmer develops a set of steps for solving a business problem, which is then programmed for the computer. The programmer sets up his or her own solution to solve a problem that may be solved in an equally satisfactory way over and over in hundreds of similar installations in banks, businesses, schools, and government agencies. This duplication of effort is wasteful.

Published standards on common business programs, such as tax preparation, financial accounting, cost accounting, real estate, loans, banking, and distribution, could reduce the wasted effort considerably. Once a common logic has been developed and accepted, it can be incorporated in programs by various firms with the assurance that their programs meet the standard.

Finally, there exists a need for a national *clearing house* of computer software and programs. Such an organization could establish documentation standards, a uniform software licensing or usage fee, and standard abstracting and indexing procedures.

In this chapter we have discussed some of the ethical issues facing society, including software piracy, electronic crime, potential risks of prolonged exposure to computers, and the need for industry standards. Many people are taking a close look at how computers are influencing our lives. As new innovations, such as robotics, artificial intelligence, automation, and voice synthesis, come into widespread use, even more ethical issues will be raised. These will need to be addressed in order for society to gain the full benefits of the computer without experiencing its potential negative impacts.

The computer raises ethical questions about the use of dragnet searches, who may access files, and when and how inaccurate or outdated information may be removed from a file. Both government and private agencies maintain databases containing millions of records. A standard universal identifier number and the social security number have been proposed as means of cataloging information in databases.

At least five major pieces of legislation have been passed since 1970 to help control the abuse and misuse of databases and credit information. Computer-related crimes, such as electronic theft, require a different approach to law enforcement and crime detection. Software piracy raises many questions regarding the fair use of computer software. Another issue raised by the computer is who shall be responsible for a software or hardware failure. Some offices use surreptitious computer monitoring as a means of tracking employee performance. To what extent should this practice be permitted, and how should the results of computer employee monitoring be used?

The extensive use of computers and VDTs raises questions about the need to study the long term health effects of exposure to VDTs or of prolonged periods spent seated at a computer keyboard. Among the emotional and psychological effects of the computer are feelings of alienation and resistance and questions related to job satisfaction and self worth. Society must ultimately decide upon the proper balance between the use of computer and human activity. There is a need for industry standards in computer hardware and software.

Selected Readings

Long, Larry. *Computers*, Prentice-Hall (1993). Chapter 18.

McKeown, Patrick G. *Living With Computers*, Harcourt Brace Jovanovich (1993). Chapters 18, 19.

O'Brien, James A. *The Nature of Computers*, Dryden Press (1993). Chapter 12.

REVIEW QUESTIONS

True or False Questions

1. The function of credit information is an ethical question raised by computer usage.
2. The International Standards Organization has promulgated a computer code of ethics.
3. Eyestrain is a possible health effect from prolonged exposure to a VDT.
4. Both computer hardware and software are areas that require industry standardization.
5. The social security number is an excellent standard universal identifier number.
6. TRW Credit Data and the Veterans Administration maintain large databases.
7. A characteristic of an ideal standard universal identifier number is the presence of an error-checking digit.
8. The Fair Credit Reporting Act was aimed at controlling abuses of databases.
9. Electronic breaking and entering is a computer crime.
10. Employee attitudes are affected when job security is threatened by the computer.

11. The issue of software piracy is not a concern today.
12. New computer systems have solved the problem of hardware and software failure.
13. The computer has virtually no effect on job performance.
14. Law enforcement agencies have changed in order to deal with electronic crimes.
15. The computer age has not led to fragmented jobs.

Completion Questions

1. Computer software _____ agreements have been employed by some companies.
2. Computer _____ measures have been employed to safeguard data.
3. Eyestrain is a potential hazard of _____.
4. The _____ notice appears on the opening screen of some programs.
5. U.S. standards have been established by _____.

ANSWER KEY

True or False Questions

1. T
2. F
3. T
4. T
5. F
6. T
7. T
8. T
9. T
10. T
11. F
12. F
13. F
14. T
15. F

Completion Questions

1. licensing
2. security
3. VDTs
4. copyright
5. ANSI

Selected Readings

Alter, Steven. *Information Systems*, Addison-Wesley (1992).

Arnold, David O. *Computers and Society Impact!*, McGraw-Hill (1991).

Burch, John G. *Systems Analysis, Design, and Implementation*, Boyd & Fraser (1992).

Capron, H. L. *Essentials of Computing*, Benjamin Cummings (1992).

Floyd, Nancy A. *Essentials of Information Processing*, Irwin (1991).

Grupe, Fritz H. *Microcomputer Applications*, W. C. Brown (1992).

Haiduk, H. Paul. *Increasing Your Productivity*, Glencoe (1991).

Hutchinson, Sarah E. *Computers*, Irwin (1992).

Kershner, Helene G. *Introduction to Computer Literacy*, D. C. Heath (1990).

Kidder, Tracy. *The Soul of a New Machine*, Avon Books (1981).

Kroenke, David M. *Database Processing*, SRA (1988).

Kroenke, David M. *Business Computer Systems*, McGraw-Hill (1990).

Leeson, Marjorie M. *Programming Logic*, SRA (1988).

Long, Larry. *Computers*, Prentice-Hall (1993).

Mandell, Steven L. *Computers and Information Processing*, West Publishing Company (1992).

Manes, Stephen. *Gates*, Doubleday (1993).

McKeown, Patrick G. *Living With Computers*, Harcourt Brace Jovanovich (1993).

O'Brien, James A. *The Nature of Computers*, Dryden Press (1993).

O'Leary, Timothy J. *Microcomputing*, McGraw-Hill (1991).

Parker, Charles S. *Understanding Computers and Information Processing*, Dryden Press (1992).

Paz, Neomi. *Programming Logic for Business Applications*, Mitchell (1988).

Rochester, Jack B. *Computers*, Irwin (1993).

Shelly, Gary B. *Systems Analysis and Design*, Boyd & Fraser (1991).

Silver, Gerald A. *Systems Analysis and Design*, Addison-Wesley (1989).

Silver, Gerald A. *Introduction to Desktop Publishing*, W. C. Brown (1990).

Silver, Gerald A. *Layout, Design, and Typography for the Desktop Publisher*, W. C. Brown (1991).

Silver, Gerald A. *Data Communications for Business*, Boyd & Fraser (1994).

Slotnick, Daniel L. *Computers and Applications*, D. C. Heath (1990).

Stair, Ralph M. *Principles of Information Systems*, Boyd & Fraser (1992).

Stamper, David A. *Business Data Communications*, Benjamin Cummings (1991).

Szymanski, Robert A. *Introduction to Computers and Information Systems*, Macmillan (1991).

Walrand, Jean. *Communication Networks*, Irwin (1991).

Glossary

Abstract A summary of a program, briefly describing its purpose, major features, options, and procedures.

Access time The time required to locate and retrieve a given piece of data from memory.

Ada A programming language sponsored by the Department of Defense and designed for use in military and business systems.

AI (Artificial Intelligence) The field of computer work involving hardware and software that simulate human intelligence, thought, and reasoning.

Algorithm A list of specific steps or a set of rules leading to the solution of a problem.

Alphanumeric Refers to a set of characters that includes letters, digits, special characters, and punctuation marks.

ALU (Arithmetic and Logic Unit) The section of the central processing unit of a computer that performs arithmetic and logic operations.

Analog computer A computer that processes data input in a continuous form or data represented as an unbroken flow of information.

Analog data Data represented in a continuous form, as contrasted with digital data represented in a discrete (discontinuous) form. Examples of analog data are physical variables measured along a continuous scale, such as voltage, resistance, and rotation.

ANSI American National Standards Institute.

APL (A Programming Language) A mathematically oriented programming language.

Applications program Software written to solve a specific problem.

Architecture The design and organization of the components of a computer system. The structure of a database.

Array A group of related numbers or words stored in the computer in adjacent memory locations.

ASCII (American Standard Code for Information Interchange) A standard system that can represent 128 different characters.

Assembler program A service program that translates assembly language into machine language.

Assembly language A low-level programming language that uses symbolic operation codes and addresses.

Asynchronous transmission A system of transmitting characters without reference to a clock or timed intervals.

ATM (Automated Teller Machine) A remote terminal that allows automated transfer of funds in bank accounts.

Audio response unit An output device that generates audible signals and tones and can synthesize the human voice.

BASIC (Beginner's All-purpose Symbolic Instruction Code) A high-level programming language used on many microcomputers.

Batch processing The processing of data at some time after a transaction has occurred. Also called off-line processing.

Binary notation A fixed-base notation in which the base is 2.

Bit The smallest unit of information that can be held in memory. Abbreviated form of the term "binary digit," a 0 or a 1.

Block A group of records, words, or characters that, for technical or logical reasons, is treated as a unit in input or output. A section of a program treated as a unit.

Block diagram A flowchart that shows the major steps or modules in the solution of a problem.

Blocking Combining two or more records into one block.

BPI (Bits Per Inch) A measure of capacity, or density, of storage media.

BPS (Bits Per Second) A measure of line capacity or data transmission speed.

Bubble memory A system in which data are stored as magnetized areas on a thin-film semiconductor.

Bug A logical or clerical error. A malfunction.

Byte A group of adjacent bits that form a character.

C A computer language particularly suited to writing operating systems and special programming applications.

CAD (Computer-Aided Design) The use of computers to prepare and test mechanical designs and make engineering drawings.

CAM (Computer-Aided Manufacturing) The application of computers to such manufacturing tasks as process control, inventory control, and scheduling of work.

Cellular storage A secondary storage system in which data are stored in cartridges that are housed in a honeycomb pattern of cells.

Check bit An extra bit added to a byte to detect an inaccuracy in transmission.

Chip *See IC (Integrated Circuit).*

Clock *See System clock.*

COBOL (Common Business-Oriented Language) A high-level programming language used in business.

CODASYL (Conference On Data Systems Languages) The group of users and manufacturers of data processing systems that developed and maintain the COBOL language.

Coding The operation of converting instructions into language commands that can be processed by a computer.

COM (Computer Output Microform) A form of output that uses miniature photographic images to store or output information.

Communications link The hardware and circuitry used to connect elements of a system in order to transmit and receive information.

Compiler A computer program that converts a program written in a high-level language into machine language.

Computer An electronic device capable of receiving input, processing data, and generating output according to stored instructions, with high speed and accuracy.

Computer word A group of bytes stored in one memory location and treated as a unit.

Control program The portion of the operating system that manages overall operations, schedules work, logs jobs, and monitors status.

Control unit The part of the computer that guides the overall operation and timing of the CPU.

Counter A component of the control unit of the central processing unit that counts and records the number of pulses sent to it.

CPU (Central Processing Unit) The portion of the computer that performs calculations, controls its operation, and contains primary memory.

CRT (Cathode ray tube) An output device that converts electric signals into visual form by means of a controlled electron beam.

Cursor A flashing pointer that can be moved about on the face of a CRT.

Cylinder The group of tracks accessed simultaneously by a set of read/write heads on a disk storage device.

Daisy wheel printer A printing device consisting of a flat wheel of spokes with a different letter or character on each spoke.

DASD (Direct Access Storage Device) A memory system that can locate or retrieve data by reference to the data's address or location.

Data Factual information of value to an individual or organization and suitable for communication, interpretation, or processing by humans or machines.

Database A collection of all the data used by an individual or organization, structured in a systematic way to eliminate duplication and to facilitate retrieval and processing for many applications.

Data communications The transmission of information between processing sites over telephone, telegraph, satellite relay, microwave, or other circuits.

Data concentrator A device that stores characters and then transmits them over a line in a high-speed burst.

Data cycle The fundamental sequence of data processing operations, composed of input, processing, and output.

Data dictionary A comprehensive list of elements in a database, usually arranged alphabetically, giving the form, function, meaning, and syntax of data.

Data input The conversion of data from source documents into a form acceptable for processing by computer or other means.

Data model The part of a database that defines information contained in a field and its format, including the type and number of characters and reference method.

Data output The reporting of information processed by computer in a form suitable for use by people.

Data processing The restructuring, manipulation, or reordering of data by people or machines to increase the data's usefulness for a particular purpose.

Data transmission The sending of data from one part of a system to another.

DBMS (Database Management System) A comprehensive set of computer programs that constructs, maintains, manipulates, and provides access to a database.

DDP (Distributed Data Processing) A system in which a network of geographically separate, stand-alone computers replaces large central computers for processing information.

Debug To detect, trace, and eliminate mistakes in computer programs or other software.

Decision table A tabular form used in preparing programs that shows conditions that may occur and actions to be taken in response.

Desktop publishing The application of computers to the preparation of typeset quality documents, including newsletters, reports, and memos.

Detail file A transaction file containing records that will be used to update a master file.

Detail flowchart A flowchart that shows every step and operation involved in solving a problem.

Diagnostic message A message printed out by the computer during compilation or execution of a program, pertaining to the diagnosis or isolation of errors in the program.

Digital computer A computer that processes data in a discrete or discontinuous form.

Digital data Data represented in discrete, discontinuous form, as contrasted with analog data represented in continuous form. Digital data are usually represented by means of coded characters, such as numbers, letters, and symbols.

Digitizer An input device that converts pictures, lines, or drawings into x-y coordinates.

Disk A metal or plastic plate coated with ferromagnetic material on which data may be recorded. A form of secondary storage. *See Diskette, Rigid disk.*

Disk pack A collection of two or more disks mounted on a common shaft.

Diskette A thin, flexible, plastic disk coated with ferromagnetic material on which data may be recorded. Also called flexible disk, floppy disk.

Document A medium and the data recorded on it for human use; for example, a report sheet or an invoice. By extension, any record that has permanence and that can be read by a person or machine.

Documentation A written record of the logic, details, and input and output specifications related to a program. User guides, manuals, and instructions available for a computer.

DOS (Disk Operating System) An operating system that stores the bulk of its instructions on magnetic disk.

Dot matrix printer An impact printout device that forms characters by striking the ends of a group of wires or rods arranged in a pattern.

Dumb terminal A computer terminal that does not contain a microcomputer or independent processing capability.

EAM (Electrical Accounting Machine) Any piece of data processing equipment that is predominantly electromechanical, such as a card punch, mechanical sorter, collator, and tabulator.

EBCDIC (Extended Binary Coded Decimal Interchange Code) A coding system that can represent 256 different characters.

Edit To prepare input data for a later operation or to change the form of output data by such operations as rearrangement or addition of data, deletion of unwanted data, format control, and code conversion.

EDP (Electronic Data Processing) Data processing largely performed by computers.

EFT (Electronic Funds Transfer) The transfer of funds by the electronic adjustment of records.

Electronic mail Messages sent by the transmission of electronic pulses rather than by the transfer of physical documents.

End-of-reel mark A reflective foil indicator that marks the end of the usable tape on a reel.

EPROM (Erasable Programmable Read Only Memory) A solid-state storage device capable of read only memory that can be removed from the computer and exposed to ultraviolet light in order to be reprogrammed.

Even parity A system for checking accuracy when transmitting digital data in which a bit is added to an array of bits (a byte) to make the sum of the bits even.

Execute To carry out an instruction or perform a routine.

Execution cycle The phase in the operating cycle of the central processing unit during which an instruction is performed or carried out.

Facsimile machine A device that scans a page, converts the data into electronic pulses, and transmits the pulses to a remote location.

Ferrite core memory A form of primary storage using a network of doughnut-shaped rings pressed from iron ferrite and strung on wires.

Fiber optics A cable consisting of bundles of glass or plastic fibers that are able to transmit data in the form of light.

Field A group of related characters, or bytes, treated as a unit.

File A collection of related records treated as a unit.

File label A magnetically recorded label before each file on a tape to give the file name and the date after which it may be destroyed. Also called header label.

File maintenance The activity of keeping a file up-to-date by adding, changing, or deleting data.

File protection ring A plastic ring that is placed on the hub of a reel of magnetic tape in order to record or erase data from the tape.

Filing The classifying and storing of information and documents for later retrieval.

Flexible disk *See Diskette.*

Floppy disk *See Diskette.*

Flowchart A graphic representation of the definition, analysis, or method of solution of a problem in which standardized symbols are used to represent operations, data flow, equipment, and so forth.

Font A set of characters molded on a printing element.

FORTRAN (FORmula TRANslating system) A programming language that resembles mathematical notation and is used primarily for scientific applications.

Full-duplex circuit A circuit in which data can flow in two directions at the same time.

Gate An electronic circuit that performs a mathematical or logical operation.

GIGO (Garbage In-Garbage Out) A term to express the fact that the quality of a computer result can be no better than the quality of the input data and the processing instructions.

Graphics Output in the form of black-and-white or color images, such as lines, plots, charts, and drawings.

Half-duplex circuit A circuit in which data flow can be shifted from one direction to the other, that is, a circuit that can receive or transmit data in one direction at a time.

Hard copy Output in a permanent physical form, such as a paper printout, that can be read or viewed by people.

Hardware The physical equipment used to input, process, and output data.

Header label *See File label.*

Hollerith card A punched card containing eighty columns and twelve rows of punch positions.

IBG (InterBlock Gap) An area on magnetic tape between blocks of records.

IC (Integrated Circuit) A solid-state device containing a complex group of transistors and electronic circuits etched on a small piece of silicon, about 1/16 inch square.

Impact printer An output device that forms characters by striking a raised letter against a ribbon, imprinting the characters on a sheet.

Information *See Data.*

Ink jet printer An output device that forms letters from a continuous stream of ink droplets.

Input *See Data input.*

Instruction cycle The phase in the operating cycle of the central processing unit during which an instruction is called from storage and the required circuitry to perform that instruction is set up.

Intelligent terminal A computer terminal equipped with an independent microprocessor capable of performing logic, decisions, and local processing.

Interactive language A language that allows programmers to communicate with computers during the execution of a program.

Interactive program A computer program that permits data to be entered or the course of programming flow to be changed during its execution.

Internally stored program A set of instructions read into computer memory that directs the computer.

Interpreter A computer program that translates statements in a programming language into machine instructions line by line.

I/O (Input/Output) A general term referring to equipment used to communicate with a computer, data involved in such communication, or media carrying the data.

IRG (InterRecord Gap) An area on magnetic tape between records.

K An abbreviation for the prefix "kilo," meaning 1,000 in decimal notation. In computer terminology, an abbreviation for a value equal to 1,024.

Kernel The center of the operating system containing routines that call in and out other software.

Kilobyte (KB) 1,024 bytes.

LAN (Local Area Network) A communications system that links workstations within a geographically limited area, usually by coaxial cable, to enable users to share computer resources.

Language translator *See Compiler.*

LCD (Liquid Crystal Display) A visual display in which output images are formed by a liquid suspended in an electrical field.

LED (Light Emitting Diode) A semiconductor device that glows and is used in displaying binary or alphanumeric information.

Library A collection of related files.

List structure A database schema that allows out-of-sequence records to be processed through the use of a system of pointers or linkage addresses to direct the computer.

Listing Loosely, a printout of all cards or records in a file or all statements in a program.

Load-point mark A reflective foil indicator that marks the beginning of the usable tape on a reel.

Longitudinal parity check An accuracy-checking system in which all bits in a track are tallied at the end of its length, and a check bit is added to generate an even or odd number of bits.

Loop structure A logic pattern in structured programming in which the computer repeats a sequence until a certain test condition prevails. Also called iteration structure.

LSI (Large-Scale Integrated circuit) A solid-state device containing thousands of electronic components manufactured on a single chip of silicon.

Machine language A language that is used directly by a machine.

Macroflowchart *See Block diagram.*

Magnetic disk *See Disk, Diskette, Rigid disk.*

Mainframe In a large computer, the central processing unit. Sometimes refers to a large computer, including its I/O devices.

Manual data processing Data processing done mentally or with paper and pencil, adding machine, or desk calculator.

Mark sense To mark a position on a punched card with an electrically conductive pencil for later conversion to machine punching.

Mass storage A secondary storage system capable of storing hundreds of millions of records.

Master file A file that is used as an authority in a given job and that is relatively permanent, even though its contents may change.

Mathematical model A planning tool in which business conditions are analyzed and solved by mathematical techniques.

Matrix *See Array.*

MB (MegaByte) About 1 million bytes, or 1,024K bytes.

Menu A list of options and choices of programs available or processing modules within a program from which users select.

MICR (Magnetic Ink Character Recognition) Recognition of characters printed with ink that contains particles of a magnetic material.

Microcomputer A miniature computer manufactured on a small chip, using solid-state integrated circuitry, that possesses characteristics of larger systems.

Microelectronics The design and construction of miniature electronic components using integrated circuits and solid state technology.

Microflowchart *See Detail flowchart.*

Microform A photographic film on which reduced images of data are stored, such as microfilm or microfiche.

Micrographics The production of greatly reduced images on photographic film.

Microprocessor The central processing unit of a computer, manufactured on a small silicon chip.

Microsecond (μs) One-millionth of a second.

Millisecond (ms) One-thousandth of a second.

Minicomputer A small, desktop digital computer with at least one I/O device and memory between 32K and 64K bytes or over.

MIPS (Millions of Instructions Per Second) A unit for measuring the speed of a computer.

Modem (MOdulator/DEModulator) A device used to connect a terminal or a computer to a transmission line. Also called a coupler.

Mouse An input device that is moved about on a tabletop and directs a pointer on a screen.

Multiplexer A device that interleaves data from several sources and sends them over a single transmission line.

Multiprocessing A system in which two or more central processing units are wired together to share processing.

Multiprogramming A mode of operation in which two or more programs are processed by one computer concurrently.

Nanosecond (ns) One-billionth of a second.

Network A system of computers or terminals interconnected by communications circuits.

Network structure A database schema using master records that may be linked to several subordinate records, each of which may be linked to several masters.

Node A central point around which are clustered a group of local terminals or workstations in a telecommunications network.

OCR (Optical Character Recognition) The ability of certain light-sensitive machines to recognize printed letters, numbers, and special characters.

Odd parity A system for checking accuracy in transmitting digital data in which a bit is added to an array of bits (a byte) to make the sum of the bits odd.

Off-line processing *See Batch processing.*

On-line processing *See Transaction-oriented processing.*

Op code (OPeration CODE) The part of a computer instruction that directs the machine to carry out a specific operation such as to add or compare data.

Operand A part of a computer instruction that describes the location where data will be found and where results will be sent.

Optical character reader An input device that can recognize certain handwritten, typed, or printed characters and convert them into electronic pulses.

Optical sense reader An input device that can interpret certain handwritten marks and convert them into electronic pulses.

OS (Operating System) Software that controls the execution of computer programs and that may provide scheduling, debugging, input/output control, accounting, compilation, storage assignment, data management, and related services.

Output *See Data output.*

Paging A procedure for expanding the memory capacity of a computer by moving data between primary memory and a secondary storage device.

Parallel output A form of output in which all characters on a line are printed at the same instant.

Parity check A system for detecting the loss or gain of a bit during transmission by checking whether the number of bits (0s or 1s) is odd or even.

Pascal A high-level programming language designed for structured programming.

Peripheral equipment Any hardware device distinct from the central processing unit that provides communications, input/output, secondary storage, or other facilities.

Pixel A spot or point that makes up the image of a picture, drawing, or line on a CRT.

PL/I (Programming Language I) A high-level programming language used for both scientific and business applications.

Plotter An output device that converts electronic signals into figures, lines, or curves by connecting point-by-point coordinate values.

Pointer A number that directs the computer to the next record in a database even though it is not in sequence.

POL (Problem-Oriented Language) Any high-level programming language that stresses problem-solving features and eliminates programming details.

Port A terminal that serves as an entry point into a telecommunications network.

Primary memory The section of the central processing unit that during processing holds program instructions, input data, calculation results, and data to be output. Also called internal storage, main memory, primary memory.

Process control A technique by which output of a system is fed back into the system as input in order to monitor, measure, or control a manufacturing process.

Program A schedule or plan that specifies the actions a computer is to take in solving a problem; a series of instructions or statements recorded in a form that can be understood by a computer.

Programmer An individual who lays out the steps in solving a problem and writes instructions for the computer.

PROM (Programmable Read Only Memory) A solid-state storage device capable of read only memory that can be programmed by the user.

Pseudocode An abbreviated, nonexecutable version of program statements, written in ordinary language as a step in program development and analysis.

Pulse An electronic signal or voltage, the presence or absence of which can be used in a computer to represent data as 1 (presence) or 0 (absence).

Pulse train A string of electronic pulses that transmit data.

RAM (Random Access Memory) A solid state storage device that enables data to be written in, changed, or read out repeatedly.

Random access storage An access mode in which records are searched for and retrieved from a secondary storage file in a nonsequential manner, usually by location. Also called direct access storage.

Read/write head That part of a magnetic tape drive that records data (in the form of electronic pulses) on tape or reads data from tape.

Real-time processing *See Transaction-oriented processing.*

Record A collection of related fields treated as a unit.

Register A storage device that holds information being processed.

Relational structure A database schema that uses a group of tables to show relationships used to search out data.

Rigid disk A round metal plate with a thin coating of ferromagnetic material on which data may be recorded. Also called disk or hard disk.

ROM (Read Only Memory) A permanently programmed semiconductor memory device that can read out data repeatedly and whose contents cannot be changed.

RPG (Report Program Generator) A high-level computer language used for processing large data files.

Scanner An input device that reads symbols or codes by passing a light or laser beam over them.

Schema The logical structure, plan, or method by which data are organized in a database system.

Scroll To move output displayed on a cathode ray tube up or down on the screen.

Secondary storage Auxiliary memory that can be accessed by the central processing unit.

Selection structure A form of program logic in which the computer branches to one of two different tracks depending upon a test condition.

Semiconductor A solid-state electronic switching device that performs functions similar to an electronic tube.

Semiconductor memory A memory system containing thousands of microscopic transistors manufactured on a chip of silicon.

Sequence structure A form of program logic in which the computer moves through a set of statements one time without branching.

Sequential access storage An access mode in which a storage medium is searched in sequence for a desired record.

Serial output A form of output in which characters are printed letter by letter, usually from left to right.

Service program The part of the operating system that contains frequently used routines and functions such as language translators.

Shell The software containing control and service programs that surround the kernel in an operating system.

Simplex circuit A circuit in which data can flow in only one direction.

Smart terminal *See Intelligent terminal.*

Software Programs, procedures, rules, and documentation that direct or relate to the operation of a computer system.

Solid-state circuit *See Semiconductor.*

Source document A record prepared at the time or location a transaction takes place that serves as a source for data to be input to a computer system.

Split screen A form of cathode ray tube display in which the screen is divided into sections for simultaneous display of different information.

Spreadsheet software A program that manipulates information and displays it in the form of an electronic ledger sheet and related graphs and charts.

Standard character set The limited collection of characters (letters, numbers, and special symbols) used to encode a program in a given language.

Standard universal identifier A number used to catalog information in a database.

Structured programming A programming technique in which steps are designed as separate, independent modules linked together by control programs.

Subroutine A sequence of statements that may be used as a whole in one or more computer programs and at one or more points in a computer program.

Synchronous transmission A system of sending and receiving characters at timed intervals.

System A collection of objects, procedures, and techniques that interact in a regulated manner to form an organized whole.

System clock A component of the control unit of the central processing unit that sends out pulses that regulate the opening and closing of electronic circuits within the CPU.

System flowchart A diagram that shows the data flow in an entire organization or system, specifying workstations, operations to be performed, communications links, and so forth.

Systems analysis The analysis of an activity to determine precisely what must be accomplished and how to accomplish it.

Telecommunications The transmission of data in digital, audio, or video form over long distances.

Teleconferencing An electronic communications system that allows individuals at different physical locations to participate in a conference.

Telecopier *See Facsimile machine.*

Teleprocessing The transmission of information in digital form through a network of computer terminals and transmission lines.

Template A pattern or guide. A plastic cutout used to draw standard flowchart symbols.

Terminal A remotely located input or output device connected to a computer.

Text editing The process of changing, adding, or deleting material to improve a text's usefulness, accuracy, or appearance.

Thermal printer An output device that forms characters by using heat and heat-sensitive paper.

Thimble A molded plastic printing element containing curved spokes, each with a different letter or character on it.

Time sharing The use of a computer system by two or more users whose programs are executed concurrently.

Topology The study of the structure, design, and layout of a network and transmission facility.

TOS (Tape Operating System) An operating system that stores the bulk of its instructions on magnetic tape.

Track The portion of a moving data medium, such as a drum, tape, or disk, that is accessible to a given reading head position.

Trailer label A magnetically recorded label that marks the end of a file on a tape and gives the file name, date on which it may be destroyed, and number of blocks or records in the file.

Trailer record A record that marks the physical end of an input file.

Transaction file *See Detail file.*

Transaction-oriented processing The processing of information at the time a transaction takes place and under direct control of the CPU. Also called on-line processing, real- time processing.

Transcribing Converting spoken or written information into keystrokes for input into a computer system; converting source data into machine-readable form.

Transistor A small, solid-state device that performs nearly all the functions of an electronic tube, especially amplification and switching.

Tree structure A database schema using master records, known as parents, which may be linked to several subordinate records, known as children, each of which is linked to only one master record.

Type element An object used in printing that contains a font of molded characters.

Type wheel A wheel with letters and numbers molded around it, used to print characters.

Unit record A punched card containing information on one transaction.

Unit record processing Processing data by using a combination of human activity and electromechanical devices.

UPC (Universal Product Code) A machine-readable code for labeling consumer products that uses parallel bars to represent digits.

Variable In a computer program, a character or group of characters that refers to a value and, in the execution of the program, corresponds to an address. A named quantity that can assume different alphabetic or numeric values.

VDT (Video Display Terminal) An output device that converts electronic pulses into visual images.

Virtual storage Computer memory expanded beyond primary memory capacity by the use of secondary storage devices and paging.

VLSI (Very Large-Scale Integrated circuit) A solid-state device containing hundreds of thousands of complex electronic circuits manufactured on one chip of silicon.

Voice recognition The conversion of tones of human speech into analog wave forms and then into a digital form that can be processed by a computer system.

Voice synthesizer A device that converts electronic pulses into audible tones that simulate the human voice.

Volume label A magnetically recorded label at the beginning of a reel of tape that indicates the volume number of that reel.

Winchester disk A system in which data are recorded on metal disks enclosed in sealed containers that are permanently mounted on the disk drive.

Word processing The recording and revising of words or phrases by machines to produce reports or documents.

Workstation A microcomputer terminal, usually equipped with secondary storage, that is part of a distributed data processing system.

Index